COMPLETE PIANO
PHOTO CHORDS

BY JONATHAN HANSEN

1 2 3 4 5 6 7 8 9 0

Visit us on the Web at www.melbay.com — E-mail us at email@melbay.com

Table of Contents

Table of Contents

About the Author

Born in 1972 in St. Louis, Missouri, Jon Hansen began playing piano at age seven. He was classically trained by several teachers and has a musical background covering classical, blues, rock, jazz, new age, country, etc. At the age of 16, he began composing music and continues to this day. Self-classified as "new-age-classical-jazz," he continues to expand his compositions into music's many different genres and facets. Jon has played informal gigs in Kansas City and St. Louis, but prefers a quiet solo career concentrating on his compositions.

From 2001 to 2005, Jon worked for Mel Bay Publications, Inc. as project coordinator and as a music editor, editing everything from piano to violin to accordion to dulcimer and so on. As project coordinator he helped hundreds of authors move their projects into the Mel Bay catalog. He was the chief editor of Mel Bay's online webzine, Creative Keyboard® and is author of several Mel Bay piano publications.

- 21008 - The Complete Piano Photo Chord Book

- 21096 - Country Piano Photo Chord Book

- 21097 - Rock Piano Photo Chord Book

- 21098 - Jazz Piano Photo Chord Book

- 21099 - Blues Piano Photo Chord Book

Acknowledgements:

I would like to thank William Bay, Doug Witherspoon, Sheri, Mig, Julie Price and everyone at Mel Bay for all their help in bringing this project to fruition. I would also like to thank my parents for all their love and support through the years; God, for without him I would not be here; and Bill W. and Dr. Bob for that very same reason. A very special thanks to Manuela, "little" Richard and "baby" Emma – they are truly the loves of my life.

Introduction

As I began playing many years ago, I was taught the scales and their respective chords unbeknownst as to how vital they would be to me in the future. Like many pianists, I was classically trained and taught to read standard notation. This has bode well for me over the years; however, as time has passed my musical tastes have grown and expanded into many genres. The talent of playing in a lead sheet format and the ability to improvise has become essential (for me). Without at least the most basic understanding and knowledge of chords and their many forms, many doors to music's ever expanding genres would be closed. Most of today's sheet music is presented in notation and, of course, chord symbols are presented above the melody line. By learning simply the chords, this music becomes available even to the most novice musician. The whole idea of music is to draw pleasure and enjoyment from the melodies which surround us all, each and every day.

How to Use the Photo Chord Book

This book will cover major, minor, augmented, diminished, extended chords, and so on. I have separated each section using the circle of fifths — C, G, D, A, E, F♯/G♭, D♭, A♭, E♭, B, and F. Each chord will contain a photo, diagram on the keyboard, chord name(s) commonly used and the spelling of the chord.

The black and white photos will show the placement of the hands on an actual keyboard. It will depict the most common fingering for each chord and the most comfortable position of the hands.

The diagram will be displayed above each photo. The notes are charted utilizing a graphic which darkens the white keys, and lightens the black keys which are to be played. You will also find the spelling of the chord below the keys in the graphic which will present the letter names of all the notes in its respective chord.

The name of the chord will be directly below the photo. You may see these chord names in sheet music, lead sheets, fake books, etc. The actual chord name will be displayed. A list of alternative chord names is also included; it would be helpful to become familiar with all these symbols.

Other Common Chord Names & Symbols

Major	M, Maj
Minor	m, min, -
Diminished	dim, °, m(♭5)
Diminished 7th	dim7, °7, dim
Half Diminished	m7(♭5), ø
Augmented	aug, (♯5), +5, +
5th	5
7th	7, dominant 7th, dom
Minor 7th	m7, min7, -7
Major 7th	Maj7, maj7, M7
Minor/major 7th	m(Maj7), m/maj7, m(M7), min(Maj7), m(+7), -(M7), min(addM7)
Suspended 4th	sus4
Suspended 2nd	sus2
7th Suspended 4th	7sus4, 7sus
7th Suspended 2nd	7sus2
Added 2nd	add2
Added 9th	add9
Added 4th	add4
6th	6, M6, maj6
Minor 6th	m6, min6, -6
6/9	6/9, 6(add9), Major6(add9), M6(add9)
9th	9, 7(add9)
Minor 9th	m9, min9, -9
Major 9th	Maj9, M9, M7(add9)
11th	11
Minor 11th	m11, min11
Major 11th	Maj11
13th	13, 7(add13), 7(add6)
Minor 13th	m13, -13, min7(add13), m7(add13)
Major 13th	Maj13, M13, Maj7(add13), M(add13), M7(add6)
7th Sharp 9th	7(♯9), 7+9
7th Flat 9th	7(♭9), 7-9, 7(add♭9)
7th Sharp 5th	7(♯5), 7+5, aug7, +7
7th Flat 5th	7(♭5), 7-5

C
Chords

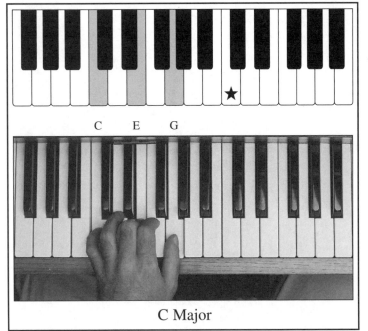

C Major

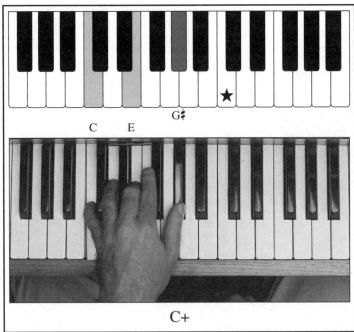

C+

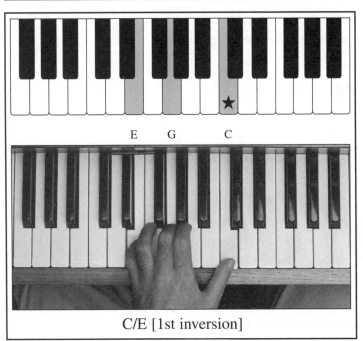

C/E [1st inversion]

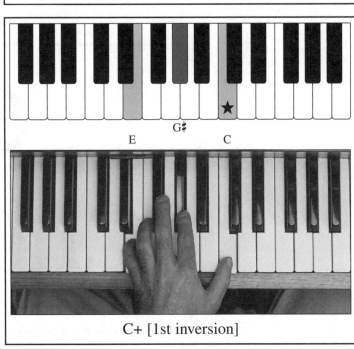

C+ [1st inversion]

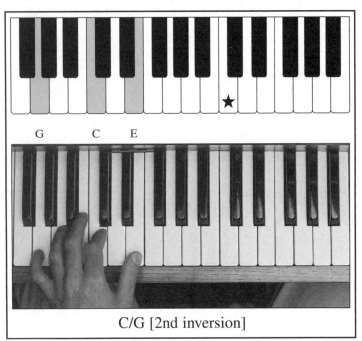

C/G [2nd inversion]

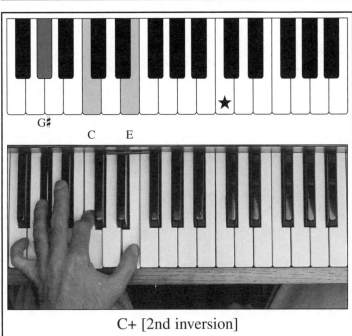

C+ [2nd inversion]

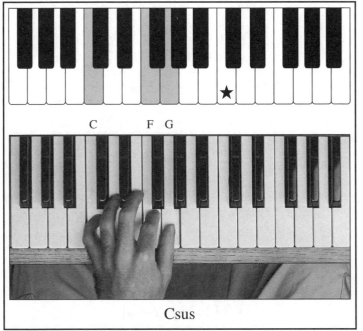

Csus

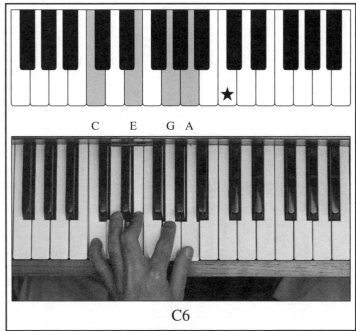

C6

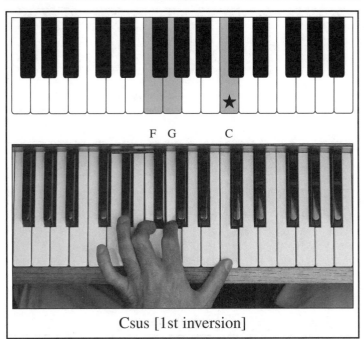

Csus [1st inversion]

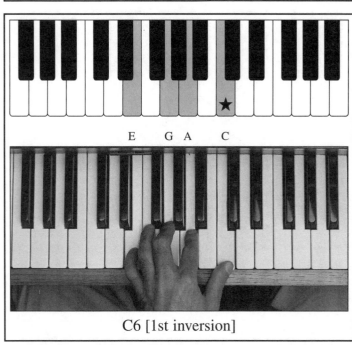

C6 [1st inversion]

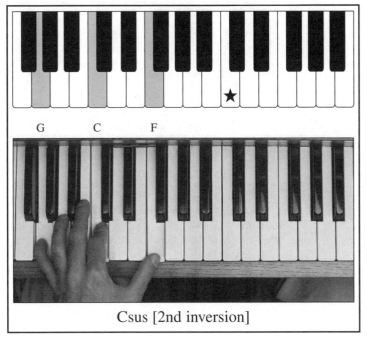

Csus [2nd inversion]

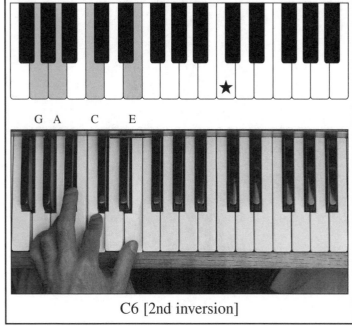

C6 [2nd inversion]

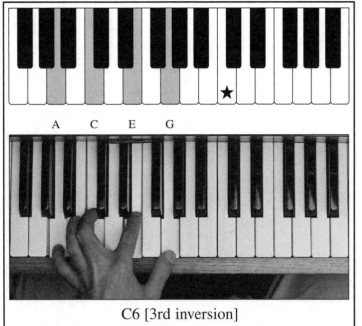

C6 [3rd inversion]

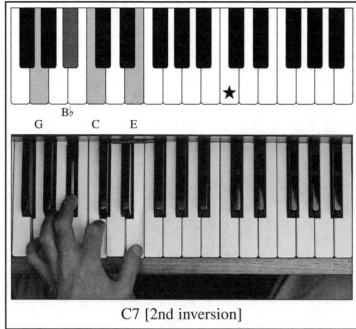

C7 [2nd inversion]

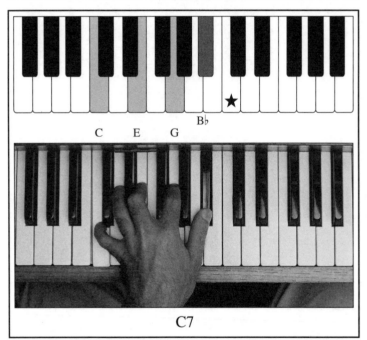

C7

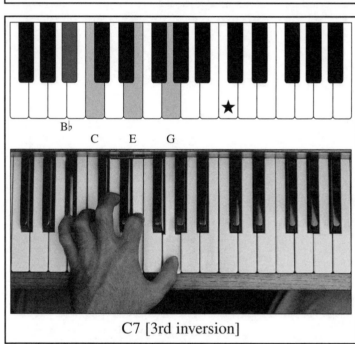

C7 [3rd inversion]

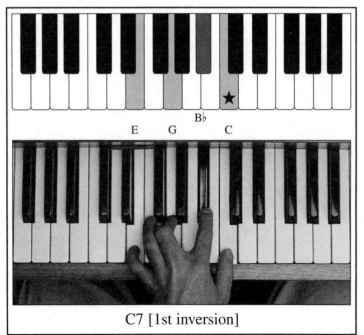

C7 [1st inversion]

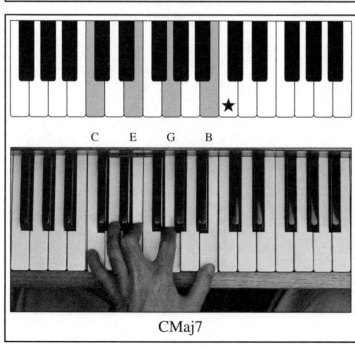

CMaj7

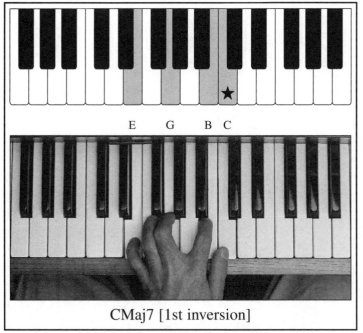

CMaj7 [1st inversion]

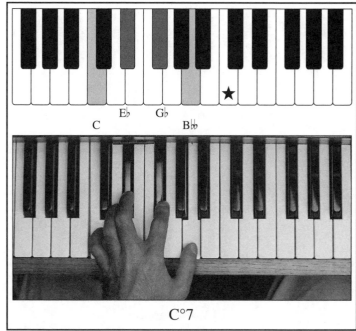

C°7

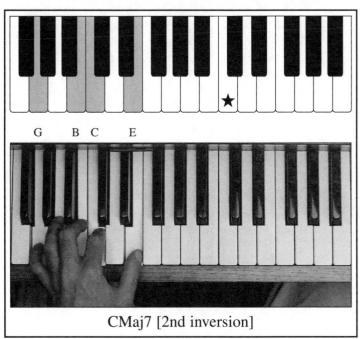

CMaj7 [2nd inversion]

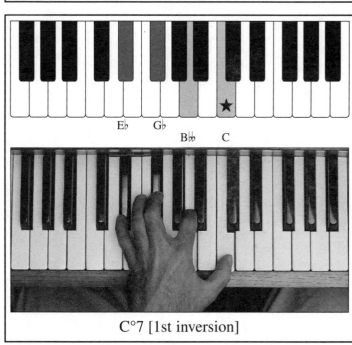

C°7 [1st inversion]

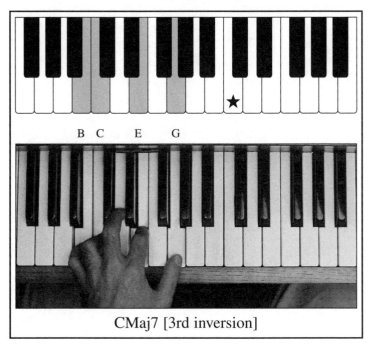

CMaj7 [3rd inversion]

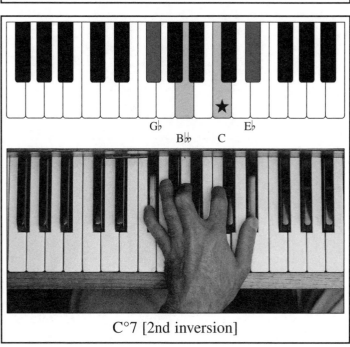

C°7 [2nd inversion]

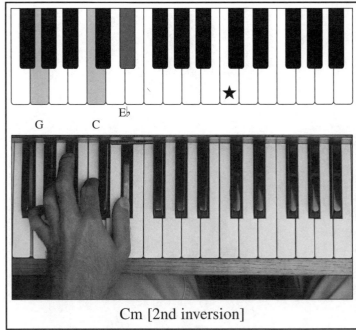

C°7 [3rd inversion]

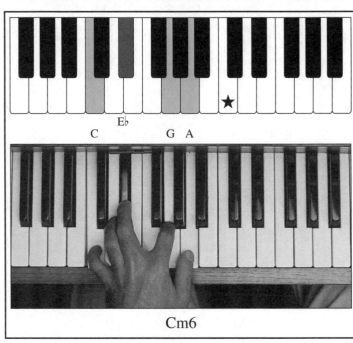

Cm [2nd inversion]

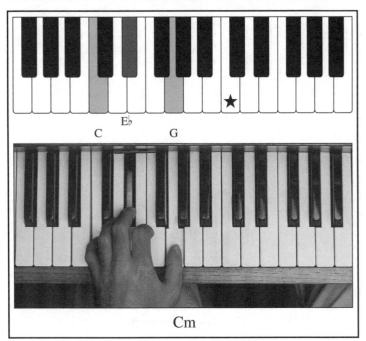

Cm

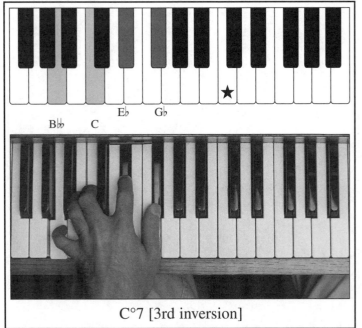

Cm6

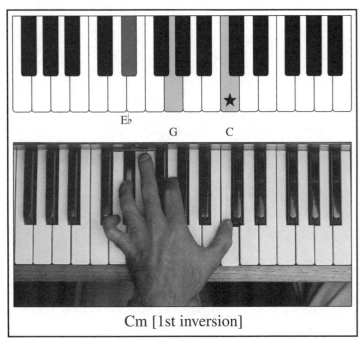

Cm [1st inversion]

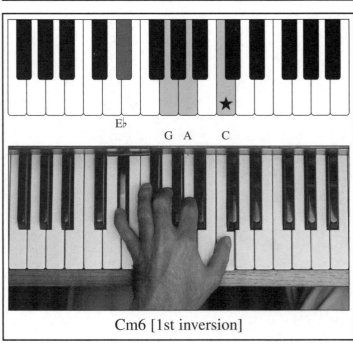

Cm6 [1st inversion]

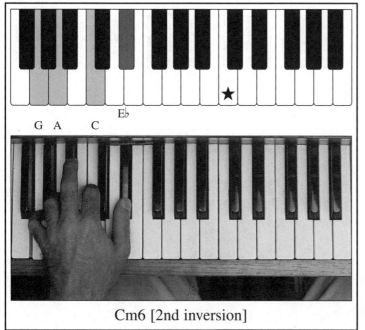

G A C
E♭

Cm6 [2nd inversion]

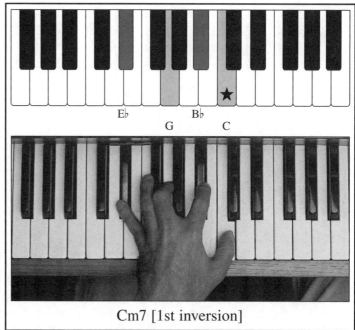

E♭
G B♭ C

Cm7 [1st inversion]

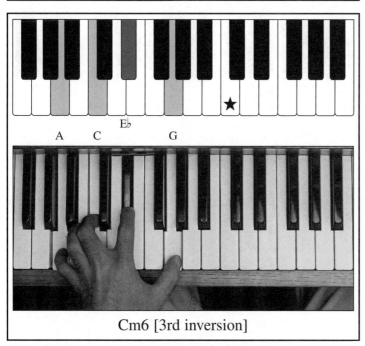

A C
E♭ G

Cm6 [3rd inversion]

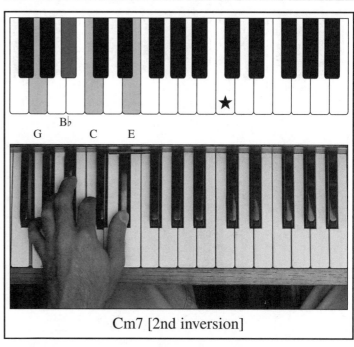

B♭
G C E

Cm7 [2nd inversion]

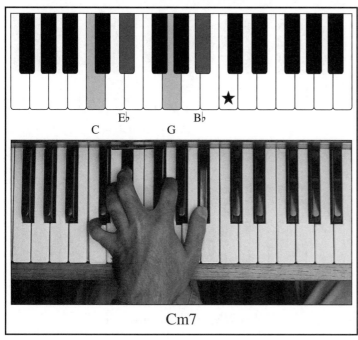

C
E♭ G B♭

Cm7

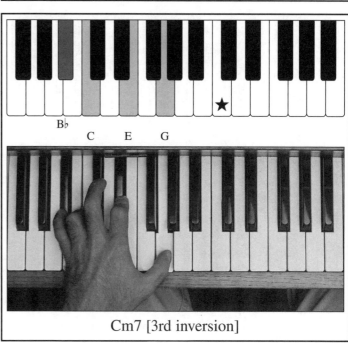

B♭ C E G

Cm7 [3rd inversion]

13

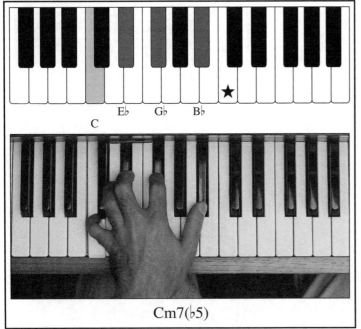

Cm7(♭5)

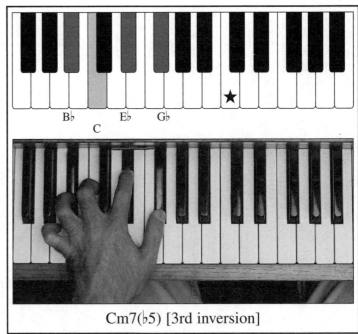

Cm7(♭5) [3rd inversion]

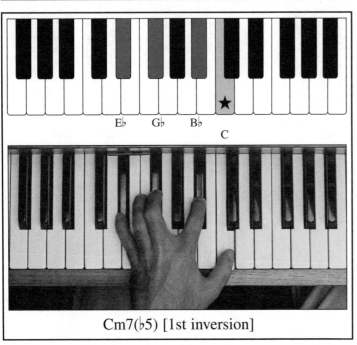

Cm7(♭5) [1st inversion]

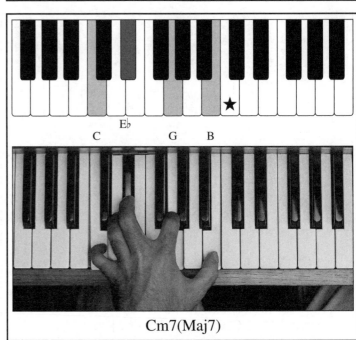

Cm7(Maj7)

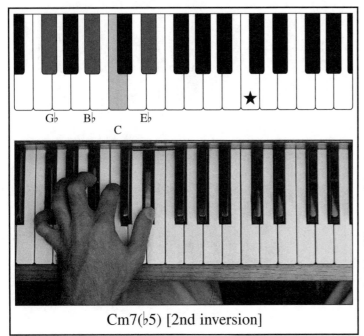

Cm7(♭5) [2nd inversion]

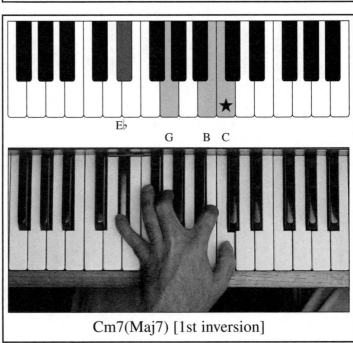

Cm7(Maj7) [1st inversion]

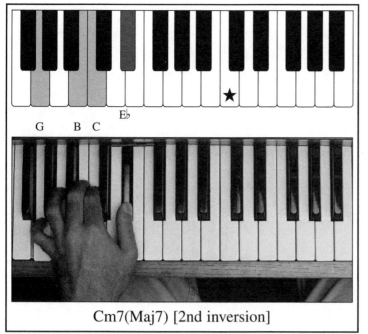

Cm7(Maj7) [2nd inversion]

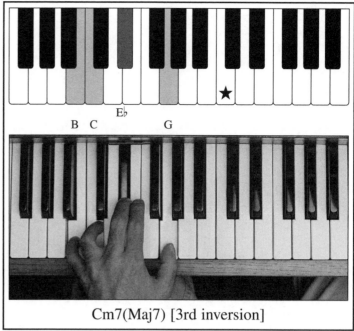

Cm7(Maj7) [3rd inversion]

See more C chords in the
***Chords for Two Hands* section**

G
Chords

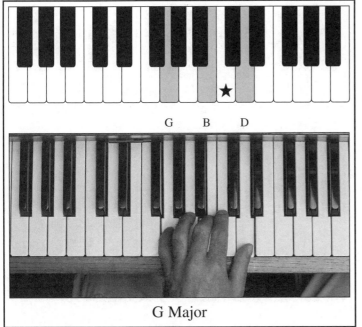

G   B   D

G Major

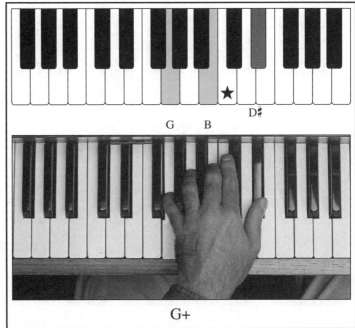

G   B   D#

G+

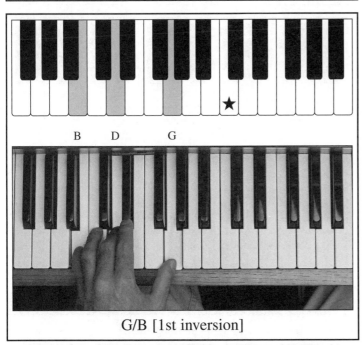

B   D   G

G/B [1st inversion]

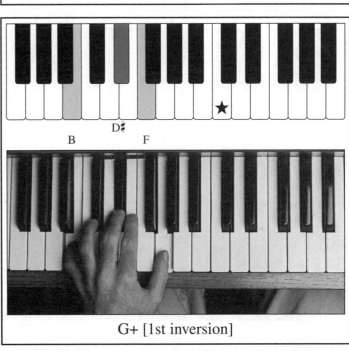

D#
B   F

G+ [1st inversion]

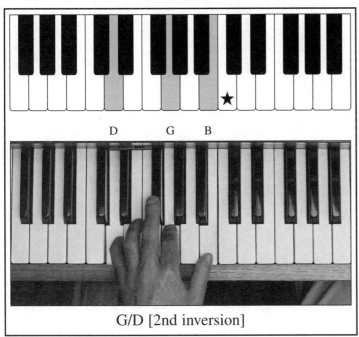

D   G   B

G/D [2nd inversion]

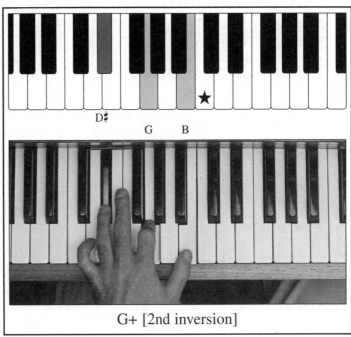

D#
G   B

G+ [2nd inversion]

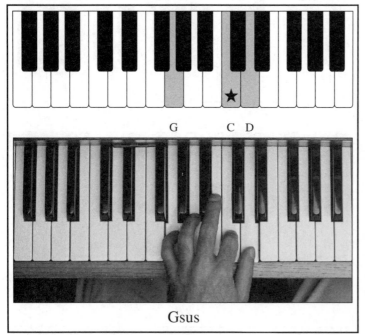

G   C D

Gsus

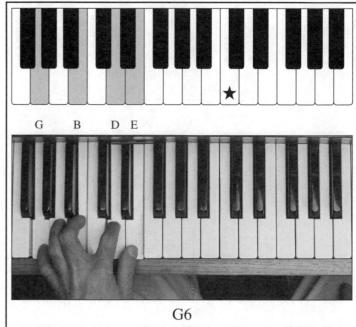

G B   D E

G6

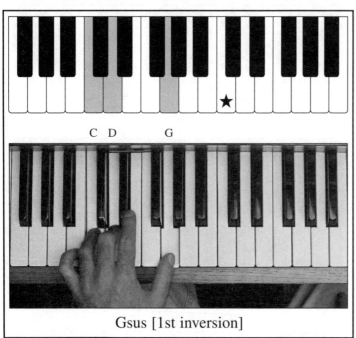

C D   G

Gsus [1st inversion]

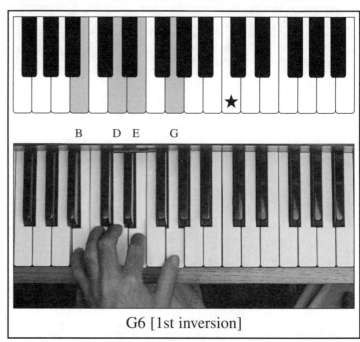

B   D E   G

G6 [1st inversion]

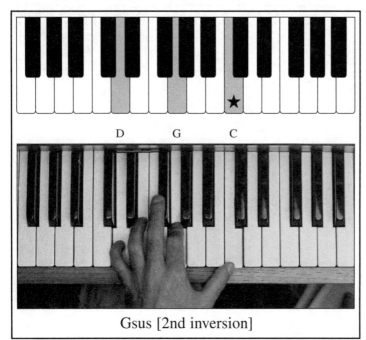

D   G   C

Gsus [2nd inversion]

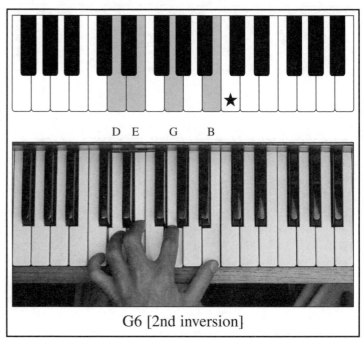

D E   G   B

G6 [2nd inversion]

18

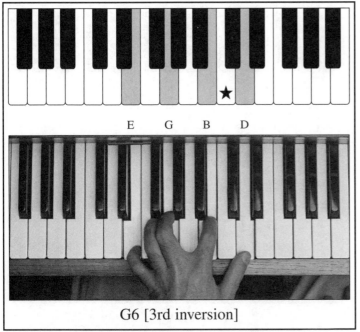

E G B D

G6 [3rd inversion]

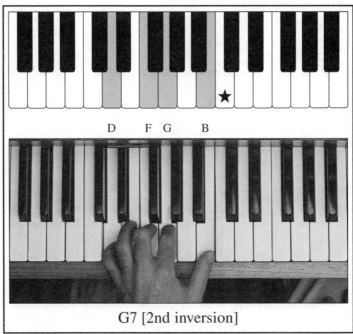

D F G B

G7 [2nd inversion]

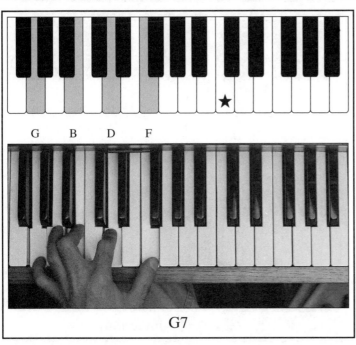

G B D F

G7

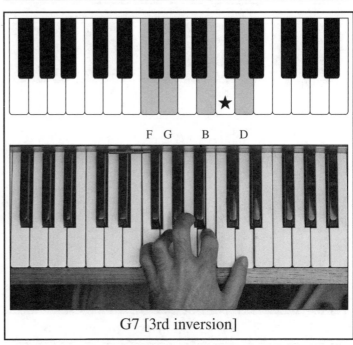

F G B D

G7 [3rd inversion]

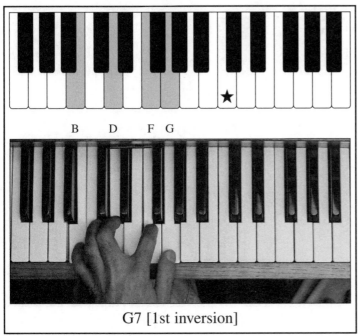

B D F G

G7 [1st inversion]

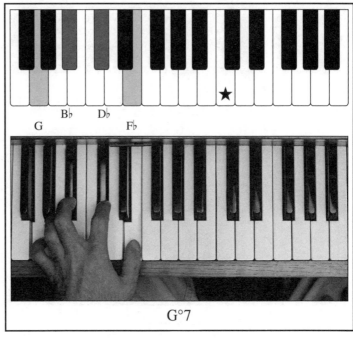

G B♭ D♭ F♭

G°7

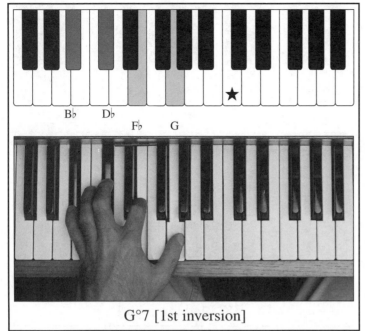

G°7 [1st inversion]

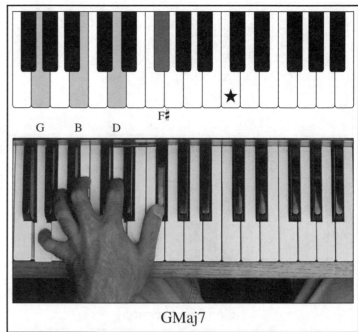

GMaj7

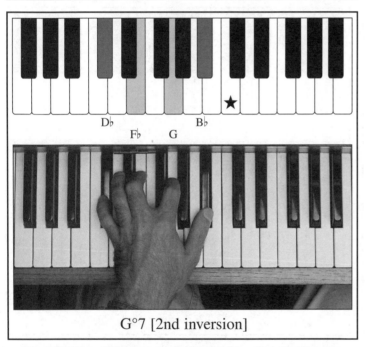

G°7 [2nd inversion]

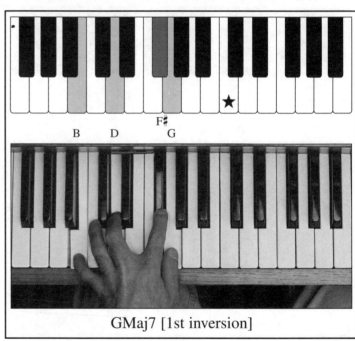

GMaj7 [1st inversion]

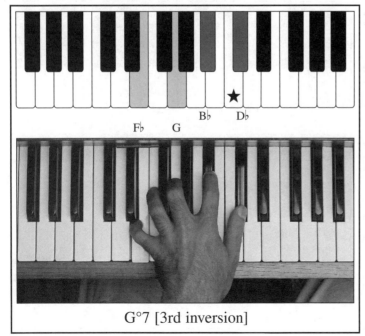

G°7 [3rd inversion]

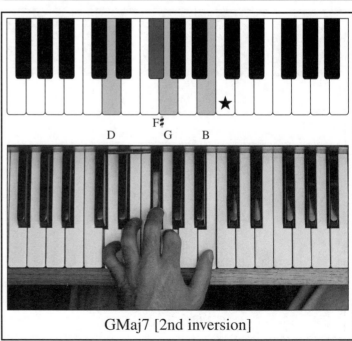

GMaj7 [2nd inversion]

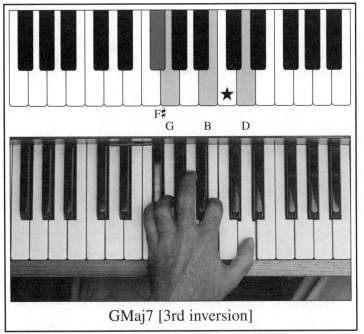

GMaj7 [3rd inversion]

Gm [2nd inversion]

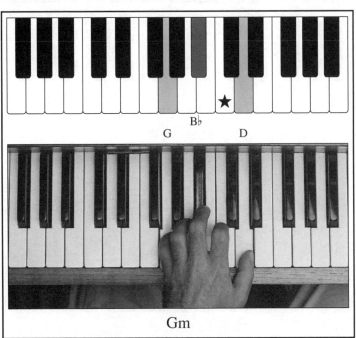

Gm

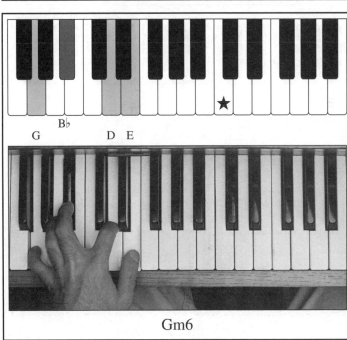

Gm6

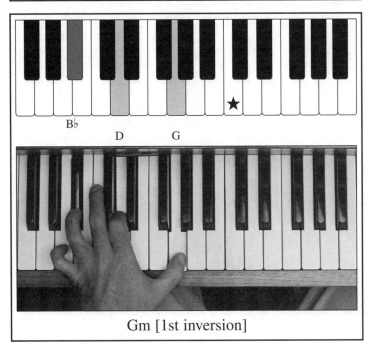

Gm [1st inversion]

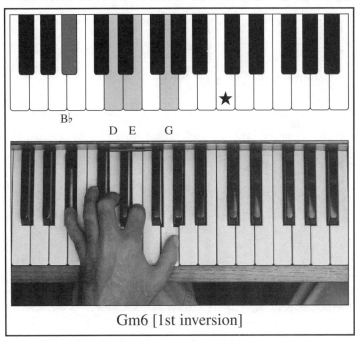

Gm6 [1st inversion]

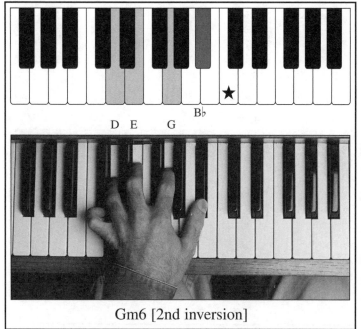

Gm6 [2nd inversion]

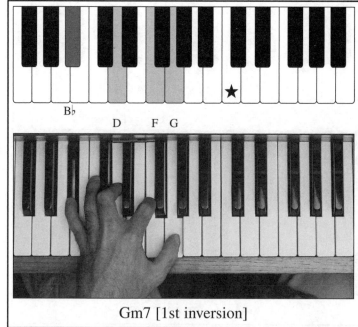

Gm7 [1st inversion]

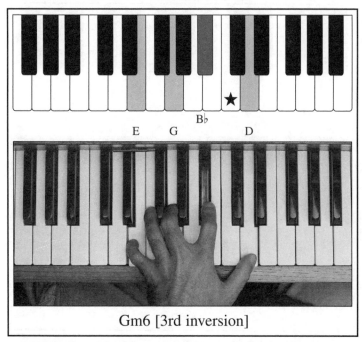

Gm6 [3rd inversion]

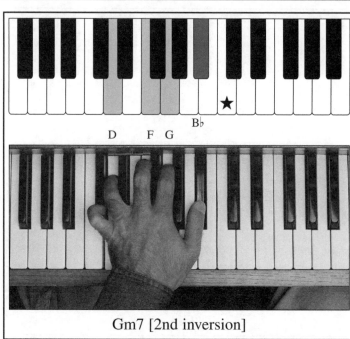

Gm7 [2nd inversion]

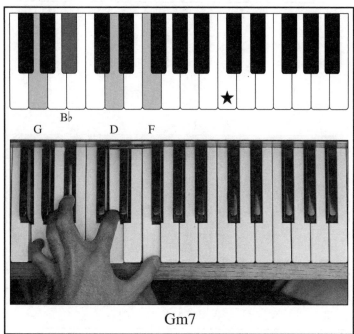

Gm7

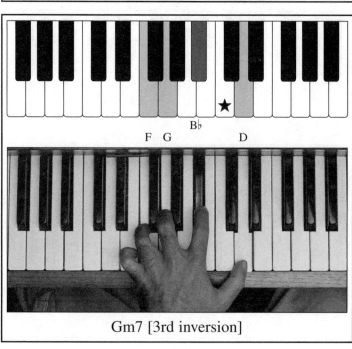

Gm7 [3rd inversion]

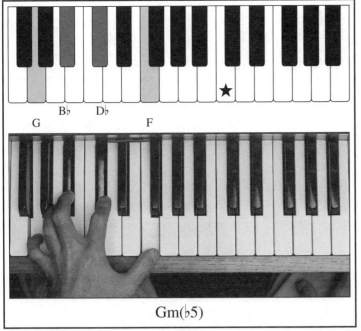

Gm(♭5)

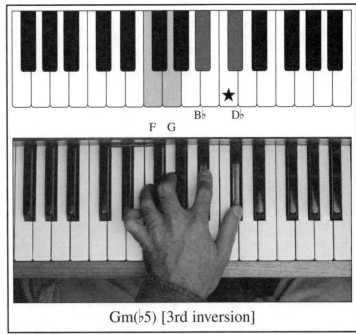

Gm(♭5) [3rd inversion]

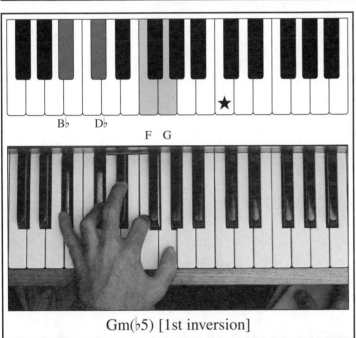

Gm(♭5) [1st inversion]

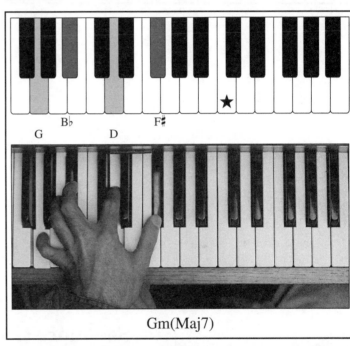

Gm(Maj7)

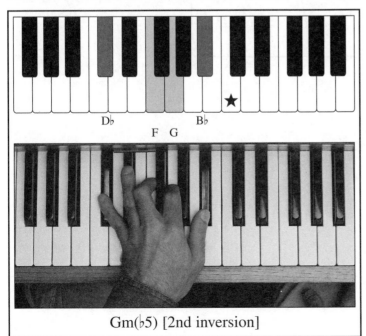

Gm(♭5) [2nd inversion]

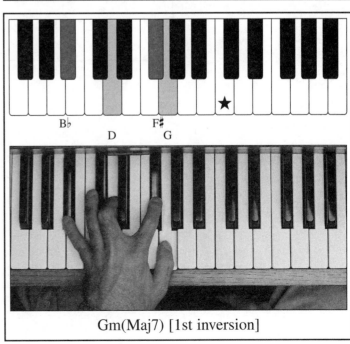

Gm(Maj7) [1st inversion]

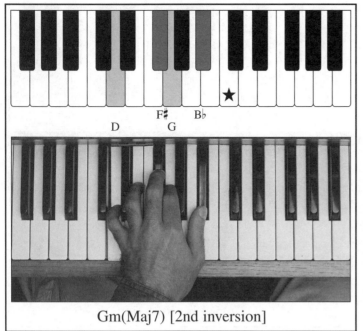

Gm(Maj7) [2nd inversion]

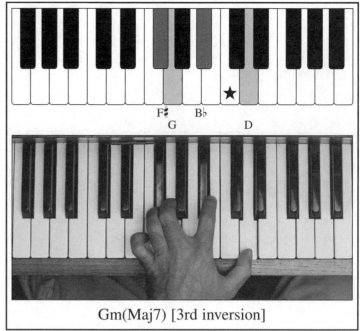

Gm(Maj7) [3rd inversion]

See more G chords in the
Chords for Two Hands **section**

D
Chords

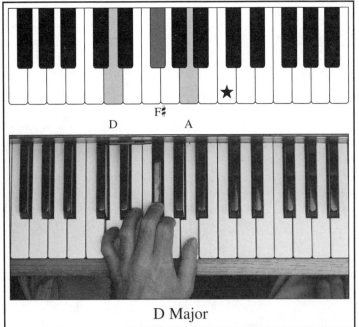

D Major

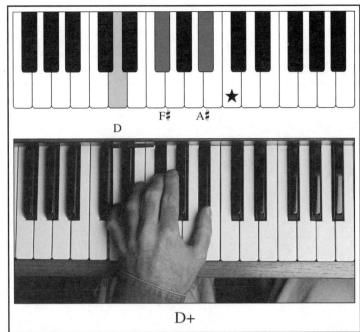

D+

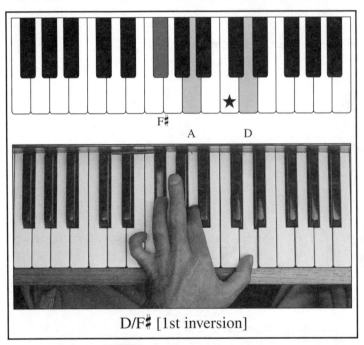

D/F♯ [1st inversion]

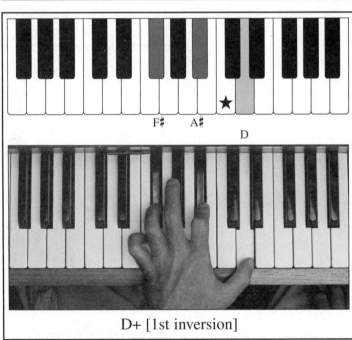

D+ [1st inversion]

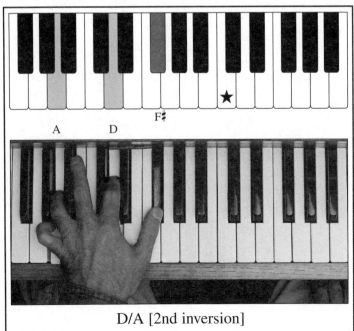

D/A [2nd inversion]

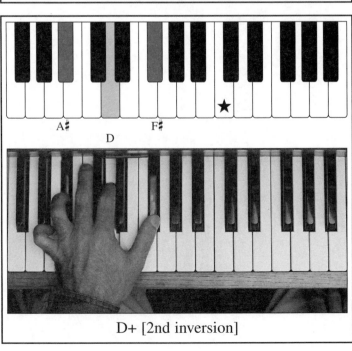

D+ [2nd inversion]

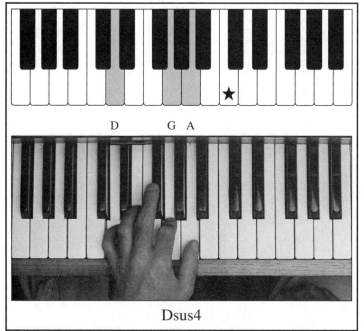

Dsus4

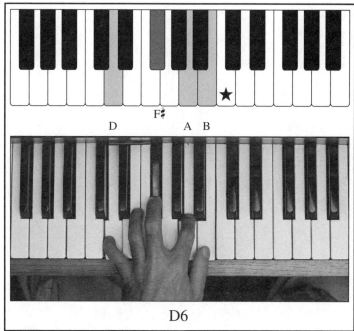

D6

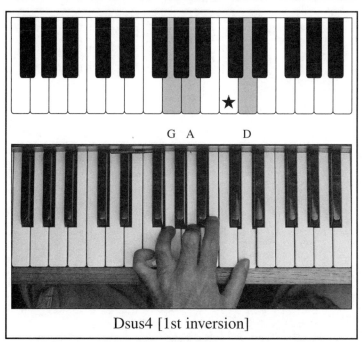

Dsus4 [1st inversion]

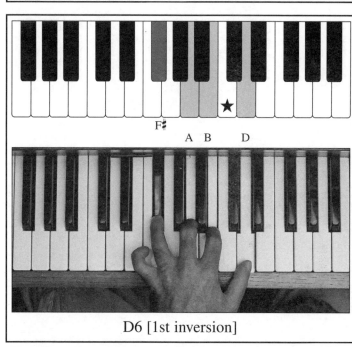

D6 [1st inversion]

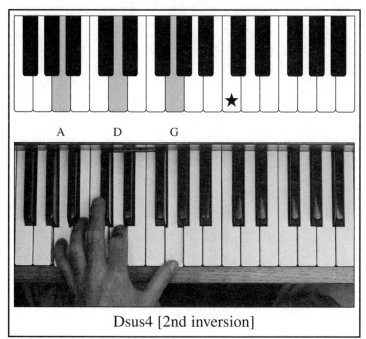

Dsus4 [2nd inversion]

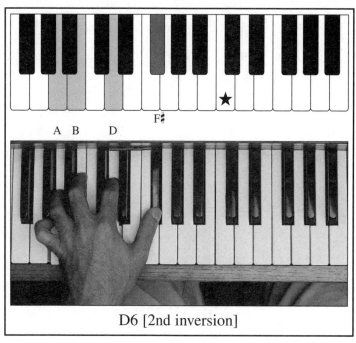

D6 [2nd inversion]

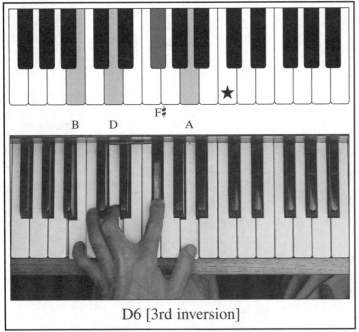

B D F♯ A

D6 [3rd inversion]

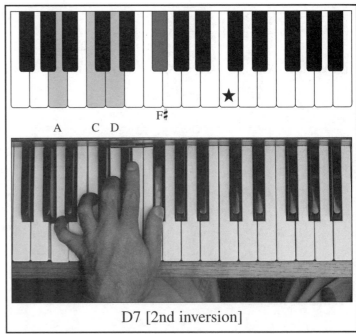

A C D F♯

D7 [2nd inversion]

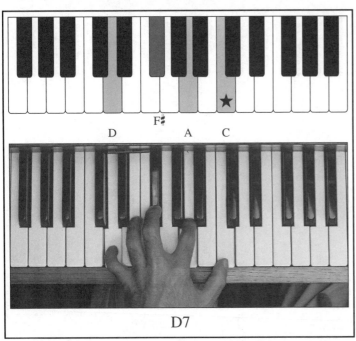

D F♯ A C

D7

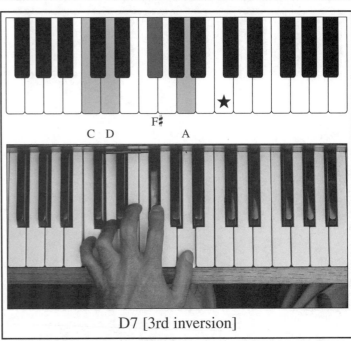

C D F♯ A

D7 [3rd inversion]

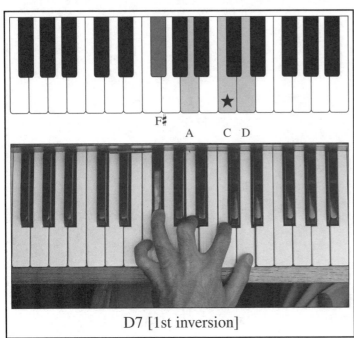

F♯ A C D

D7 [1st inversion]

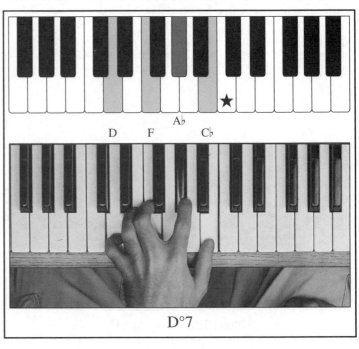

D F A♭ C♭

D°7

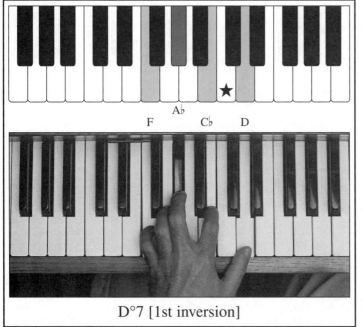

D°7 [1st inversion]

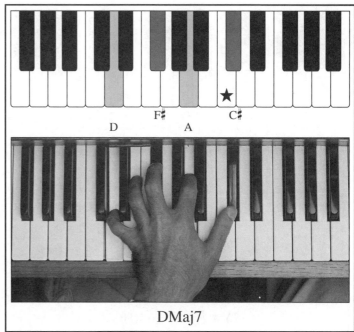

DMaj7

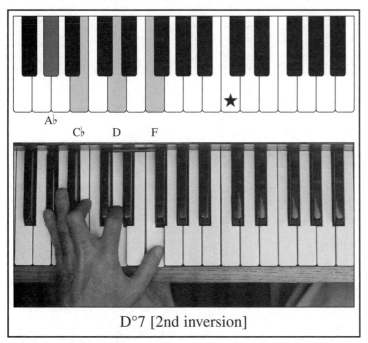

D°7 [2nd inversion]

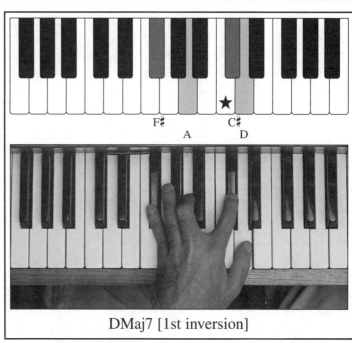

DMaj7 [1st inversion]

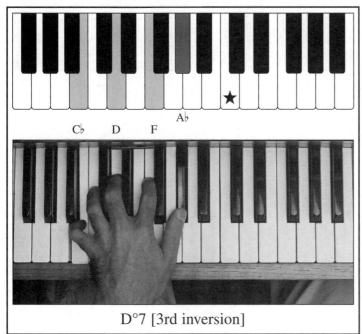

D°7 [3rd inversion]

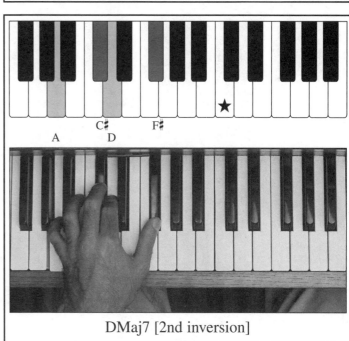

DMaj7 [2nd inversion]

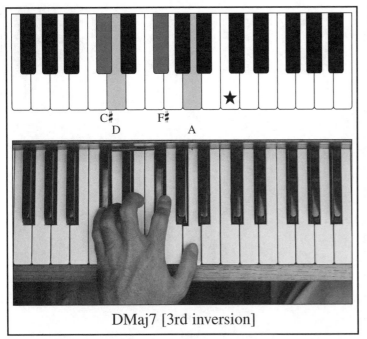

DMaj7 [3rd inversion]

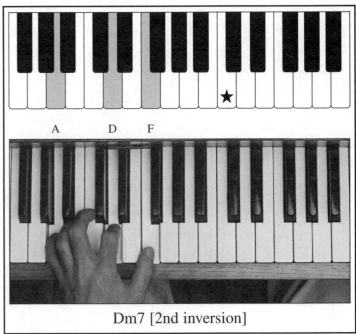

Dm7 [2nd inversion]

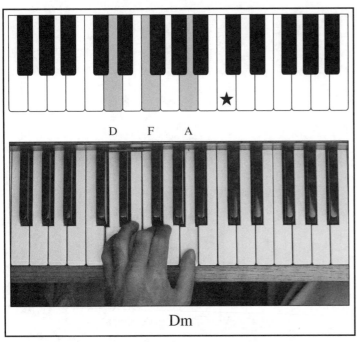

Dm

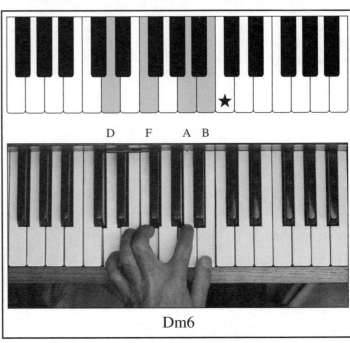

Dm6

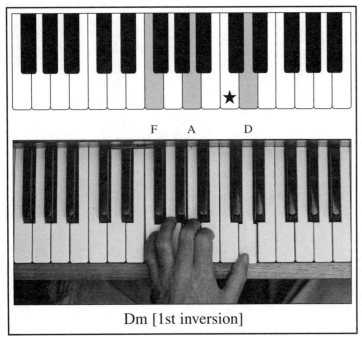

Dm [1st inversion]

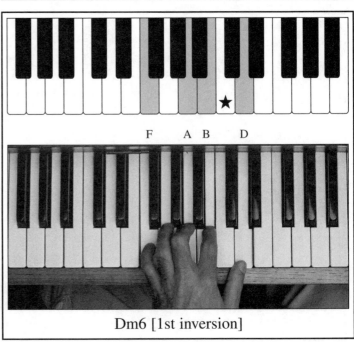

Dm6 [1st inversion]

A B D F

Dm6 [2nd inversion]

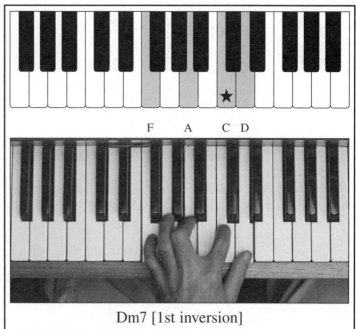

F A C D

Dm7 [1st inversion]

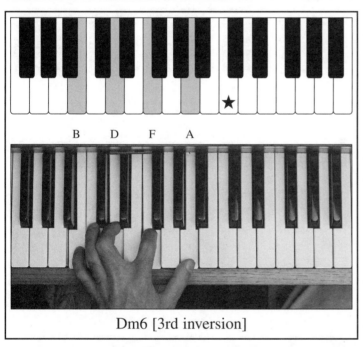

B D F A

Dm6 [3rd inversion]

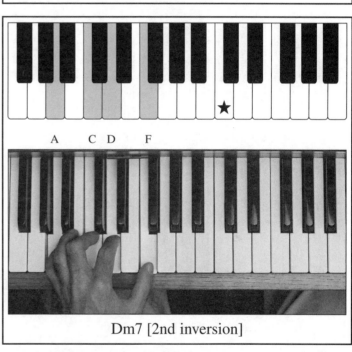

A C D F

Dm7 [2nd inversion]

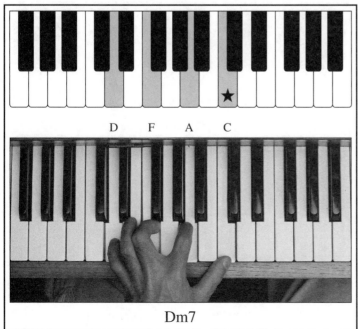

D F A C

Dm7

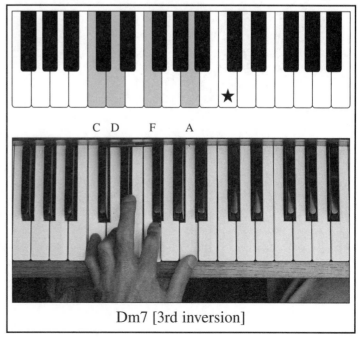

C D F A

Dm7 [3rd inversion]

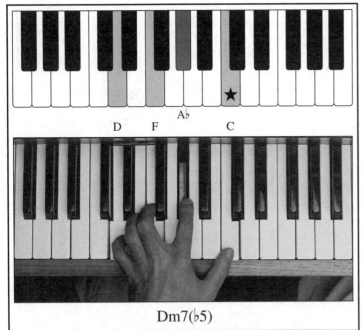

Dm7(♭5)

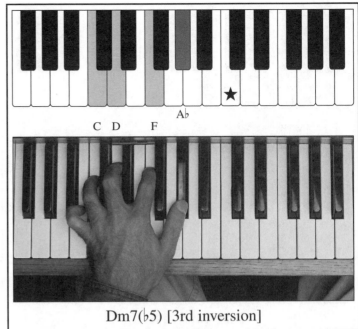

Dm7(♭5) [3rd inversion]

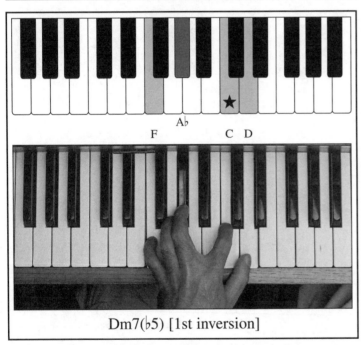

Dm7(♭5) [1st inversion]

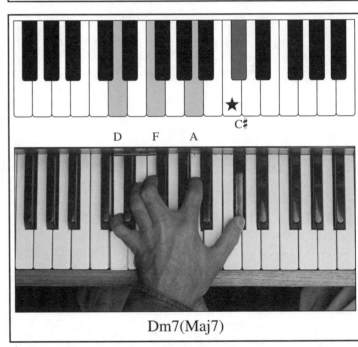

Dm7(Maj7)

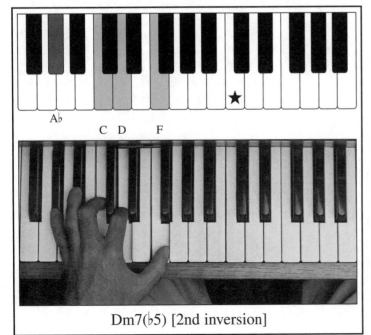

Dm7(♭5) [2nd inversion]

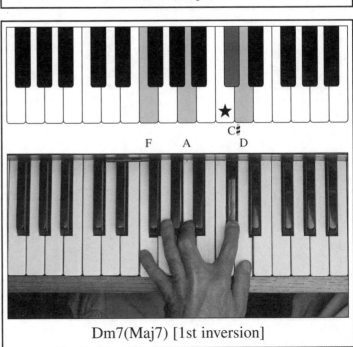

Dm7(Maj7) [1st inversion]

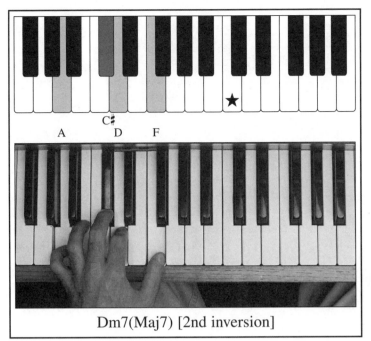

Dm7(Maj7) [2nd inversion]

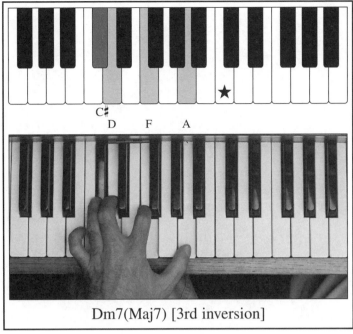

Dm7(Maj7) [3rd inversion]

See more D chords in the *Chords for Two Hands* section

A
Chords

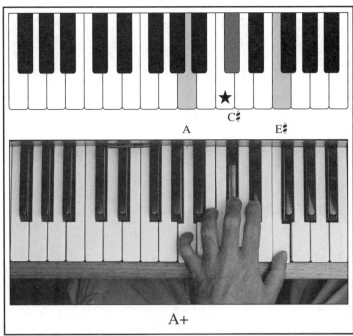

A Major

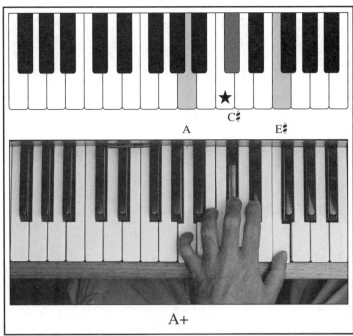

A+

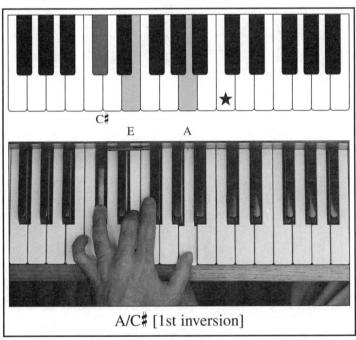

A/C♯ [1st inversion]

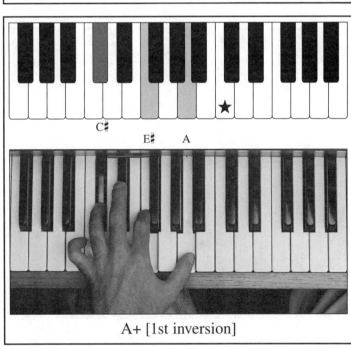

A+ [1st inversion]

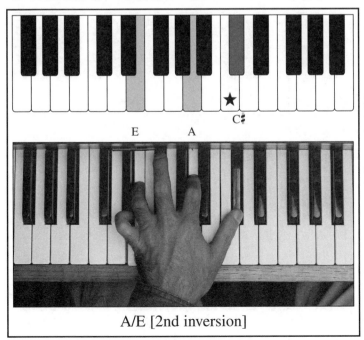

A/E [2nd inversion]

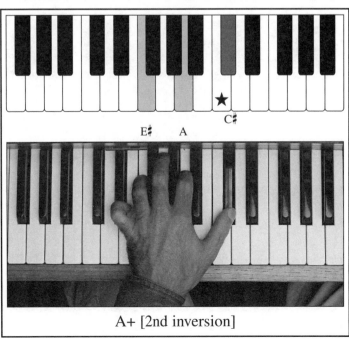

A+ [2nd inversion]

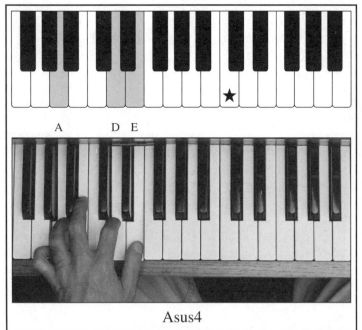

Asus4

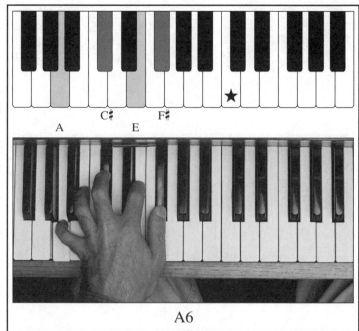

A6

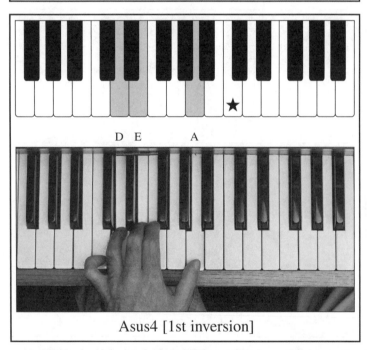

Asus4 [1st inversion]

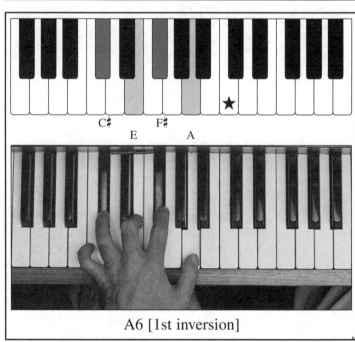

A6 [1st inversion]

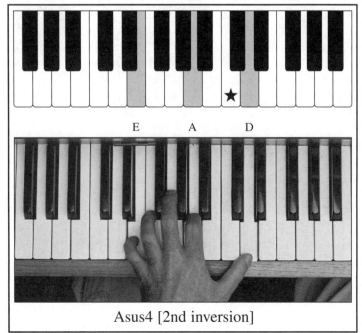

Asus4 [2nd inversion]

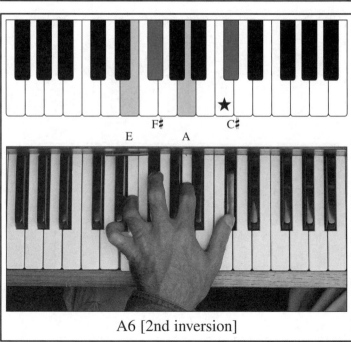

A6 [2nd inversion]

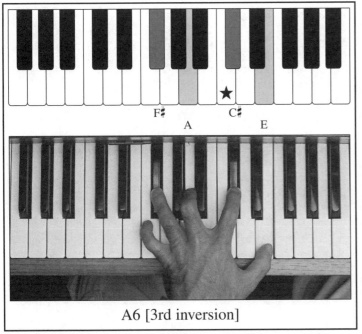

A6 [3rd inversion]

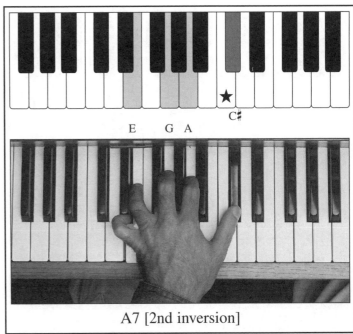

A7 [2nd inversion]

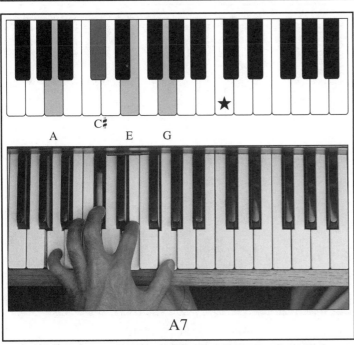

A7

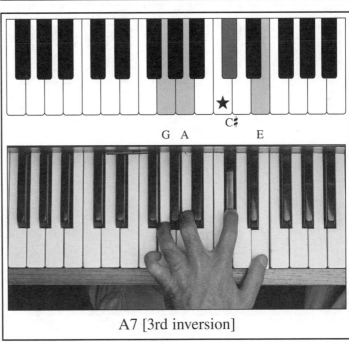

A7 [3rd inversion]

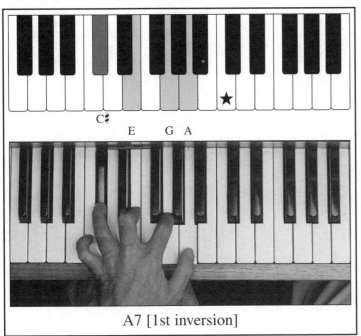

A7 [1st inversion]

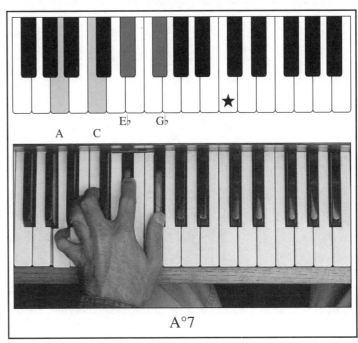

A°7

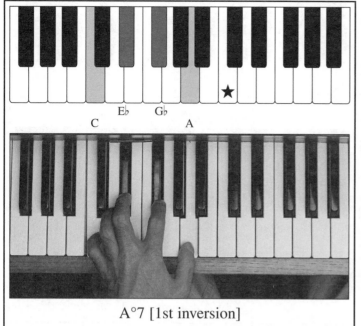

A°7 [1st inversion]

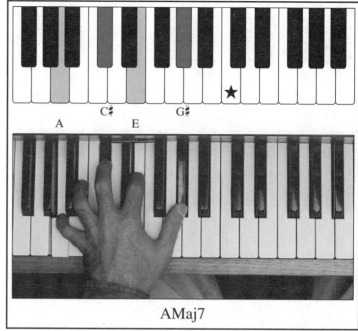

AMaj7

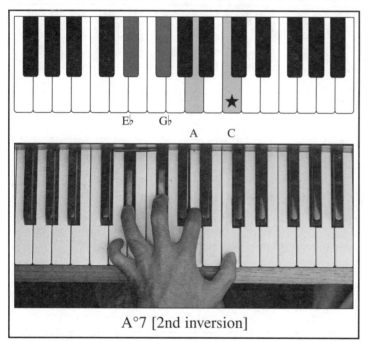

A°7 [2nd inversion]

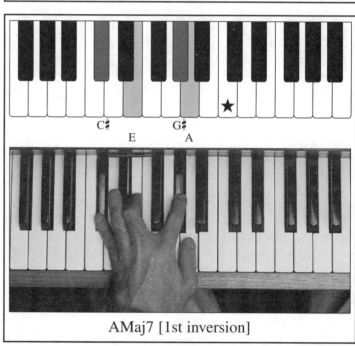

AMaj7 [1st inversion]

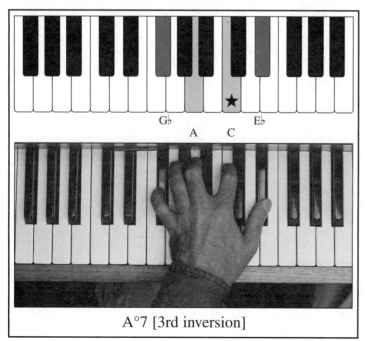

A°7 [3rd inversion]

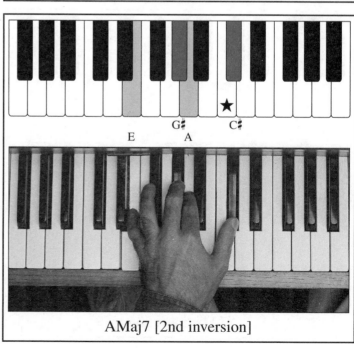

AMaj7 [2nd inversion]

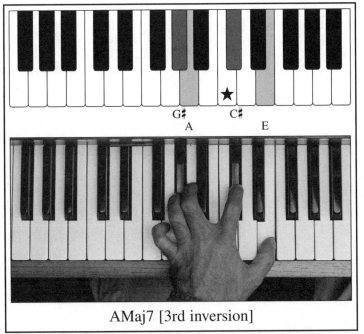

AMaj7 [3rd inversion]

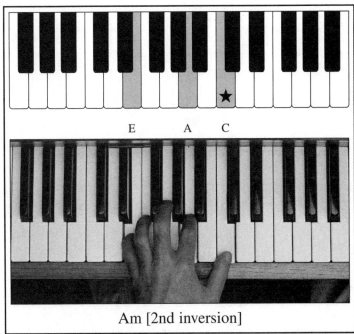

Am [2nd inversion]

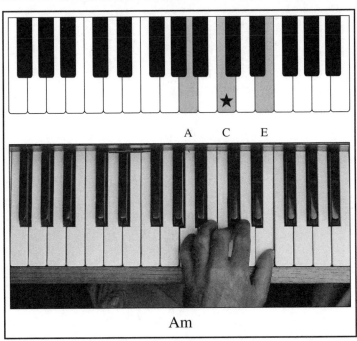

Am

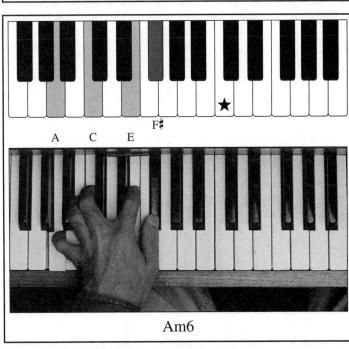

Am6

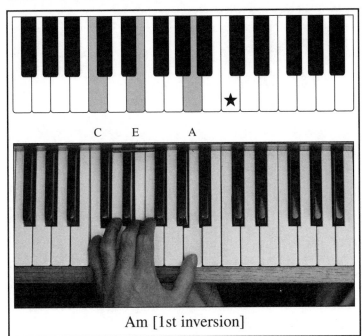

Am [1st inversion]

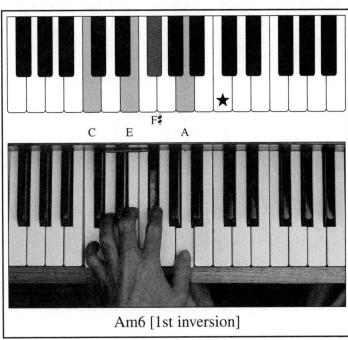

Am6 [1st inversion]

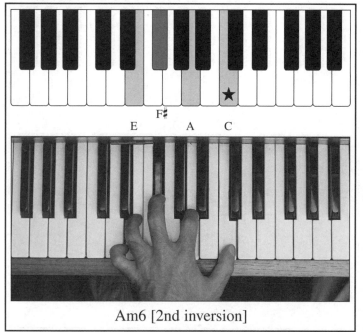

F#
E   A   C

Am6 [2nd inversion]

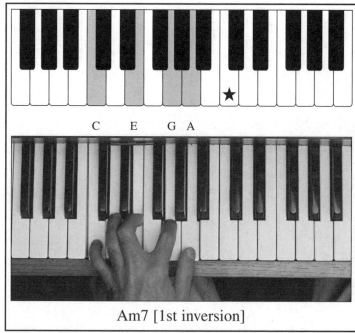

C   E   G A

Am7 [1st inversion]

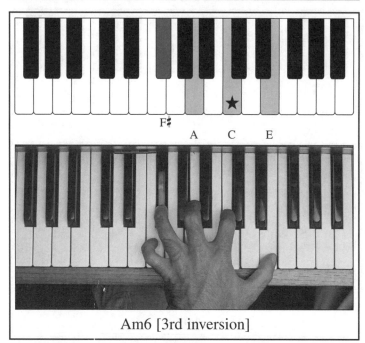

F#
A   C   E

Am6 [3rd inversion]

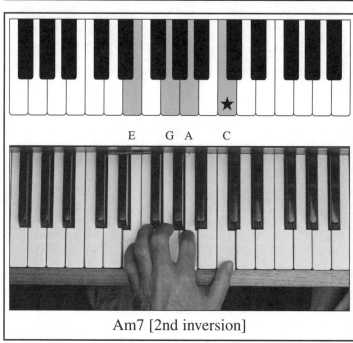

E   G A   C

Am7 [2nd inversion]

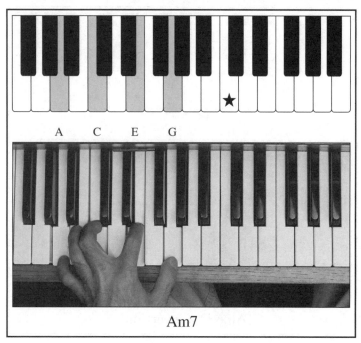

A   C   E   G

Am7

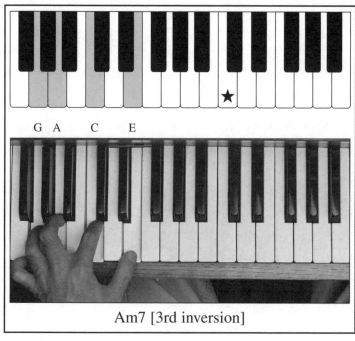

G A   C   E

Am7 [3rd inversion]

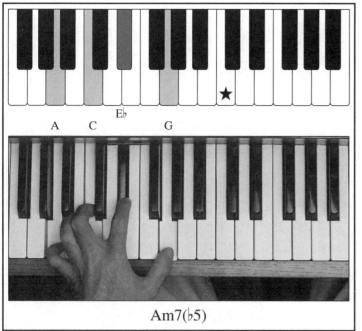

Am7(♭5)

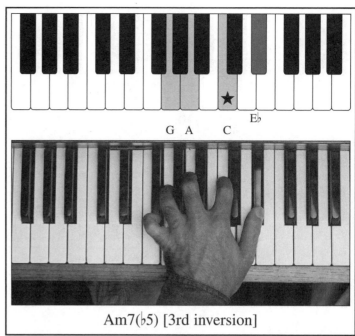

Am7(♭5) [3rd inversion]

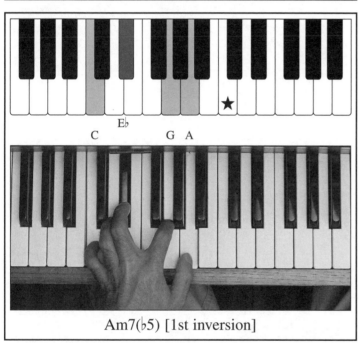

Am7(♭5) [1st inversion]

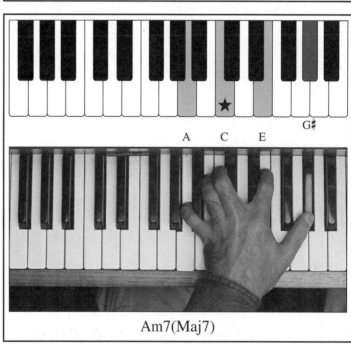

Am7(Maj7)

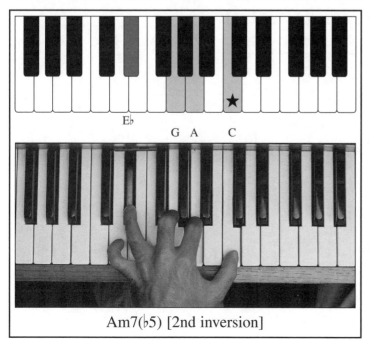

Am7(♭5) [2nd inversion]

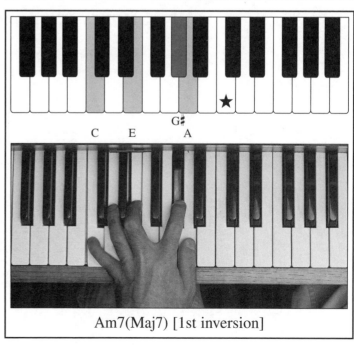

Am7(Maj7) [1st inversion]

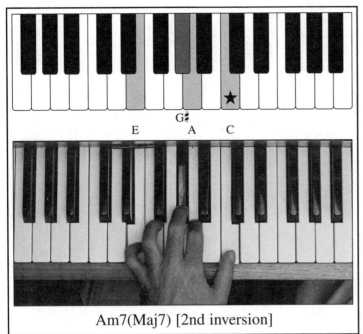

Am7(Maj7) [2nd inversion]

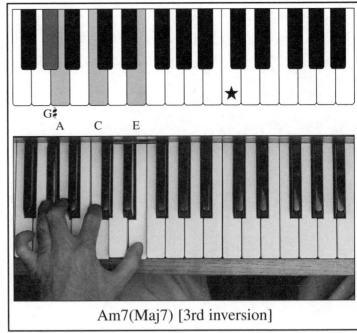

Am7(Maj7) [3rd inversion]

See more A chords in the
Chords for Two Hands **section**

E
Chords

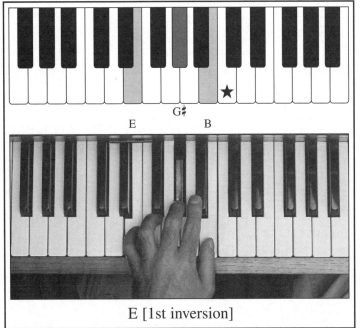

E [1st inversion]

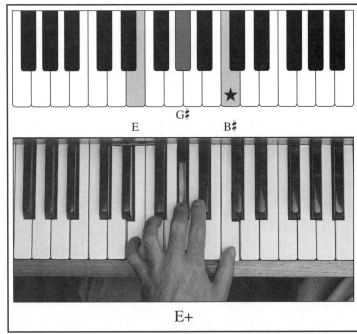

E+

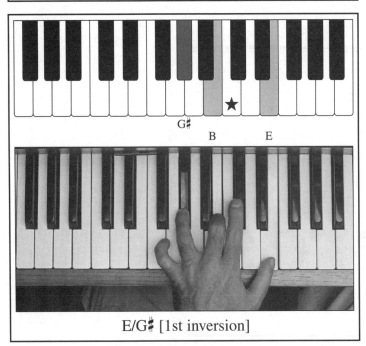

E/G♯ [1st inversion]

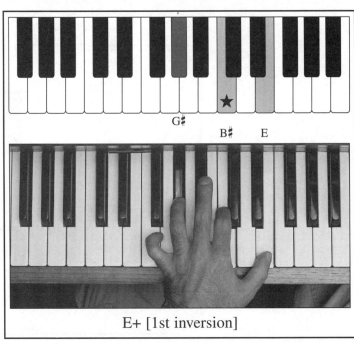

E+ [1st inversion]

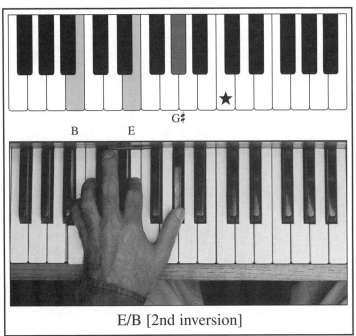

E/B [2nd inversion]

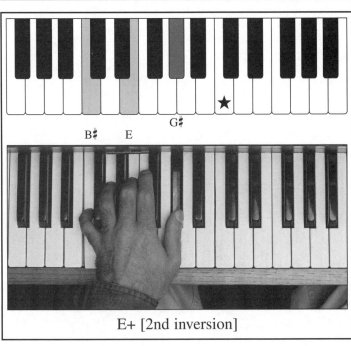

E+ [2nd inversion]

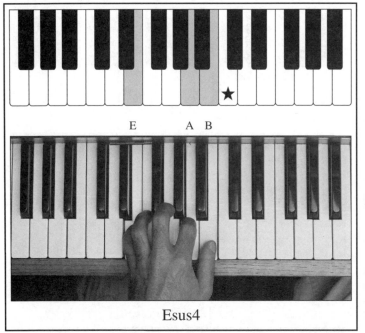

Esus4

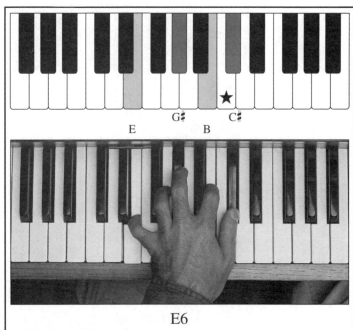

E6

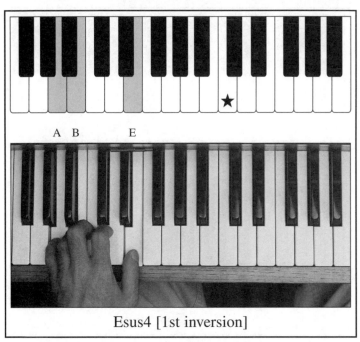

Esus4 [1st inversion]

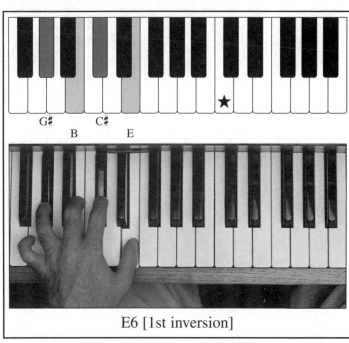

E6 [1st inversion]

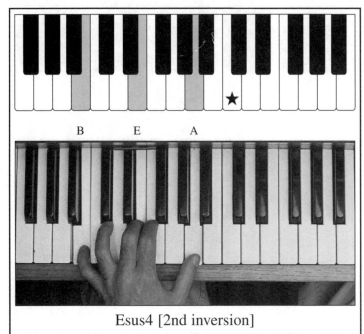

Esus4 [2nd inversion]

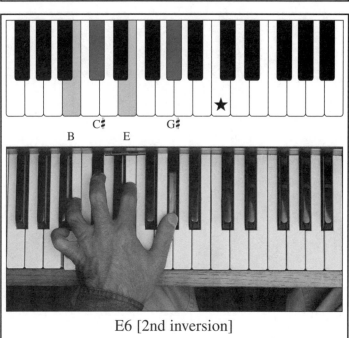

E6 [2nd inversion]

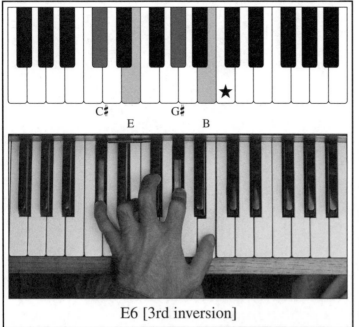

E6 [3rd inversion]

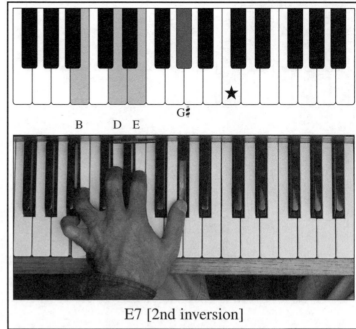

E7 [2nd inversion]

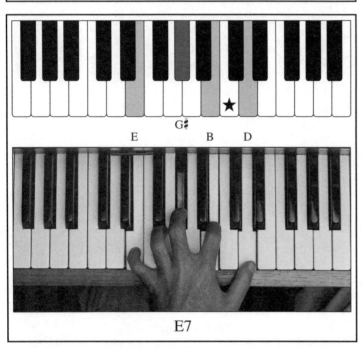

E7

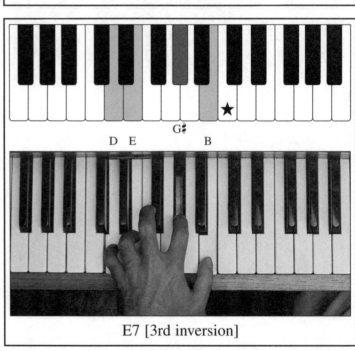

E7 [3rd inversion]

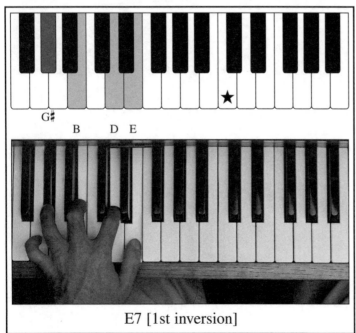

E7 [1st inversion]

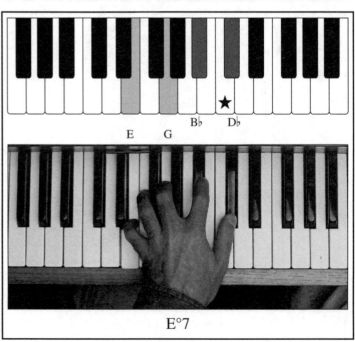

E°7

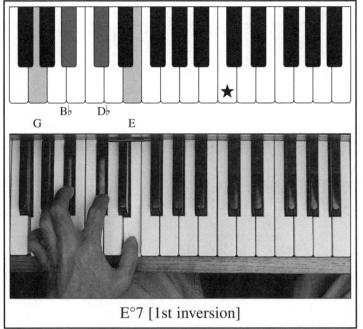

E°7 [1st inversion]

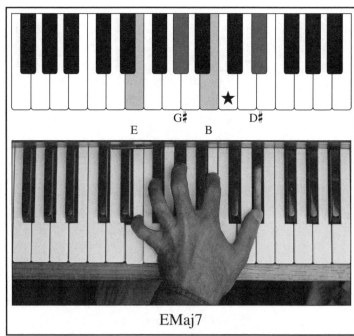

EMaj7

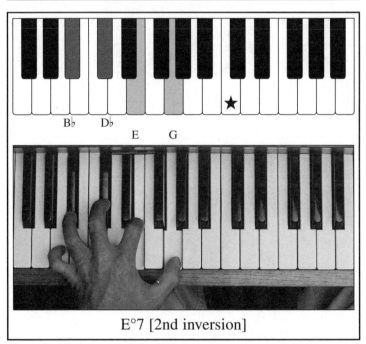

E°7 [2nd inversion]

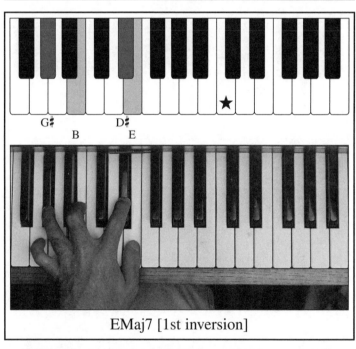

EMaj7 [1st inversion]

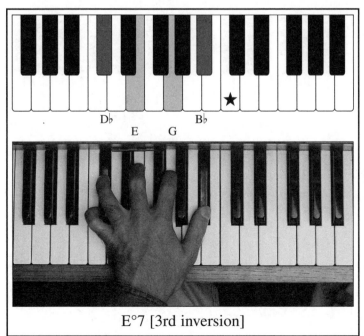

E°7 [3rd inversion]

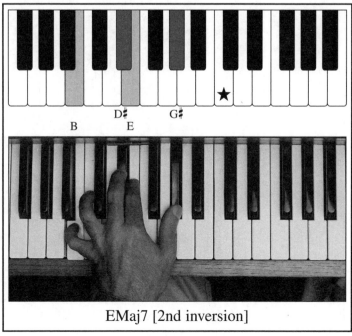

EMaj7 [2nd inversion]

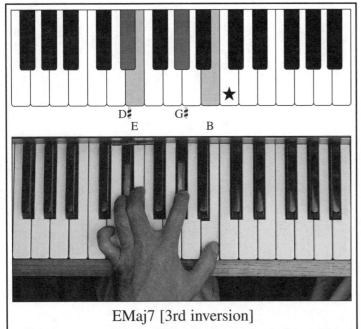

EMaj7 [3rd inversion]

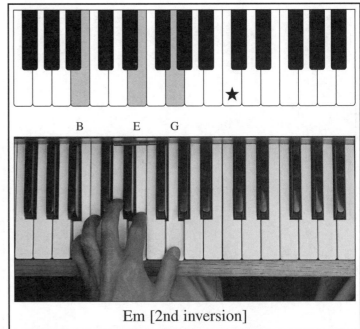

Em [2nd inversion]

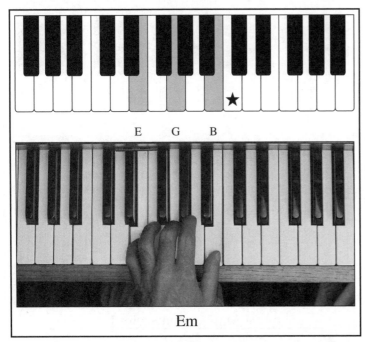

Em

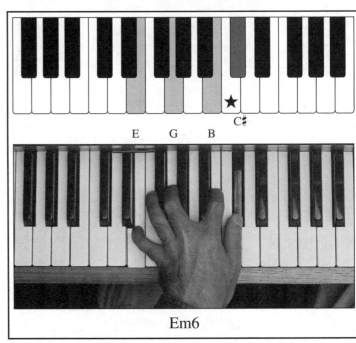

Em6

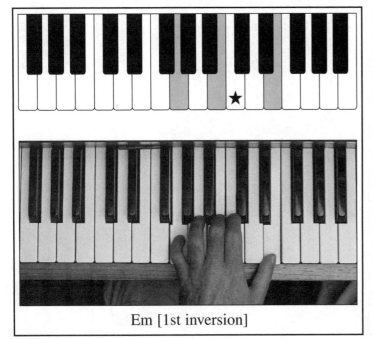

Em [1st inversion]

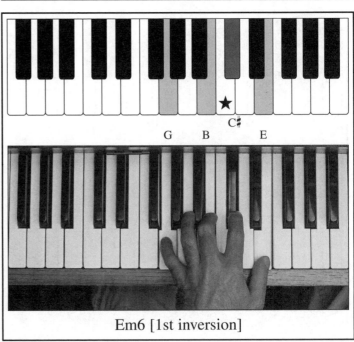

Em6 [1st inversion]

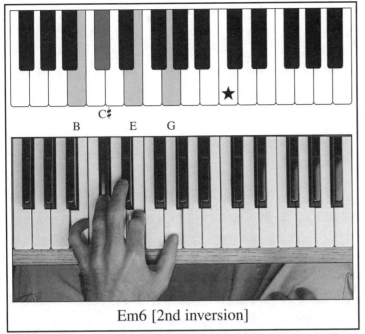

Em6 [2nd inversion]

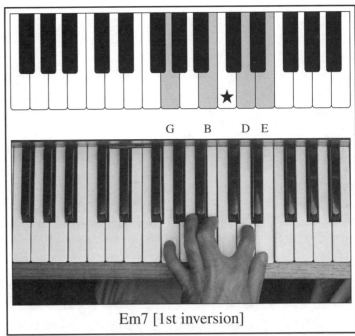

Em7 [1st inversion]

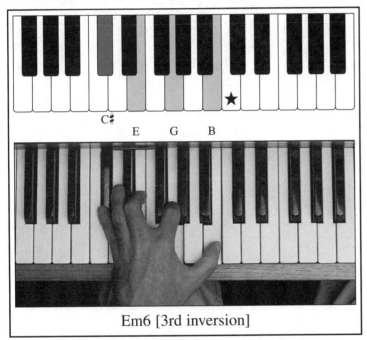

Em6 [3rd inversion]

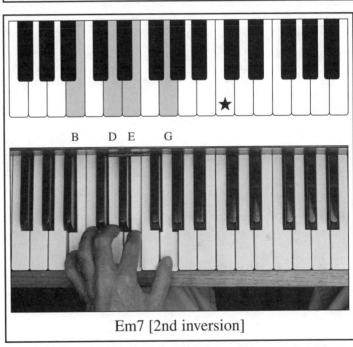

Em7 [2nd inversion]

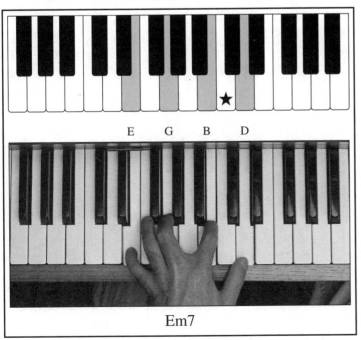

Em7

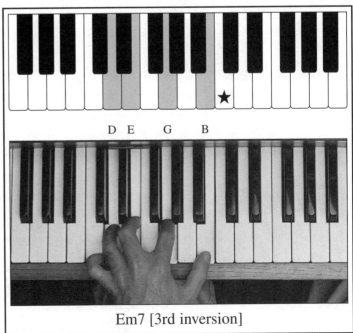

Em7 [3rd inversion]

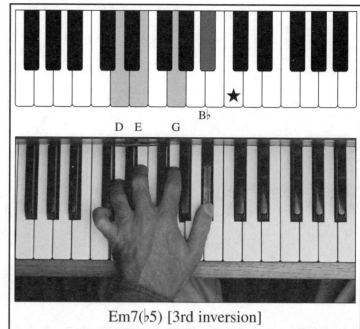

Em7(♭5)

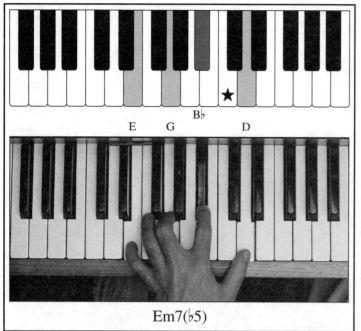

Em7(♭5) [3rd inversion]

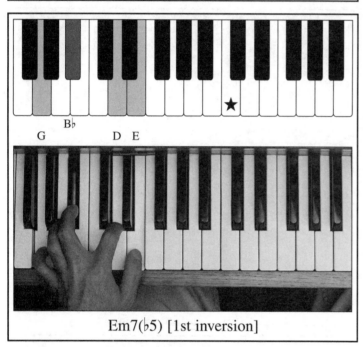

Em7(♭5) [1st inversion]

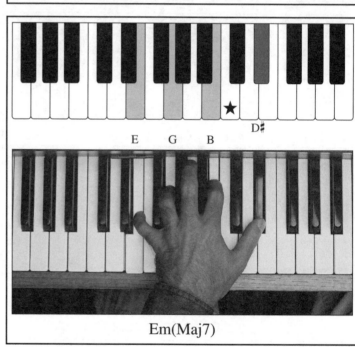

Em(Maj7)

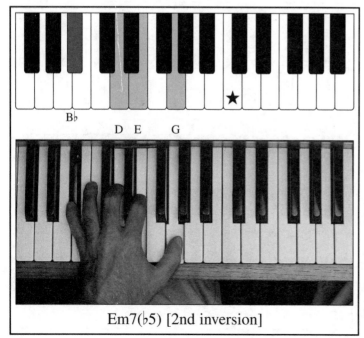

Em7(♭5) [2nd inversion]

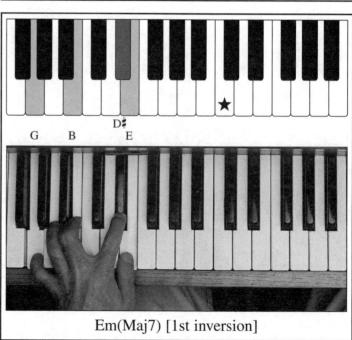

Em(Maj7) [1st inversion]

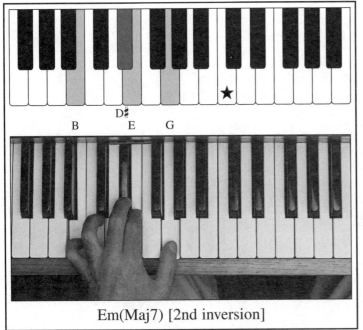

Em(Maj7) [2nd inversion]

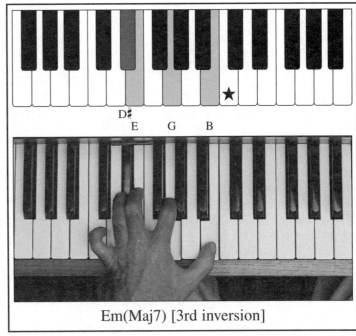

Em(Maj7) [3rd inversion]

See more E chords in the
Chords for Two Hands **section**

B
Chords

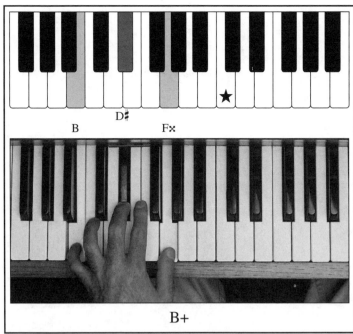

B Major

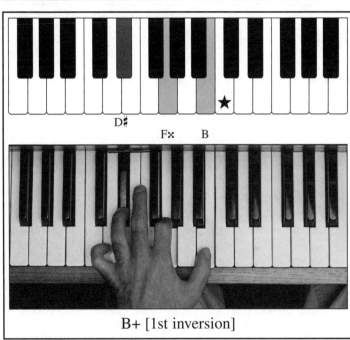

B+

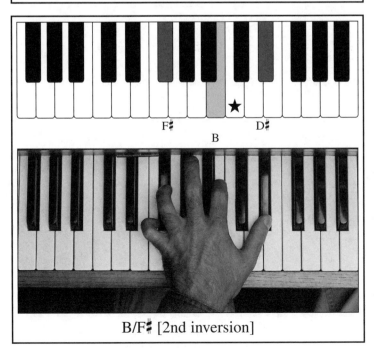

B/D♯ [1st inversion]

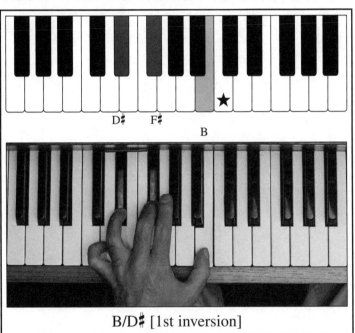

B+ [1st inversion]

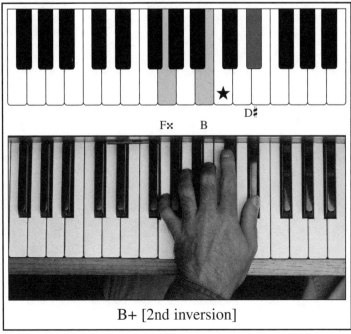

B/F♯ [2nd inversion]

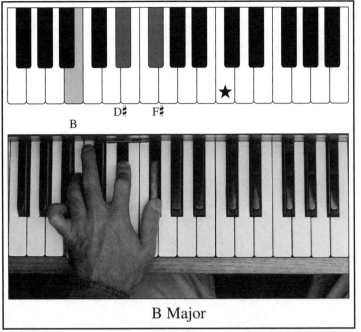

B+ [2nd inversion]

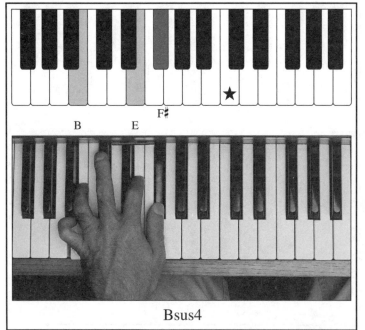

Bsus4

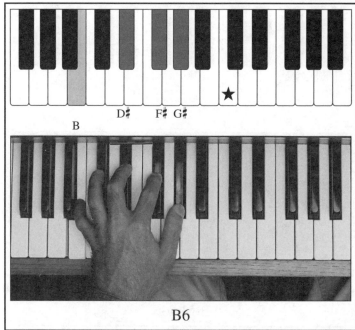

B6

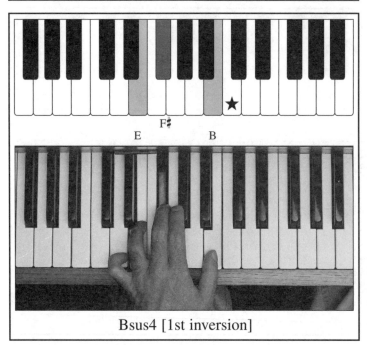

Bsus4 [1st inversion]

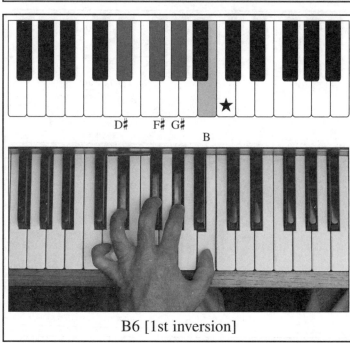

B6 [1st inversion]

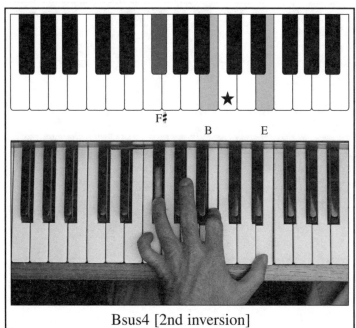

Bsus4 [2nd inversion]

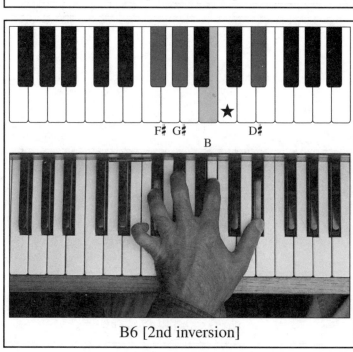

B6 [2nd inversion]

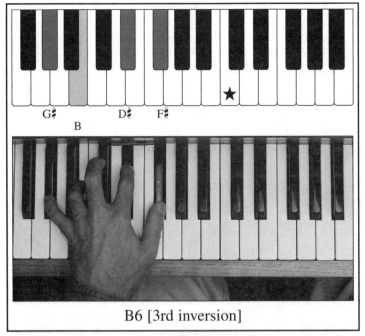

B6 [3rd inversion]

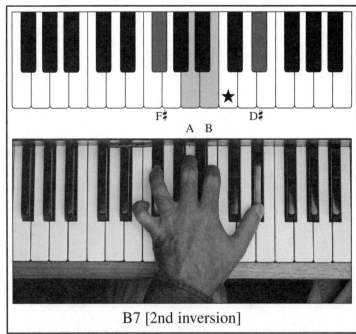

B7 [2nd inversion]

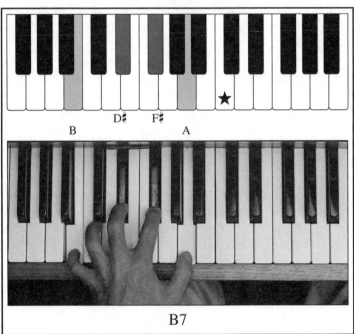

B7

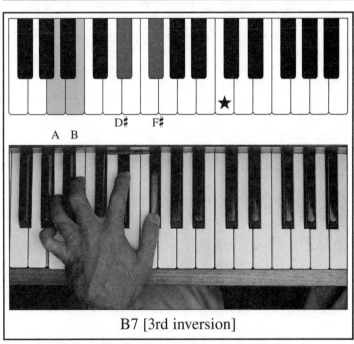

B7 [3rd inversion]

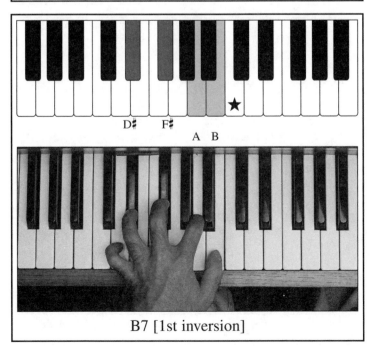

B7 [1st inversion]

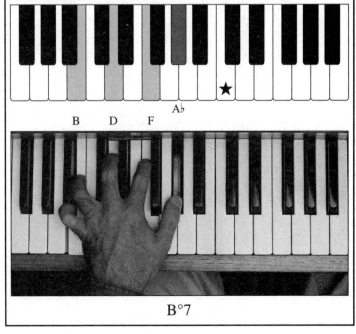

B°7

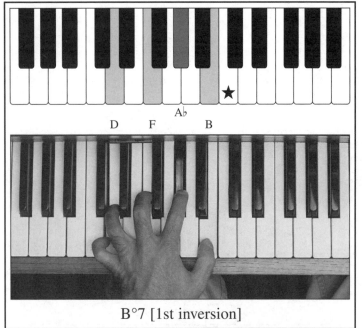

B°7 [1st inversion]

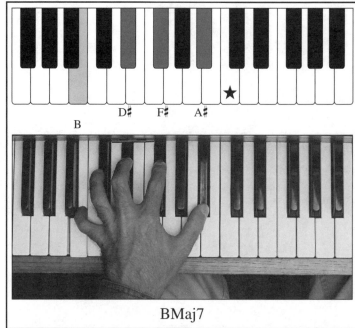

BMaj7

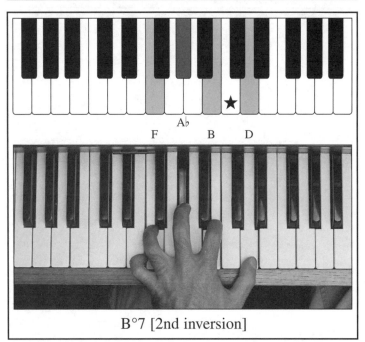

B°7 [2nd inversion]

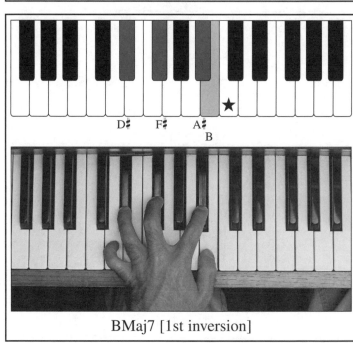

BMaj7 [1st inversion]

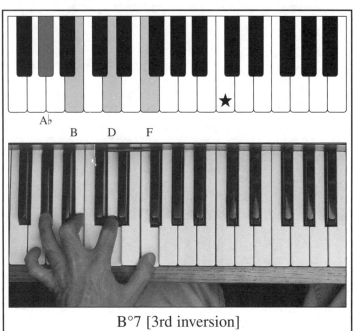

B°7 [3rd inversion]

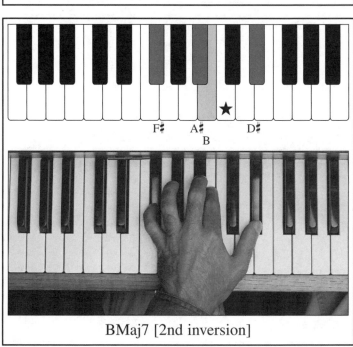

BMaj7 [2nd inversion]

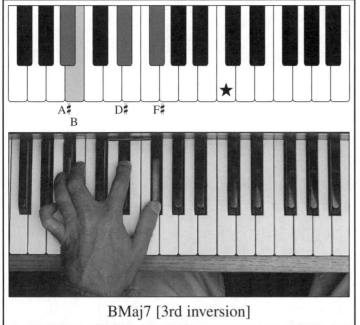

BMaj7 [3rd inversion]

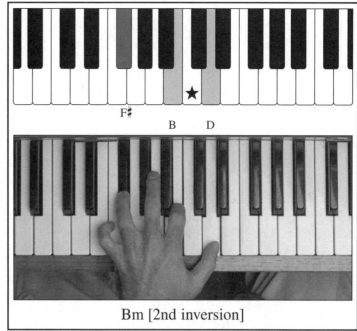

Bm [2nd inversion]

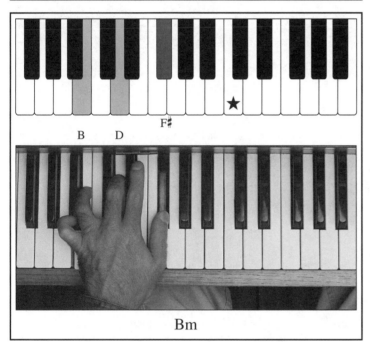

Bm

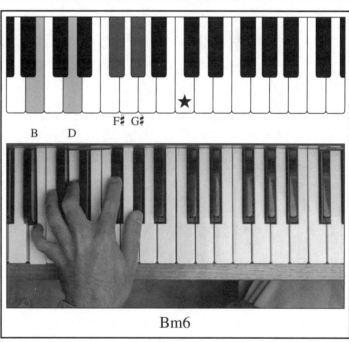

Bm6

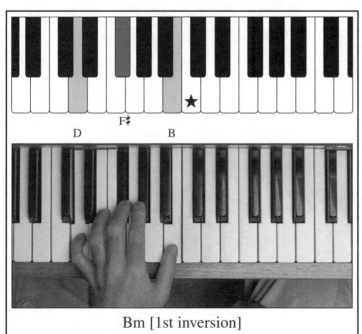

Bm [1st inversion]

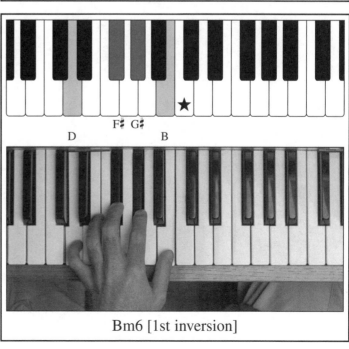

Bm6 [1st inversion]

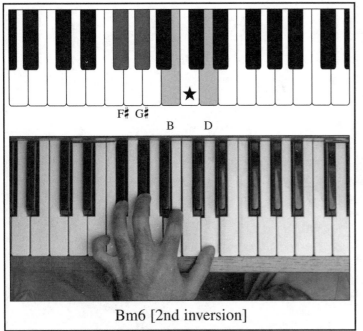

Bm6 [2nd inversion]

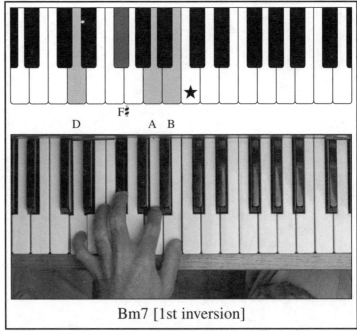

Bm7 [1st inversion]

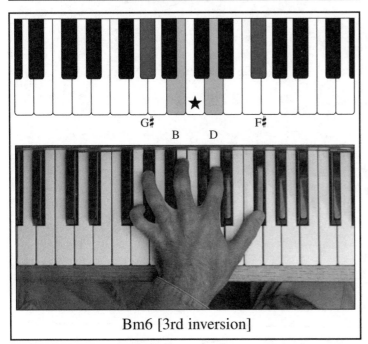

Bm6 [3rd inversion]

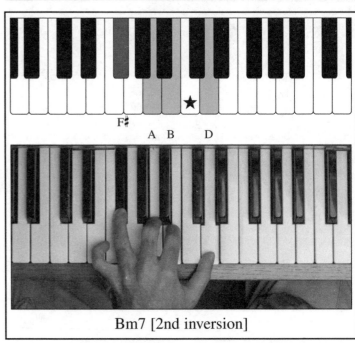

Bm7 [2nd inversion]

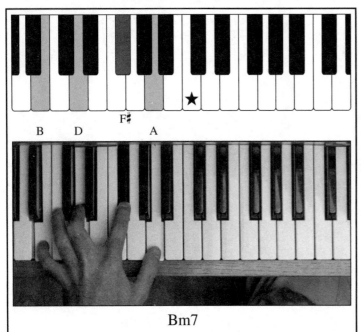

Bm7

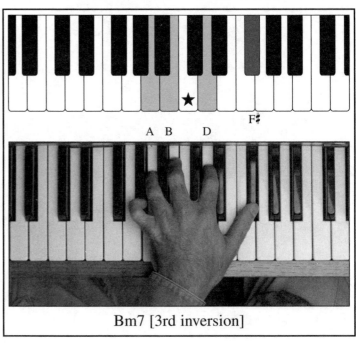

Bm7 [3rd inversion]

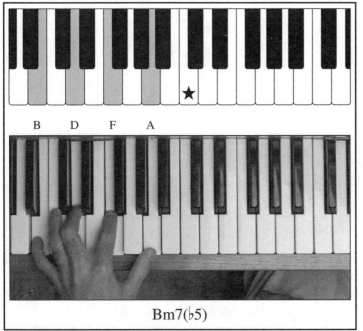

Bm7(♭5)

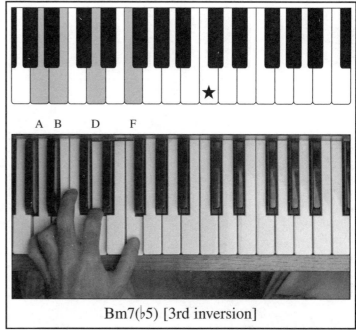

Bm7(♭5) [3rd inversion]

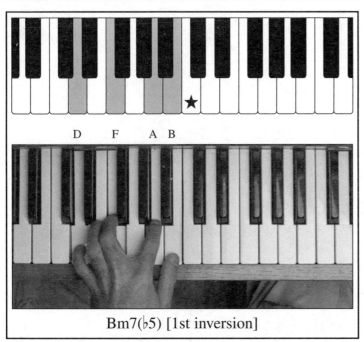

Bm7(♭5) [1st inversion]

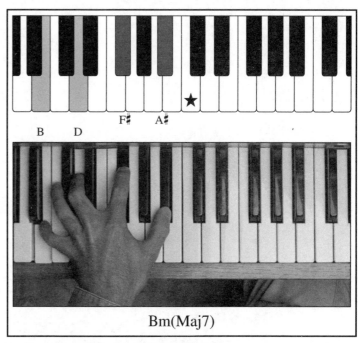

Bm(Maj7)

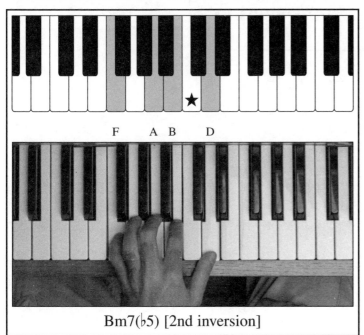

Bm7(♭5) [2nd inversion]

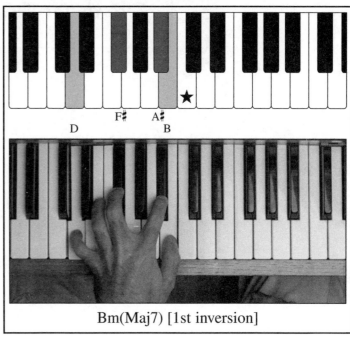

Bm(Maj7) [1st inversion]

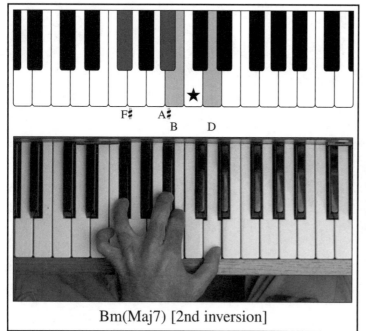

Bm(Maj7) [2nd inversion]

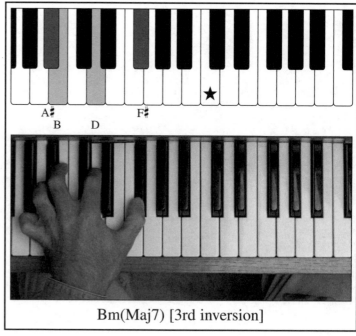

Bm(Maj7) [3rd inversion]

See more B chords in the
Chords for Two Hands **section**

F♯

Chords

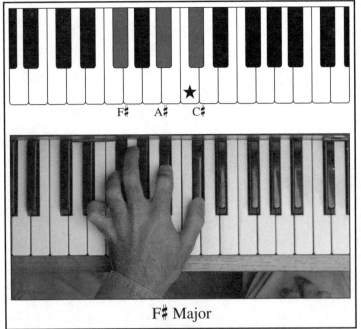

F♯ Major

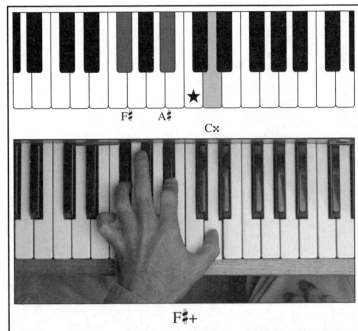

F♯+

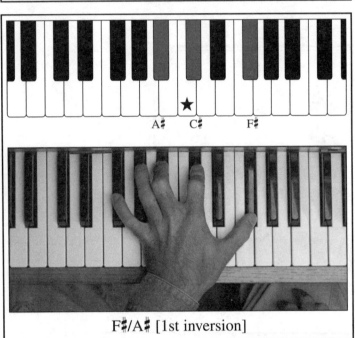

F♯/A♯ [1st inversion]

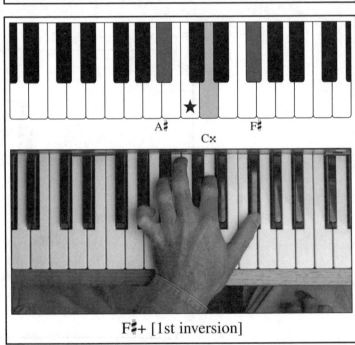

F♯+ [1st inversion]

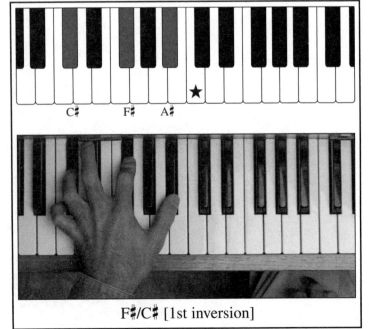

F♯/C♯ [1st inversion]

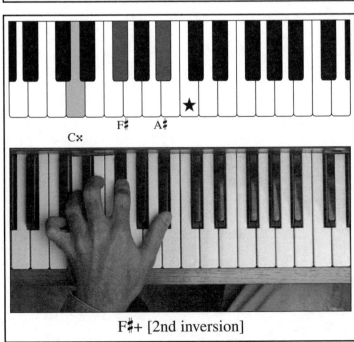

F♯+ [2nd inversion]

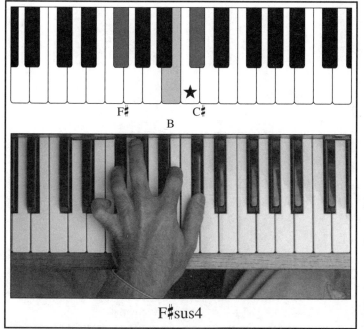

F#sus4

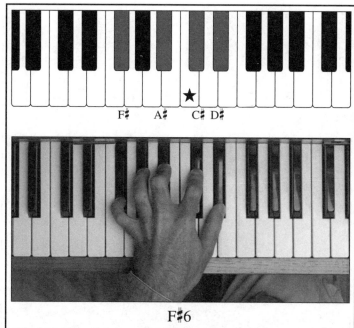

F#6

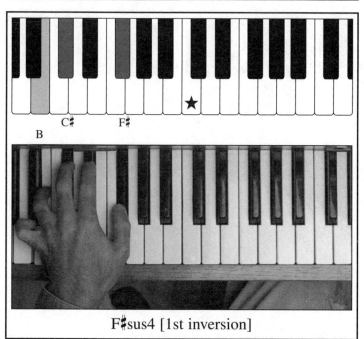

F#sus4 [1st inversion]

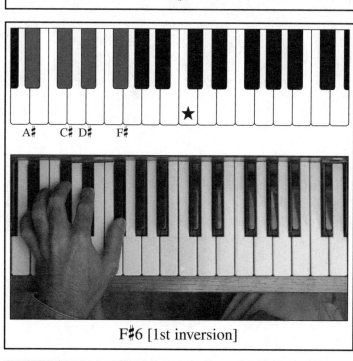

F#6 [1st inversion]

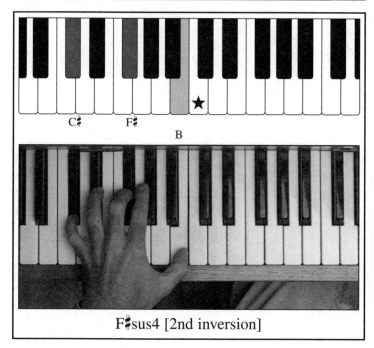

F#sus4 [2nd inversion]

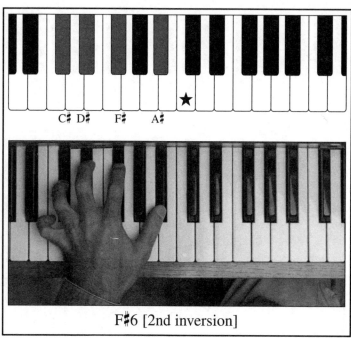

F#6 [2nd inversion]

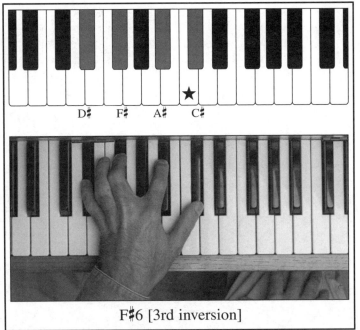

F#6 [3rd inversion]

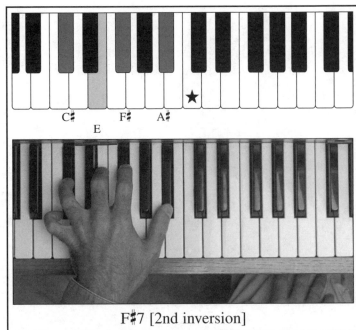

F#7 [2nd inversion]

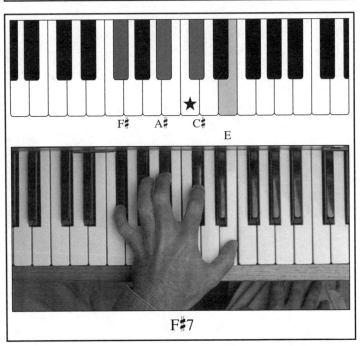

F#7

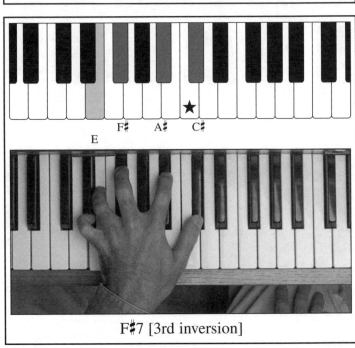

F#7 [3rd inversion]

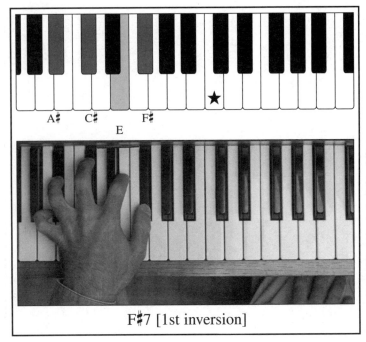

F#7 [1st inversion]

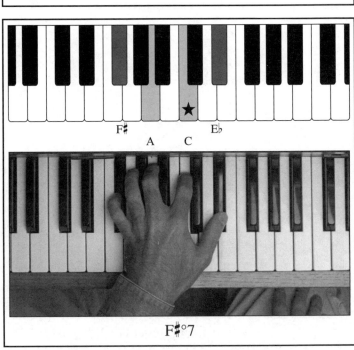

F#°7

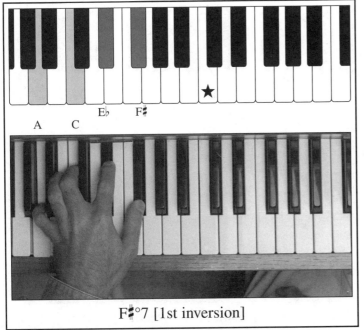

F#°7 [1st inversion]

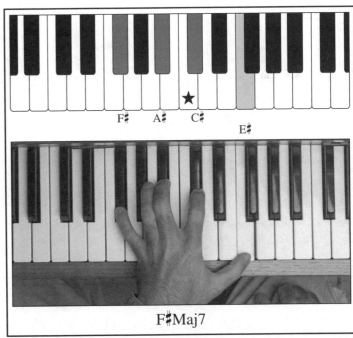

F#Maj7

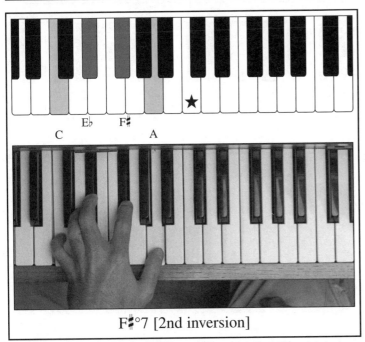

F#°7 [2nd inversion]

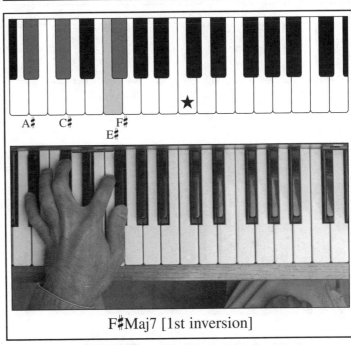

F#Maj7 [1st inversion]

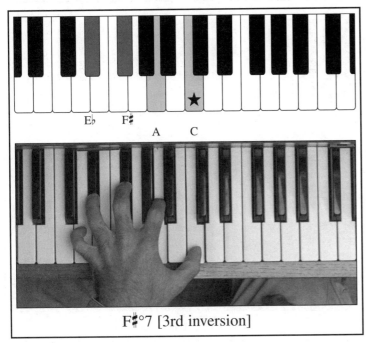

F#°7 [3rd inversion]

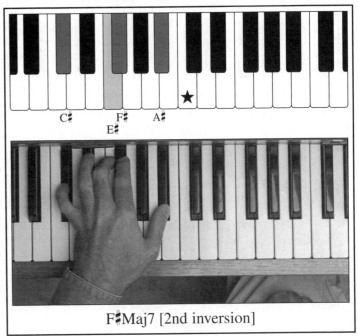

F#Maj7 [2nd inversion]

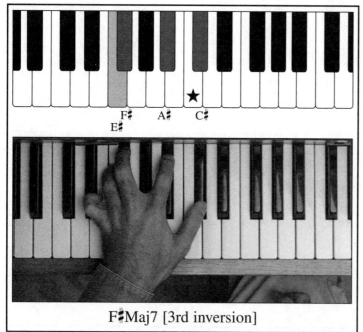

F#Maj7 [3rd inversion]

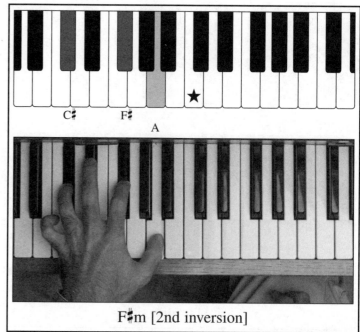

F#m [2nd inversion]

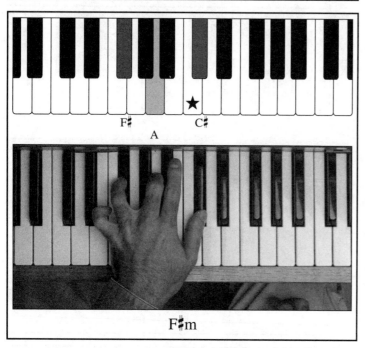

F#m

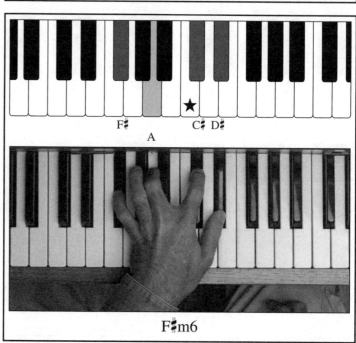

F#m6

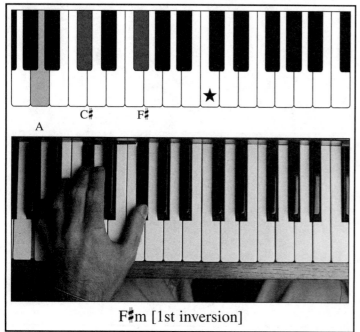

F#m [1st inversion]

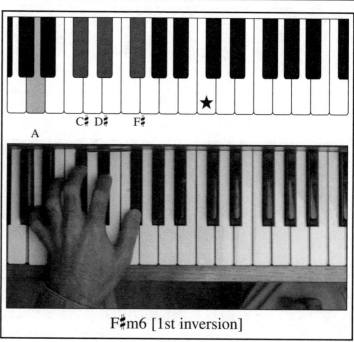

F#m6 [1st inversion]

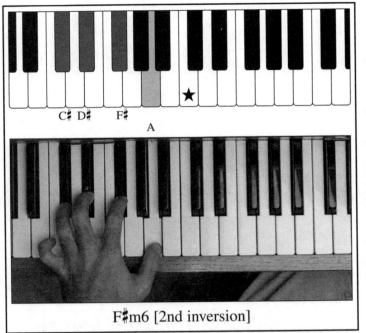

F#m6 [2nd inversion]

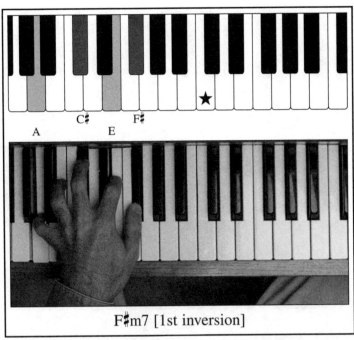

F#m7 [1st inversion]

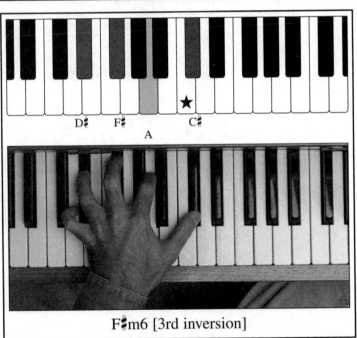

F#m6 [3rd inversion]

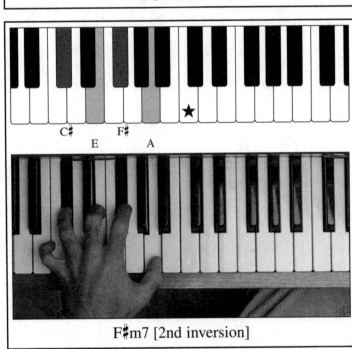

F#m7 [2nd inversion]

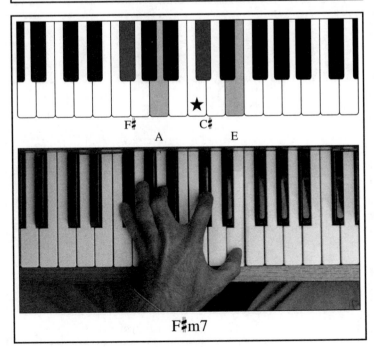

F#m7

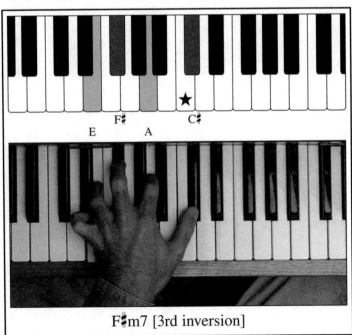

F#m7 [3rd inversion]

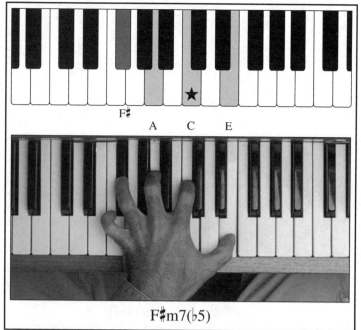

F#m7(♭5)

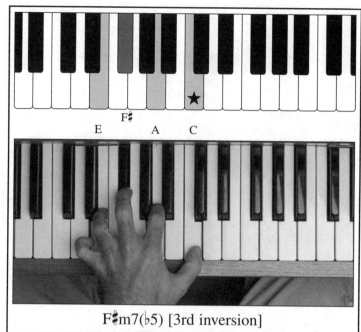

F#m7(♭5) [3rd inversion]

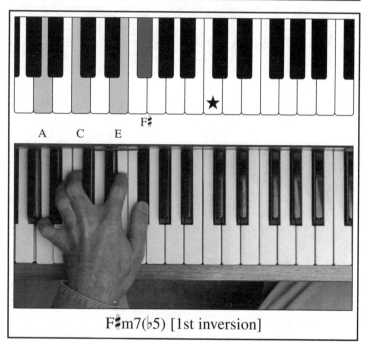

F#m7(♭5) [1st inversion]

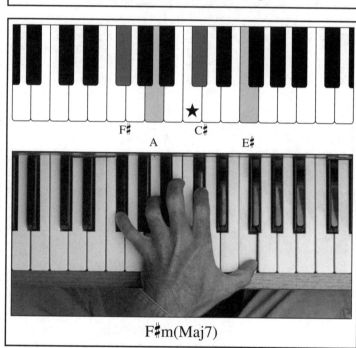

F#m(Maj7)

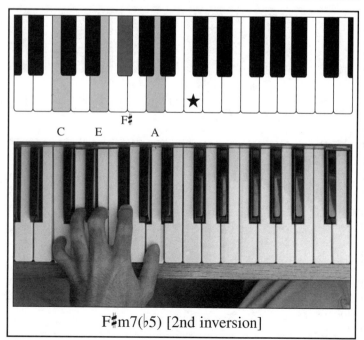

F#m7(♭5) [2nd inversion]

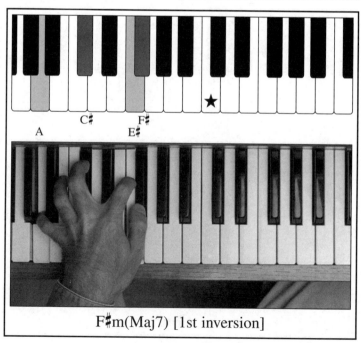

F#m(Maj7) [1st inversion]

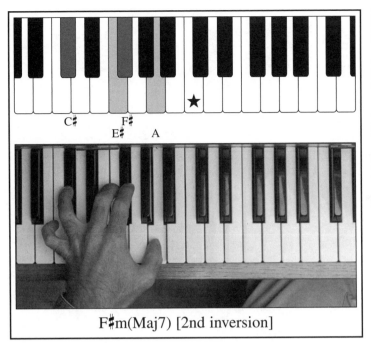

F#m(Maj7) [2nd inversion]

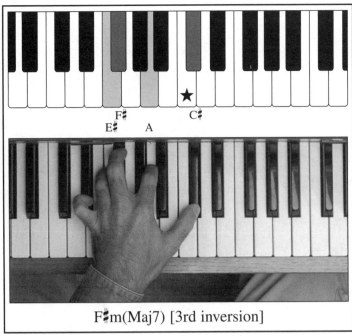

F#m(Maj7) [3rd inversion]

See more F# chords in the
***Chords for Two Hands* section**

D♭
Chords

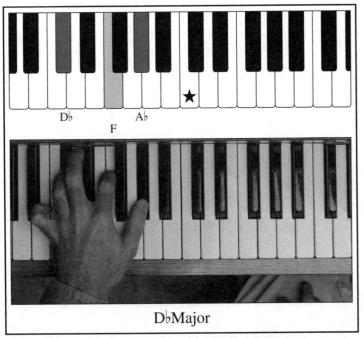

DbMajor

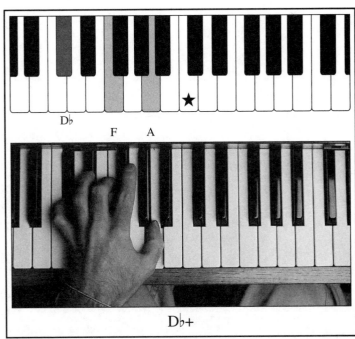

Db+

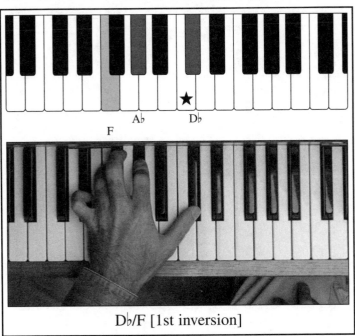

Db/F [1st inversion]

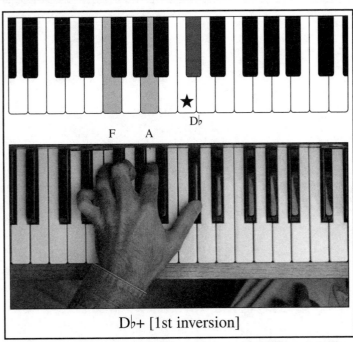

Db+ [1st inversion]

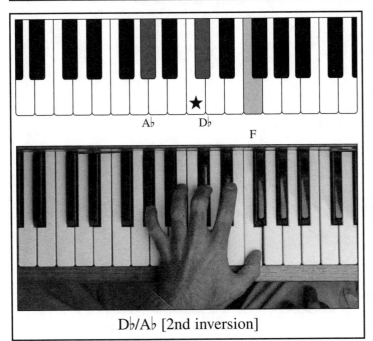

Db/Ab [2nd inversion]

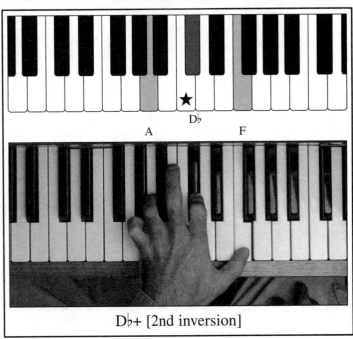

Db+ [2nd inversion]

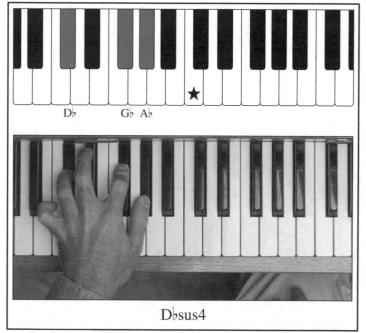

D♭sus4

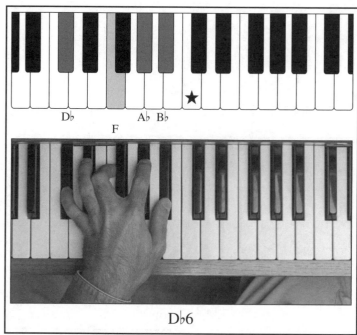

D♭6

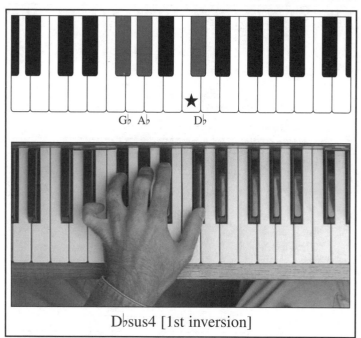

D♭sus4 [1st inversion]

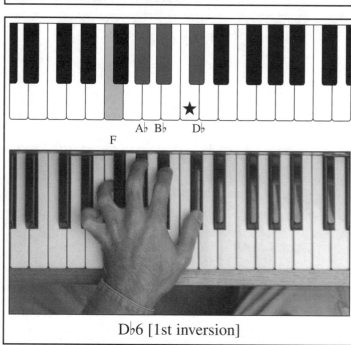

D♭6 [1st inversion]

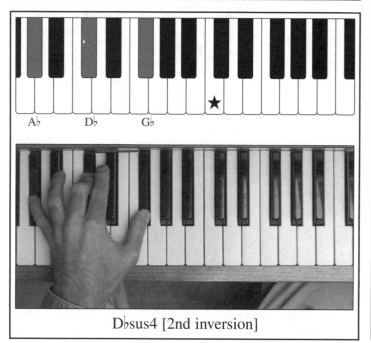

D♭sus4 [2nd inversion]

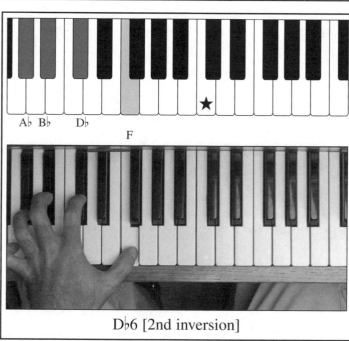

D♭6 [2nd inversion]

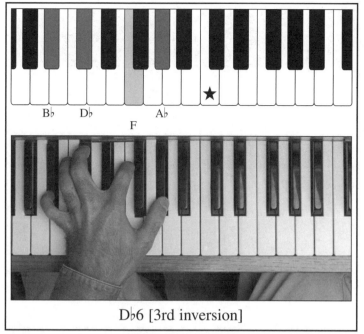

Db6 [3rd inversion]

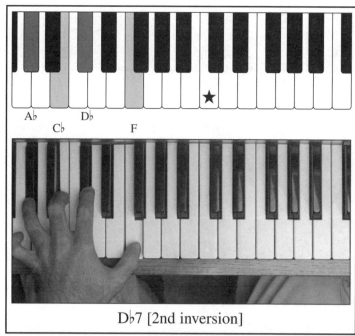

Db7 [2nd inversion]

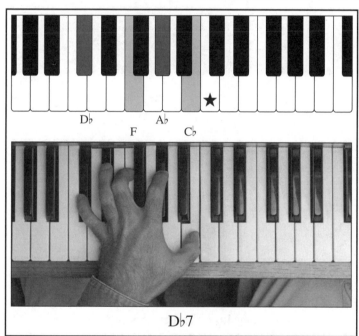

Db7

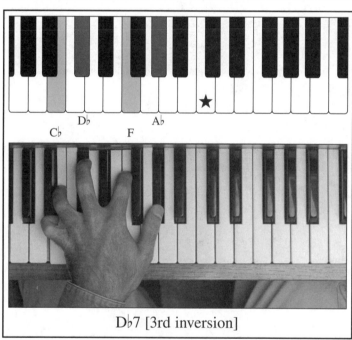

Db7 [3rd inversion]

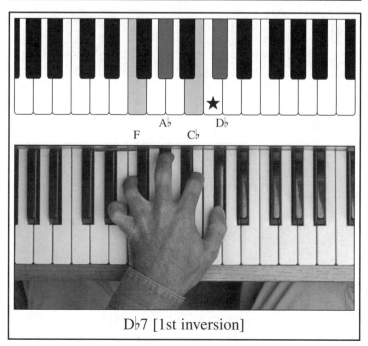

Db7 [1st inversion]

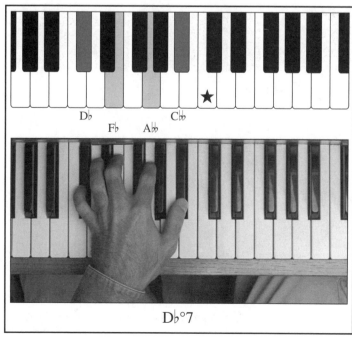

Db°7

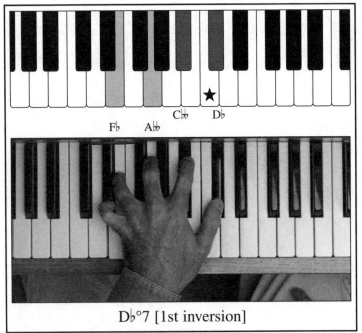

D♭°7 [1st inversion]

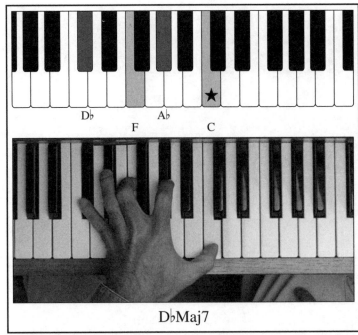

D♭Maj7

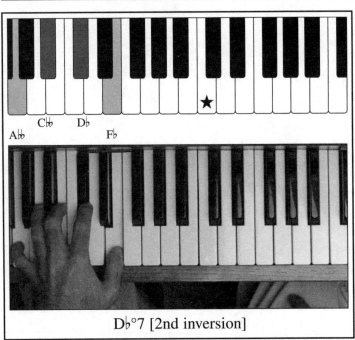

D♭°7 [2nd inversion]

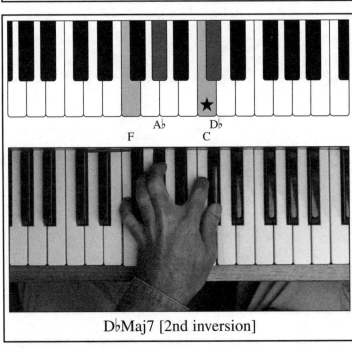

D♭Maj7 [2nd inversion]

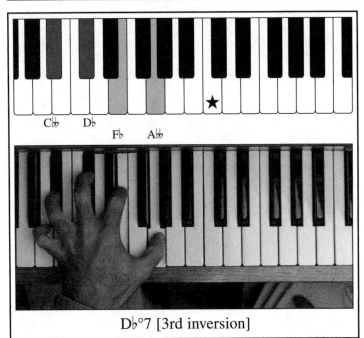

D♭°7 [3rd inversion]

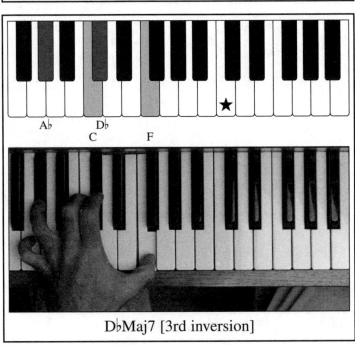

D♭Maj7 [3rd inversion]

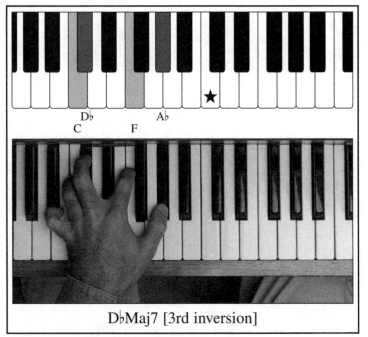

D♭Maj7 [3rd inversion]

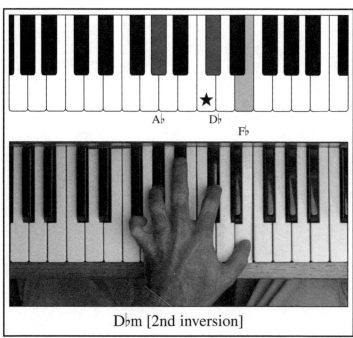

D♭m [2nd inversion]

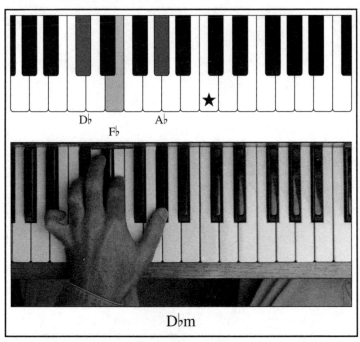

D♭m

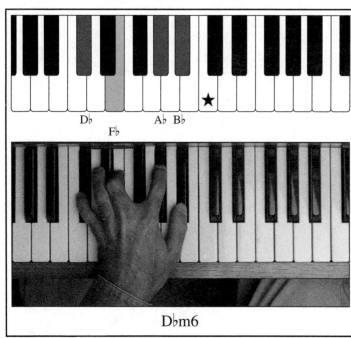

D♭m6

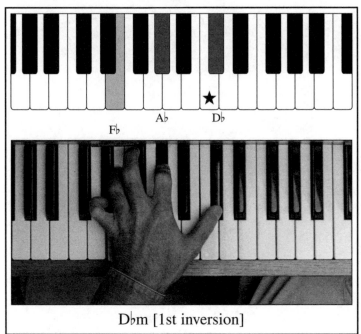

D♭m [1st inversion]

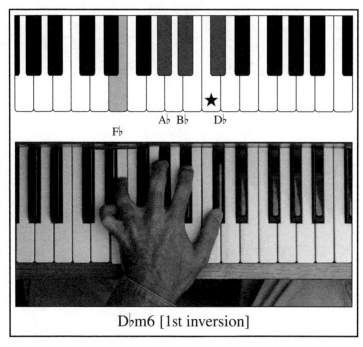

D♭m6 [1st inversion]

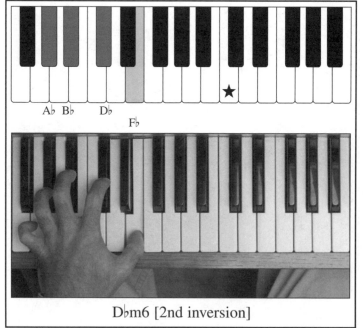

D♭m6 [2nd inversion]

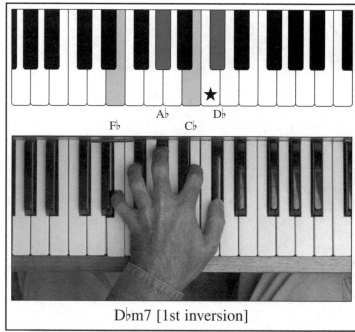

D♭m7 [1st inversion]

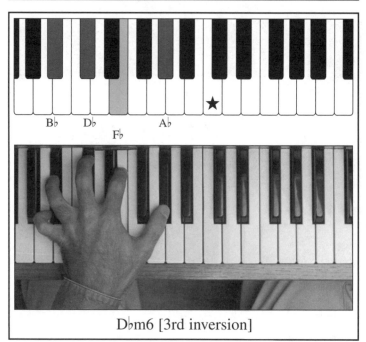

D♭m6 [3rd inversion]

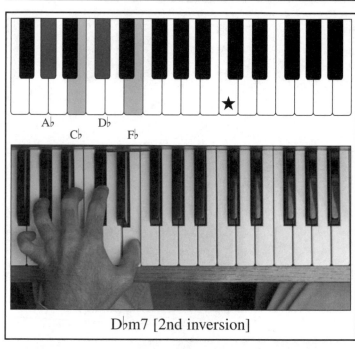

D♭m7 [2nd inversion]

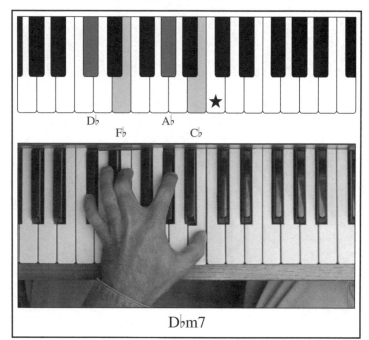

D♭m7

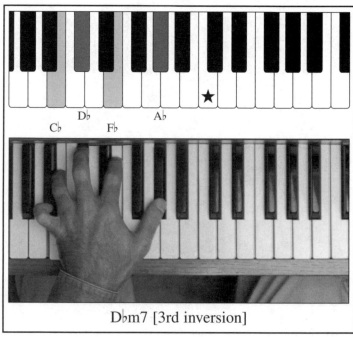

D♭m7 [3rd inversion]

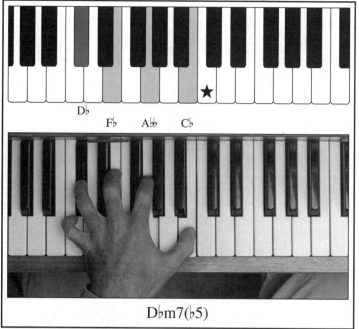

D♭m7(♭5)

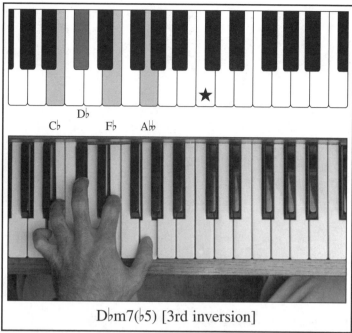

D♭m7(♭5) [3rd inversion]

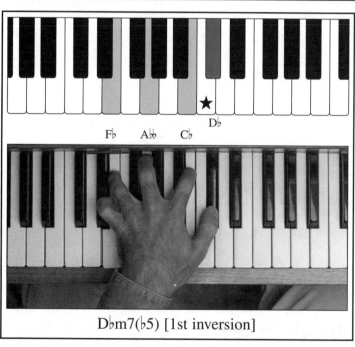

D♭m7(♭5) [1st inversion]

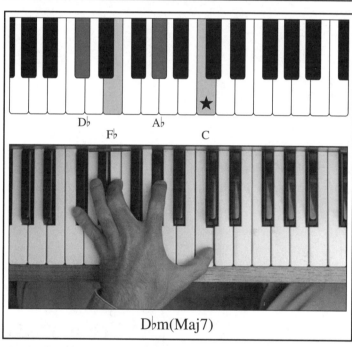

D♭m(Maj7)

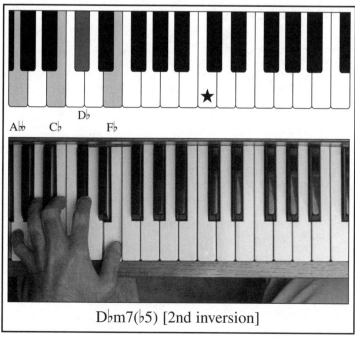

D♭m7(♭5) [2nd inversion]

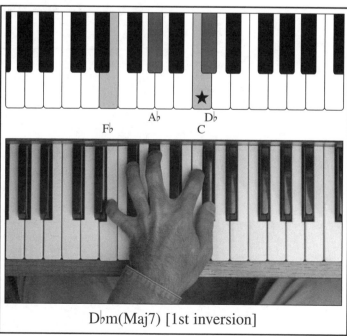

D♭m(Maj7) [1st inversion]

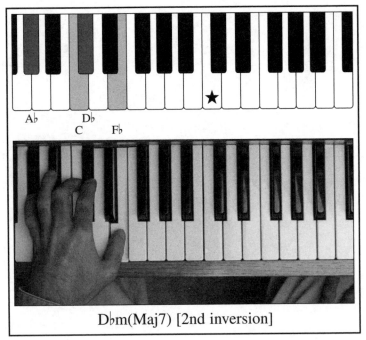

Dbm(Maj7) [2nd inversion]

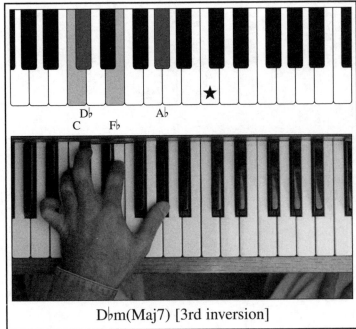

Dbm(Maj7) [3rd inversion]

See more Db chords in the
***Chords for Two Hands* section**

A♭ Chords

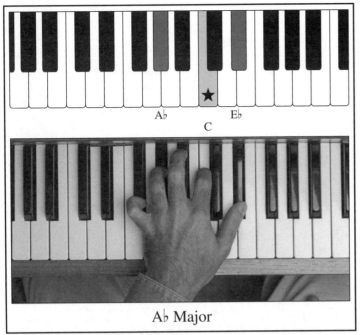

Ab Major

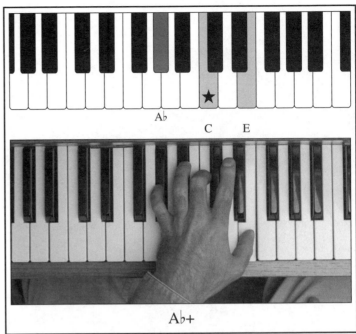

Ab+

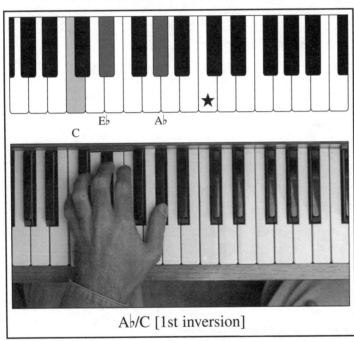

Ab/C [1st inversion]

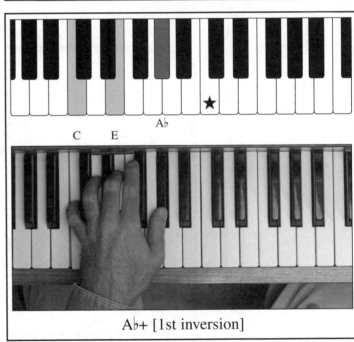

Ab+ [1st inversion]

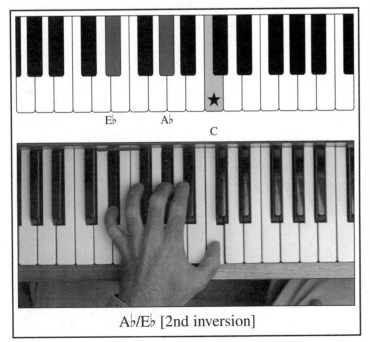

Ab/Eb [2nd inversion]

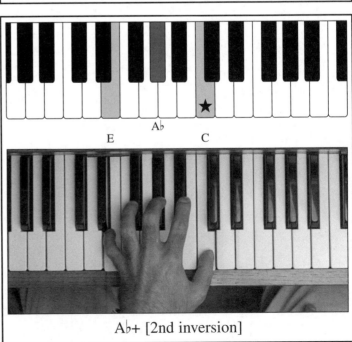

Ab+ [2nd inversion]

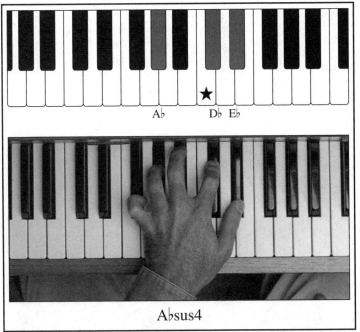

Absus4

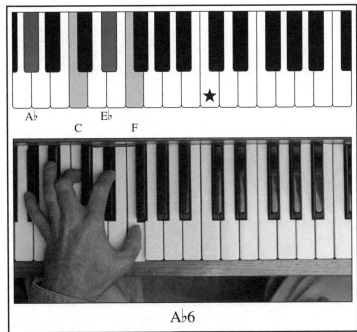

Ab6

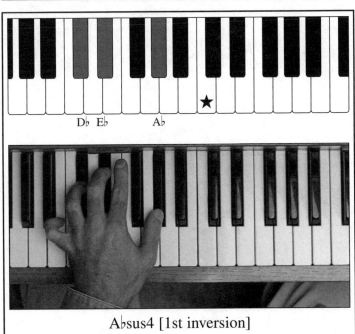

Absus4 [1st inversion]

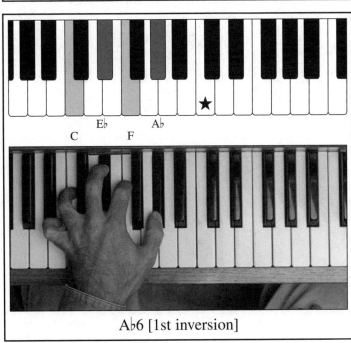

Ab6 [1st inversion]

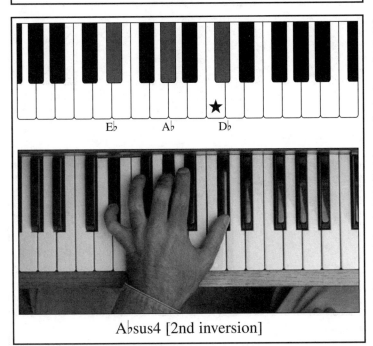

Absus4 [2nd inversion]

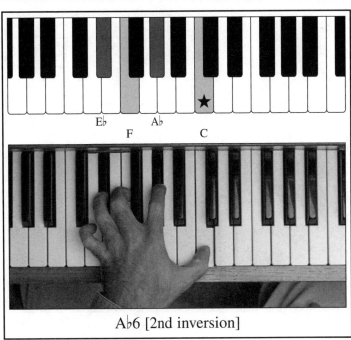

Ab6 [2nd inversion]

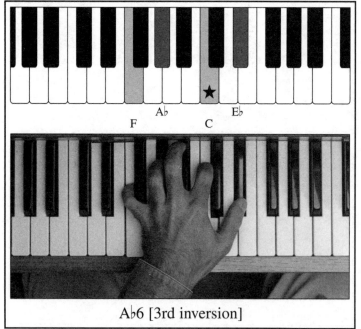

Ab6 [3rd inversion]

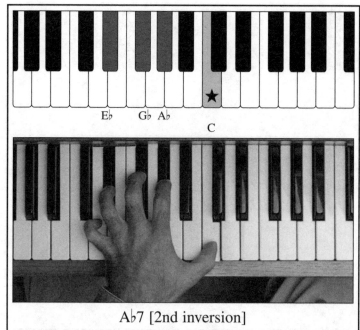

Ab7 [2nd inversion]

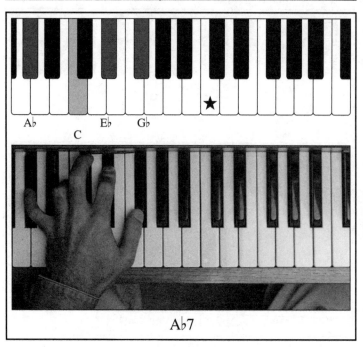

Ab7

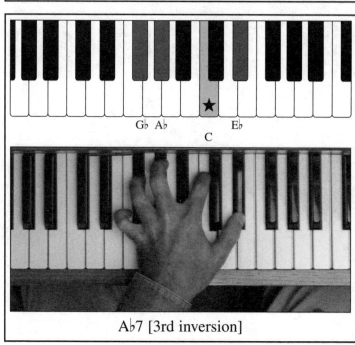

Ab7 [3rd inversion]

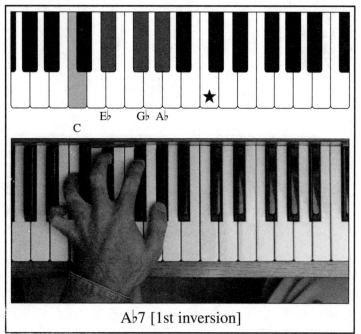

Ab7 [1st inversion]

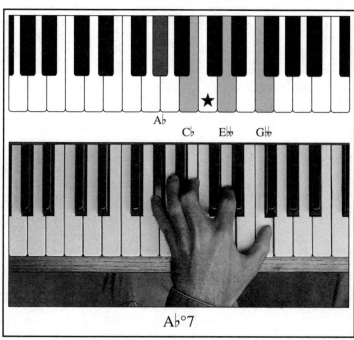

Ab°7

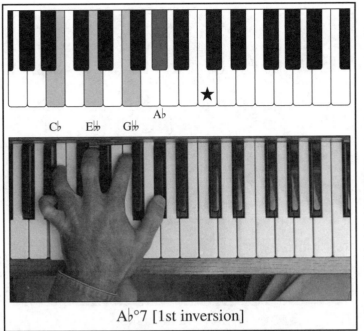

Ab°7 [1st inversion]

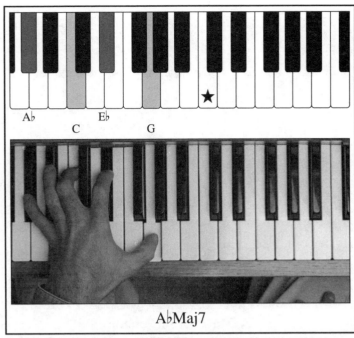

AbMaj7

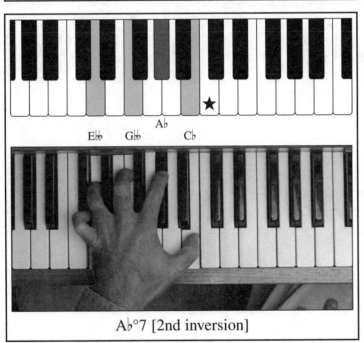

Ab°7 [2nd inversion]

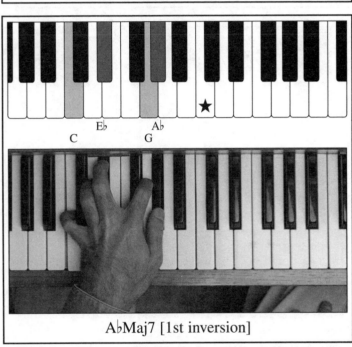

AbMaj7 [1st inversion]

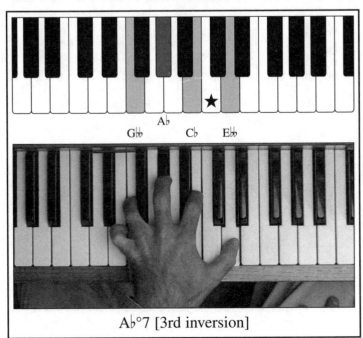

Ab°7 [3rd inversion]

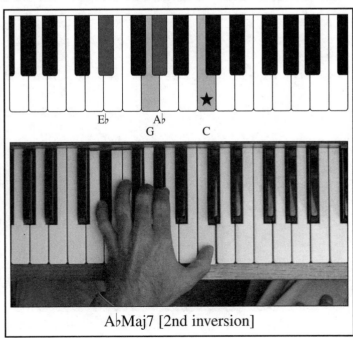

AbMaj7 [2nd inversion]

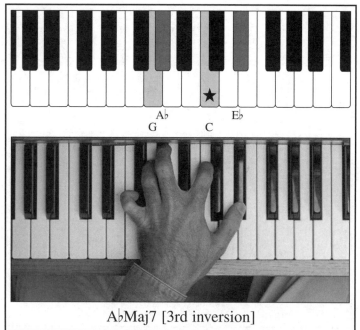

AbMaj7 [3rd inversion]

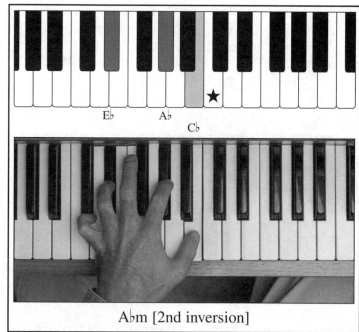

Abm [2nd inversion]

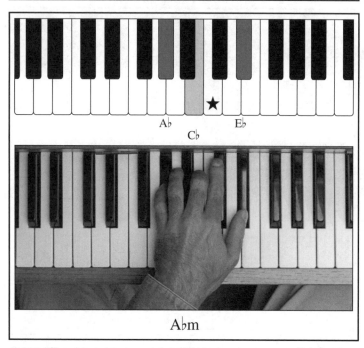

Abm

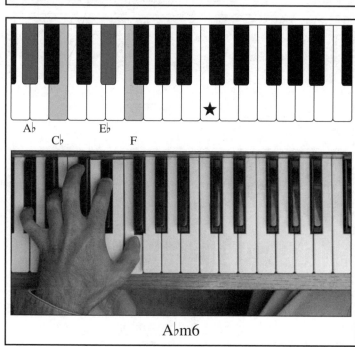

Abm6

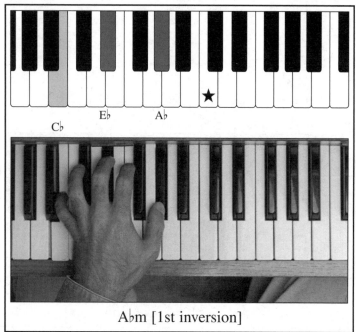

Abm [1st inversion]

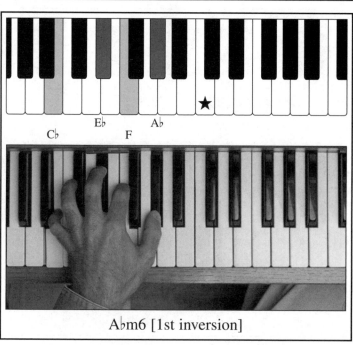

Abm6 [1st inversion]

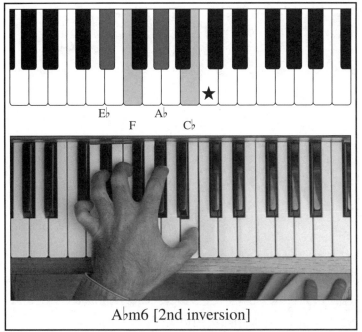

Abm6 [2nd inversion]

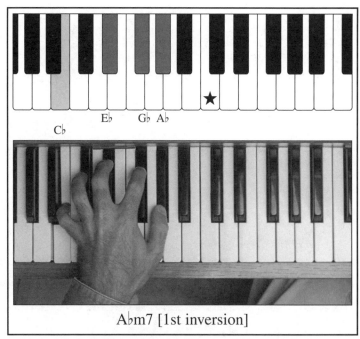

Abm7 [1st inversion]

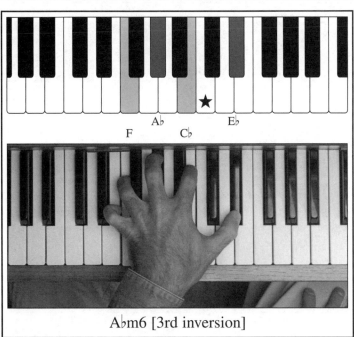

Abm6 [3rd inversion]

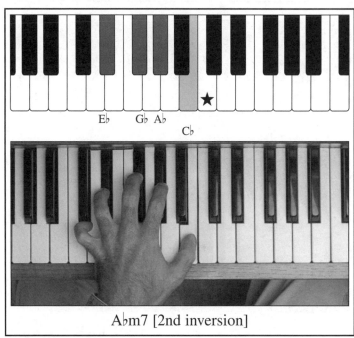

Abm7 [2nd inversion]

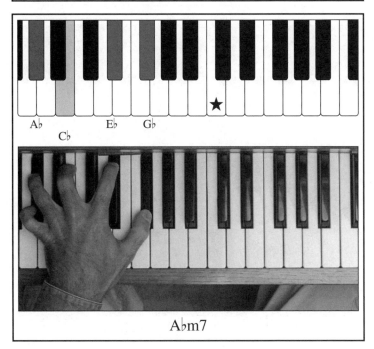

Abm7

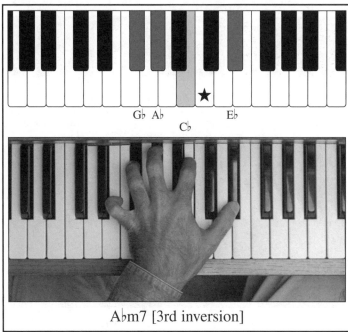

Abm7 [3rd inversion]

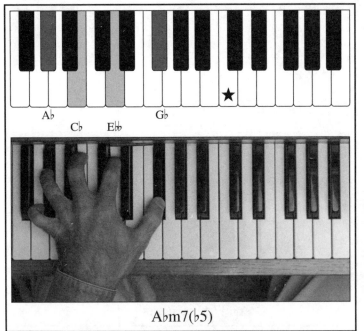

Abm7(b5)

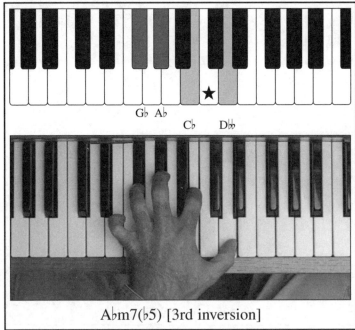

Abm7(b5) [3rd inversion]

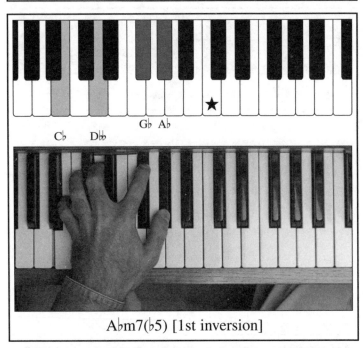

Abm7(b5) [1st inversion]

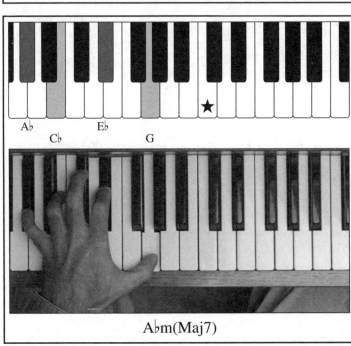

Abm(Maj7)

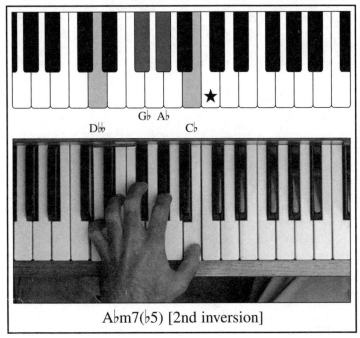

Abm7(b5) [2nd inversion]

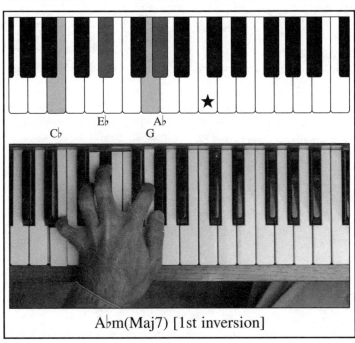

Abm(Maj7) [1st inversion]

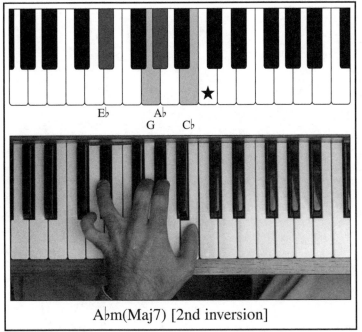

Abm(Maj7) [2nd inversion]

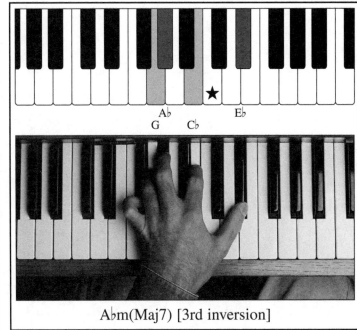

Abm(Maj7) [3rd inversion]

See more A♭ chords in the
***Chords for Two Hands* section**

E♭
Chords

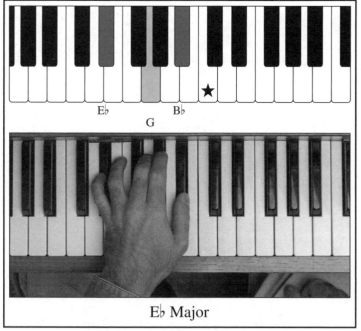

Eb Major

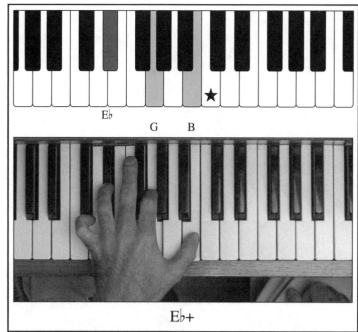

Eb+

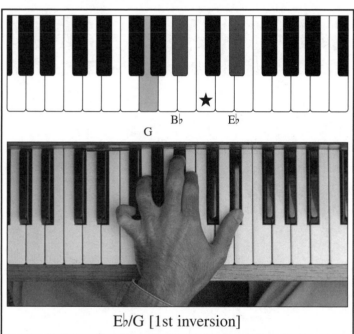

Eb/G [1st inversion]

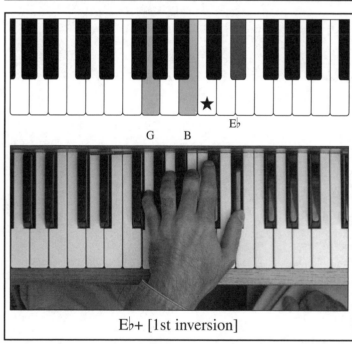

Eb+ [1st inversion]

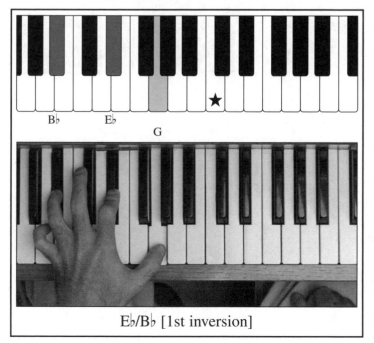

Eb/Bb [1st inversion]

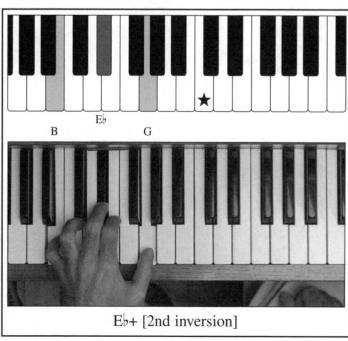

Eb+ [2nd inversion]

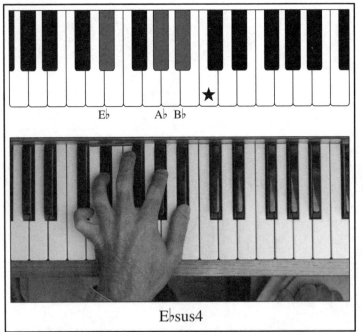

Ebsus4

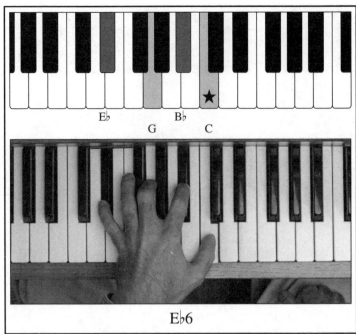

Eb6

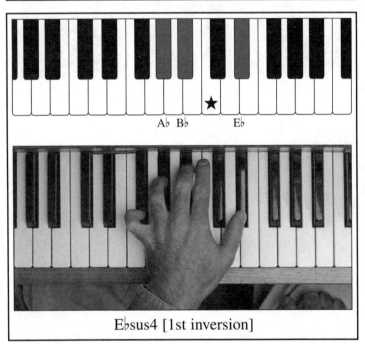

Ebsus4 [1st inversion]

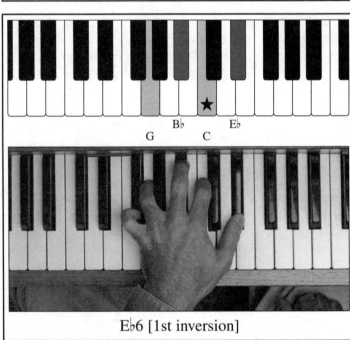

Eb6 [1st inversion]

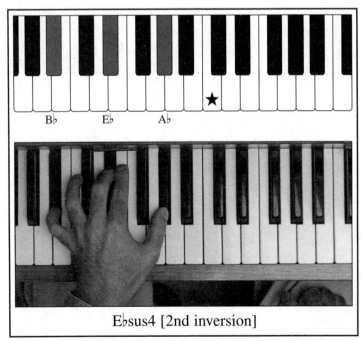

Ebsus4 [2nd inversion]

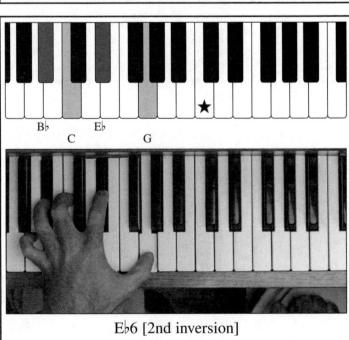

Eb6 [2nd inversion]

90

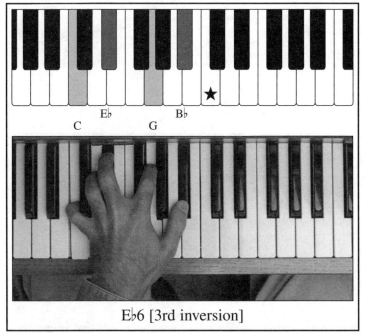

Eb6 [3rd inversion]

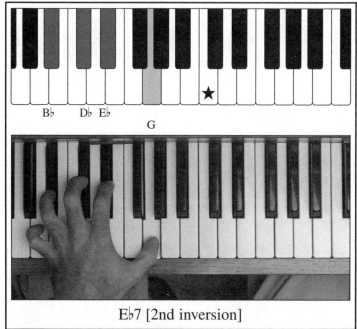

Eb7 [2nd inversion]

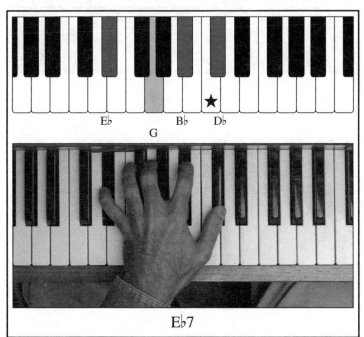

Eb7

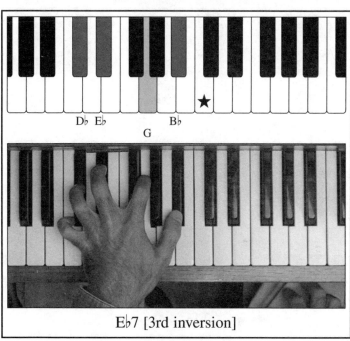

Eb7 [3rd inversion]

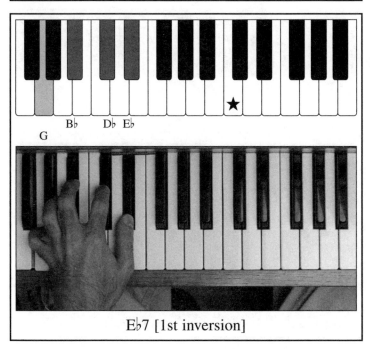

Eb7 [1st inversion]

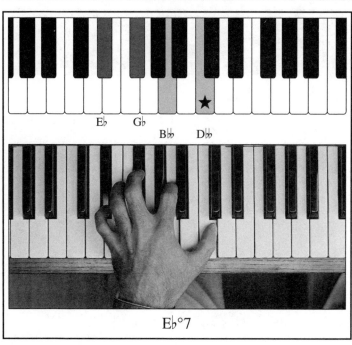

Eb°7

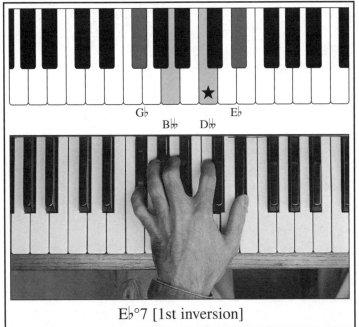

Eb°7 [1st inversion]

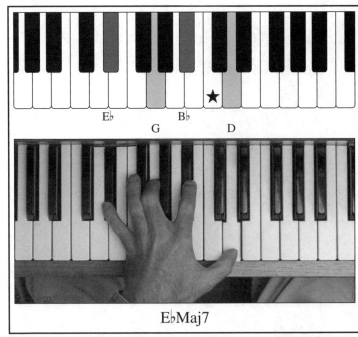

EbMaj7

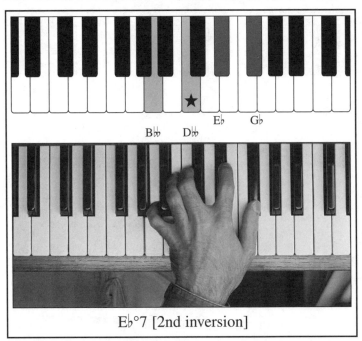

Eb°7 [2nd inversion]

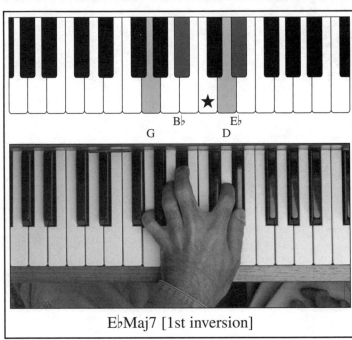

EbMaj7 [1st inversion]

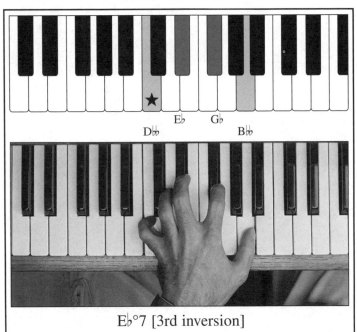

Eb°7 [3rd inversion]

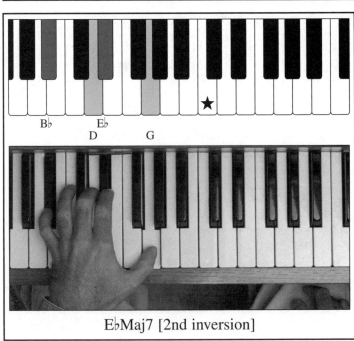

EbMaj7 [2nd inversion]

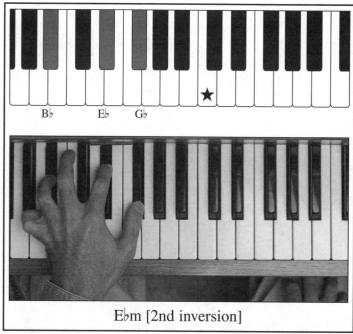

E♭Maj7 [3rd inversion]

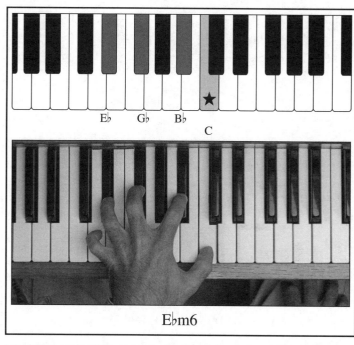

E♭m [2nd inversion]

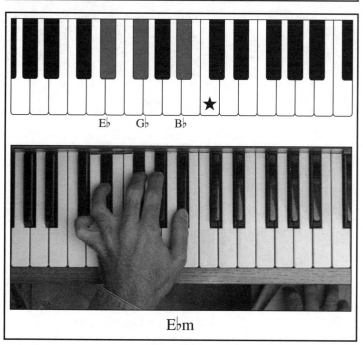

E♭m

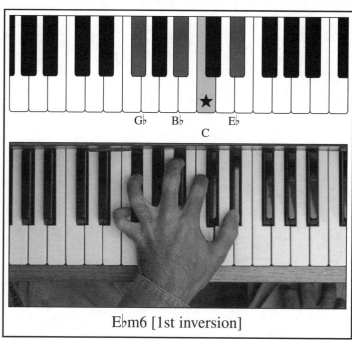

E♭m6

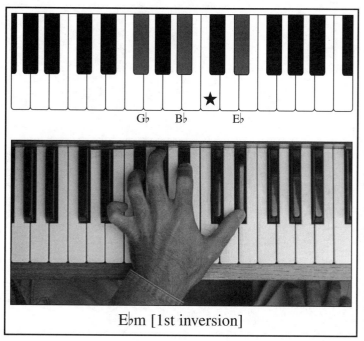

E♭m [1st inversion]

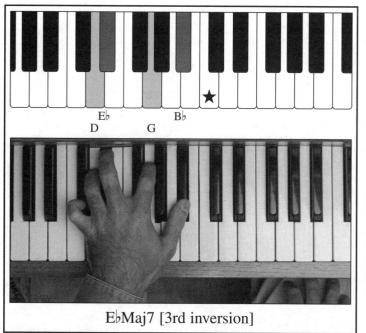

E♭m6 [1st inversion]

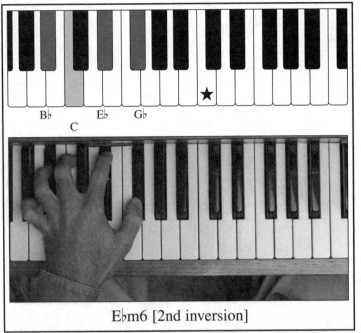

E♭m6 [2nd inversion]

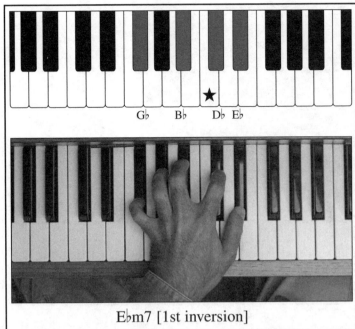

E♭m7 [1st inversion]

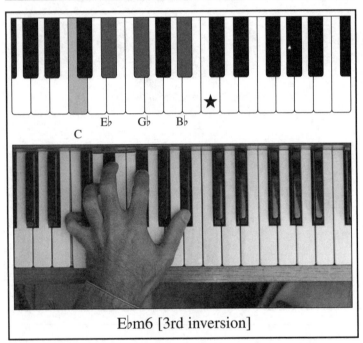

E♭m6 [3rd inversion]

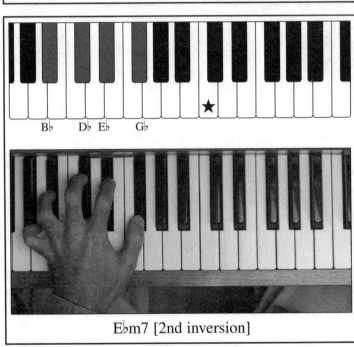

E♭m7 [2nd inversion]

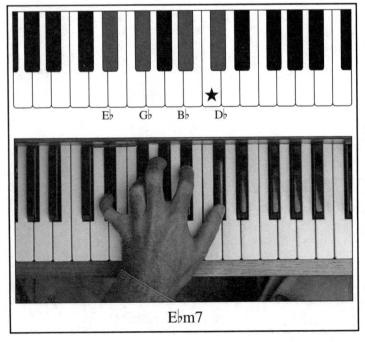

E♭m7

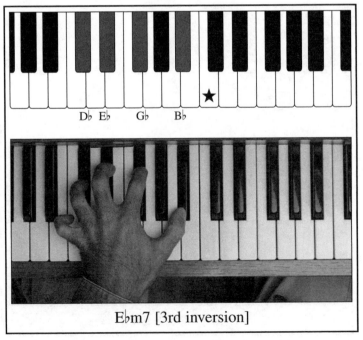

E♭m7 [3rd inversion]

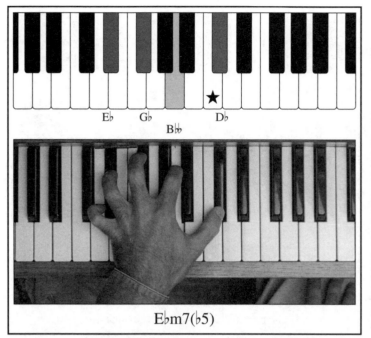

Ebm7(b5)

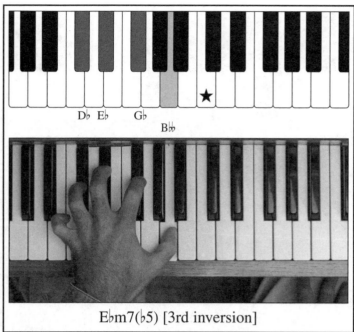

Ebm7(b5) [3rd inversion]

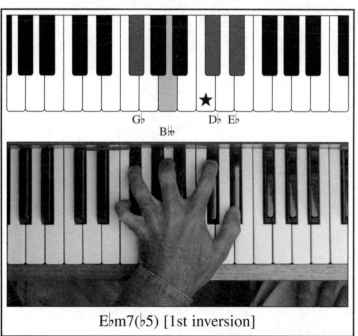

Ebm7(b5) [1st inversion]

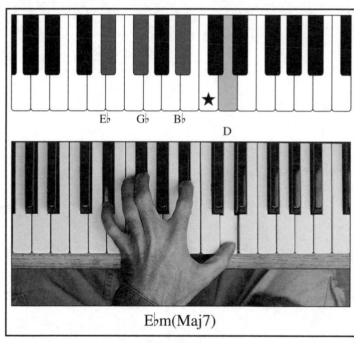

Ebm(Maj7)

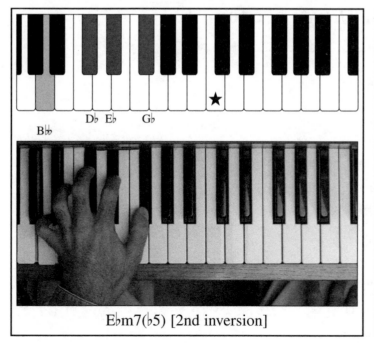

Ebm7(b5) [2nd inversion]

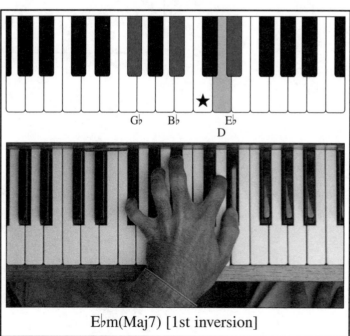

Ebm(Maj7) [1st inversion]

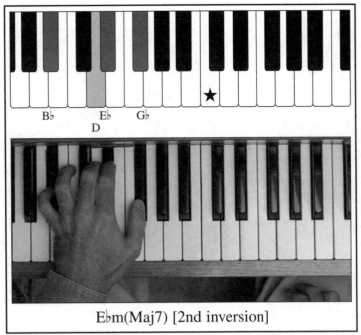

Ebm(Maj7) [2nd inversion]

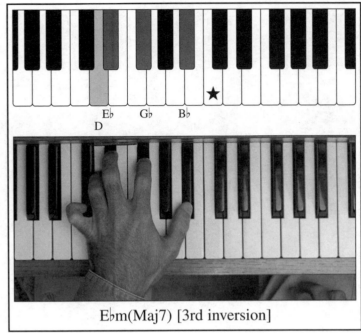

Ebm(Maj7) [3rd inversion]

See more E♭ chords in the
***Chords for Two Hands* section**

B♭ Chords

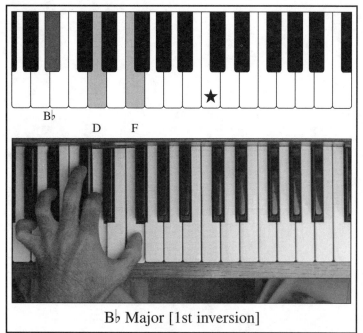

Bb Major [1st inversion]

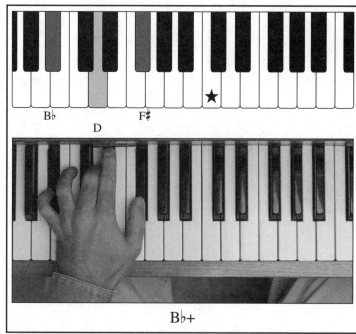

Bb+

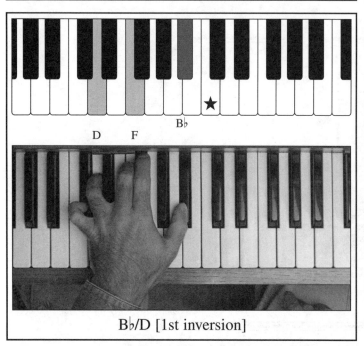

Bb/D [1st inversion]

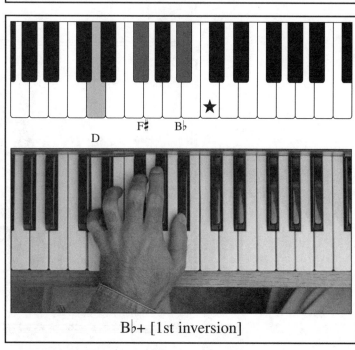

Bb+ [1st inversion]

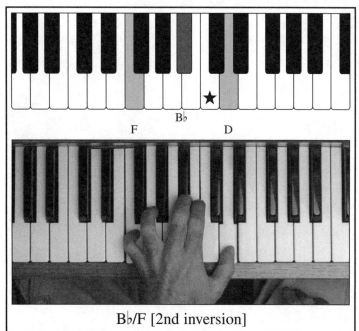

Bb/F [2nd inversion]

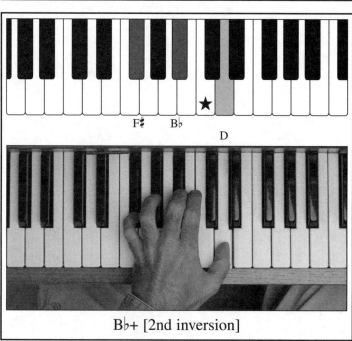

Bb+ [2nd inversion]

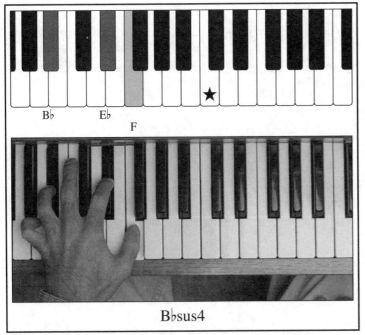

B♭sus4

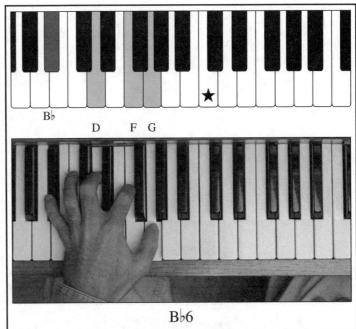

B♭6

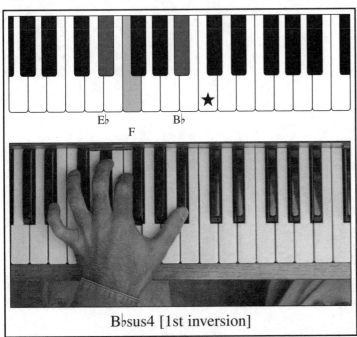

B♭sus4 [1st inversion]

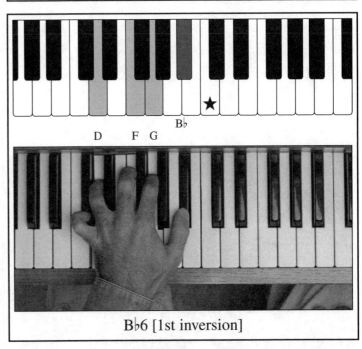

B♭6 [1st inversion]

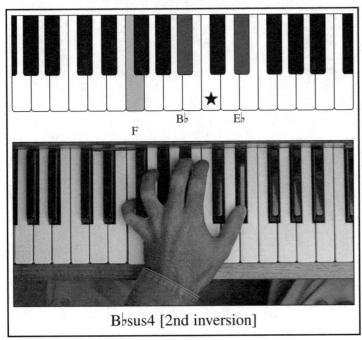

B♭sus4 [2nd inversion]

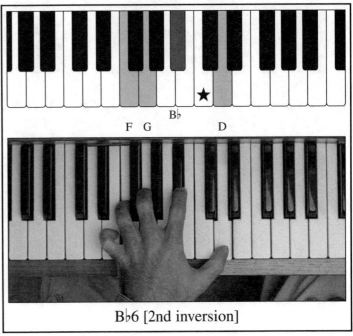

B♭6 [2nd inversion]

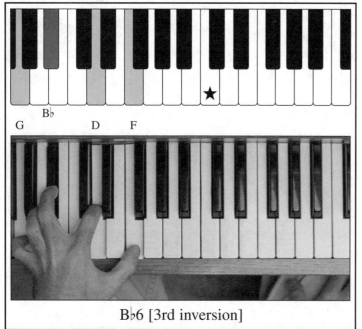

Bb6 [3rd inversion]

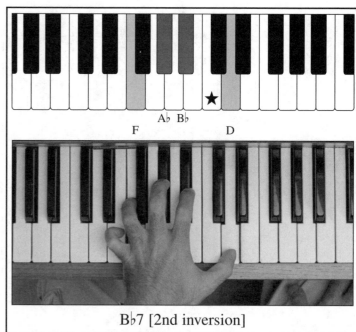

Bb7 [2nd inversion]

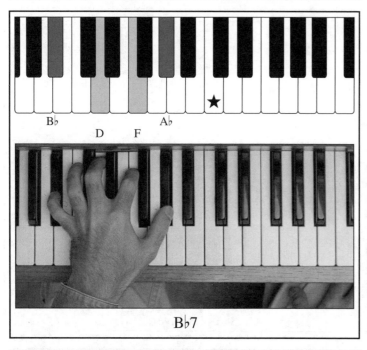

Bb7

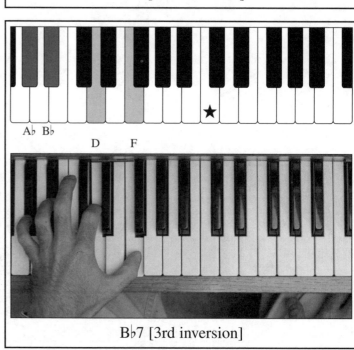

Bb7 [3rd inversion]

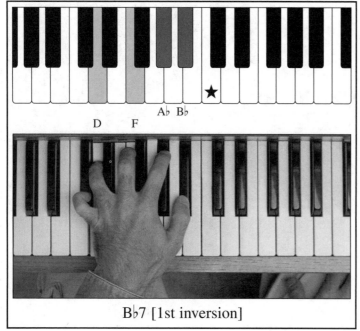

Bb7 [1st inversion]

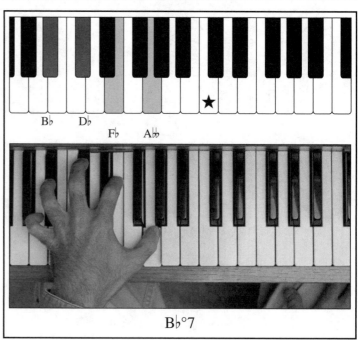

Bb°7

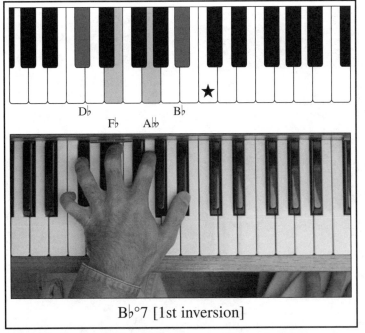

Bb°7 [1st inversion]

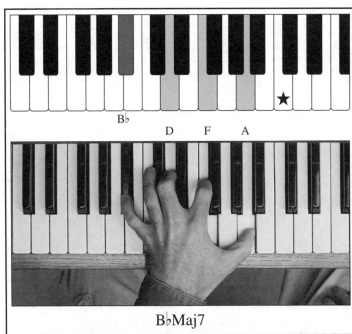

BbMaj7

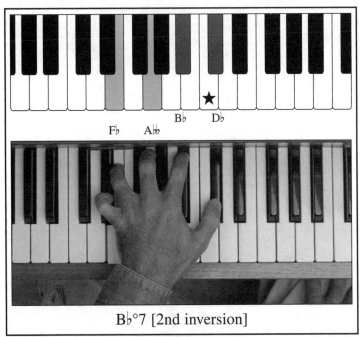

Bb°7 [2nd inversion]

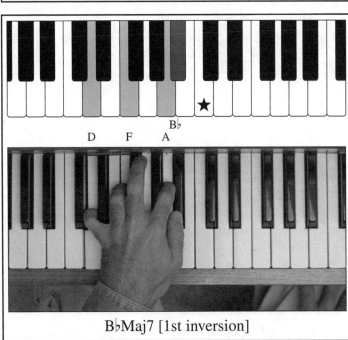

BbMaj7 [1st inversion]

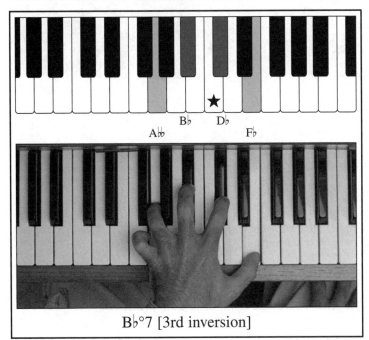

Bb°7 [3rd inversion]

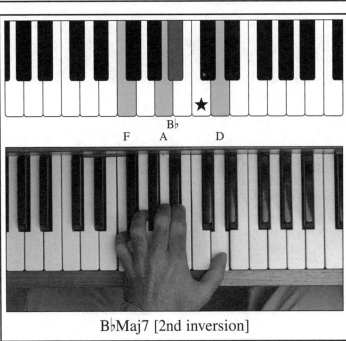

BbMaj7 [2nd inversion]

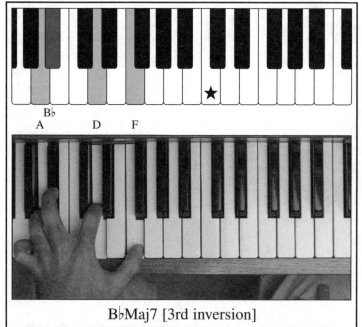

B♭Maj7 [3rd inversion]

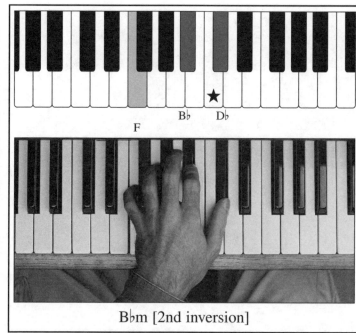

B♭m [2nd inversion]

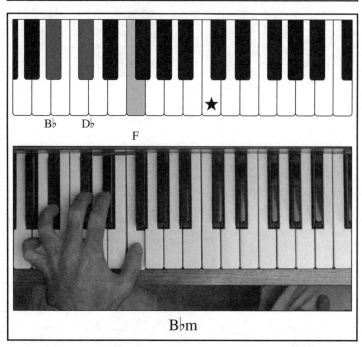

B♭m

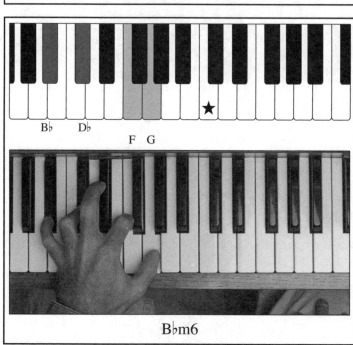

B♭m6

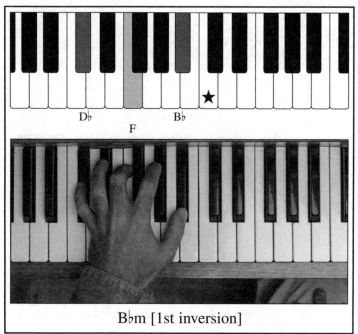

B♭m [1st inversion]

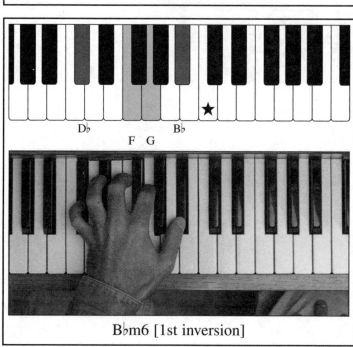

B♭m6 [1st inversion]

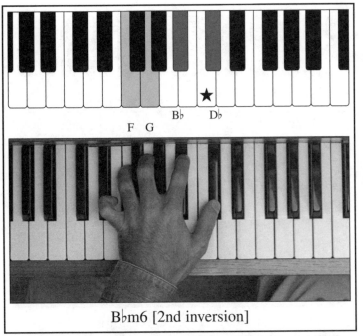

Bbm6 [2nd inversion]

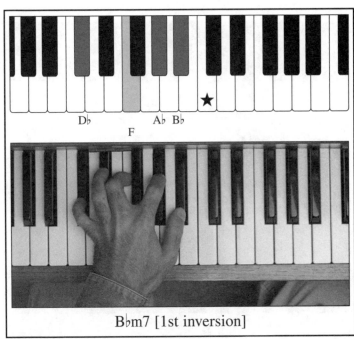

Bbm7 [1st inversion]

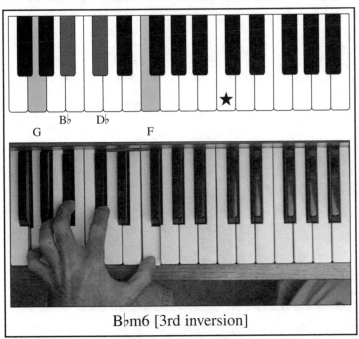

Bbm6 [3rd inversion]

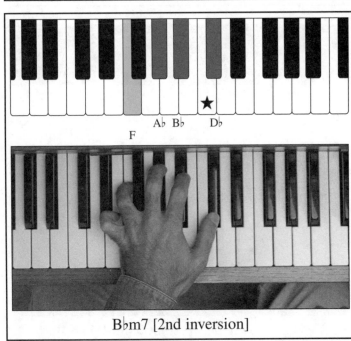

Bbm7 [2nd inversion]

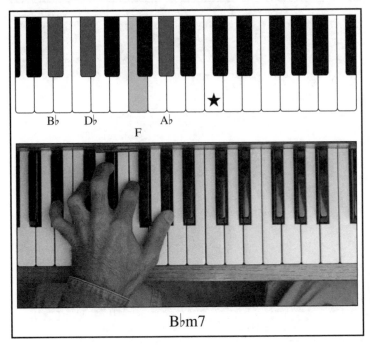

Bbm7

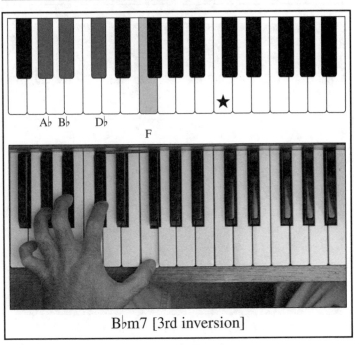

Bbm7 [3rd inversion]

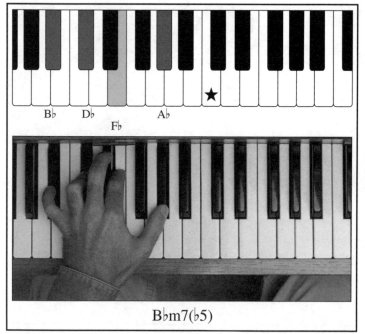

B♭m7(♭5)

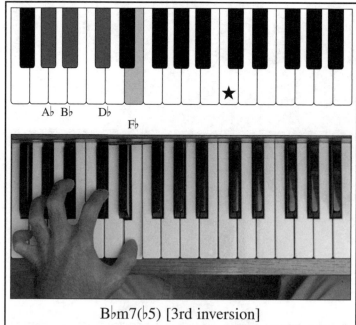

B♭m7(♭5) [3rd inversion]

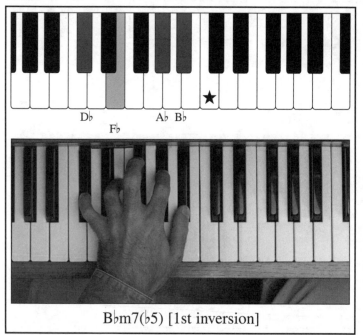

B♭m7(♭5) [1st inversion]

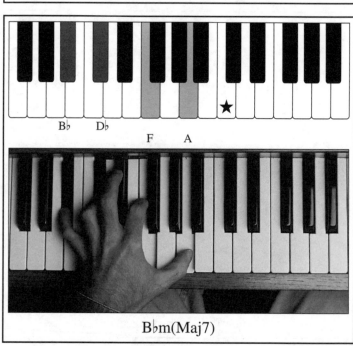

B♭m(Maj7)

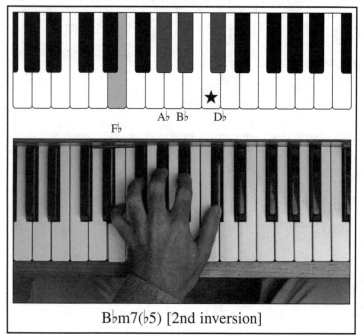

B♭m7(♭5) [2nd inversion]

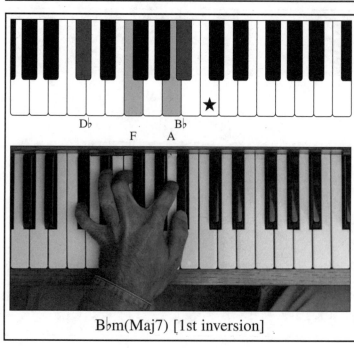

B♭m(Maj7) [1st inversion]

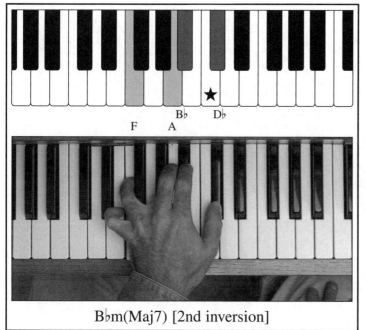

B♭m(Maj7) [2nd inversion]

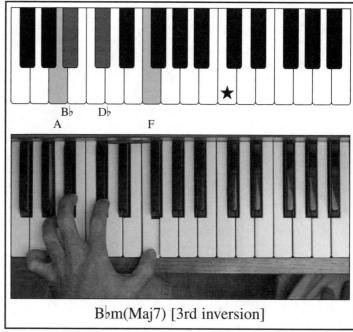

B♭m(Maj7) [3rd inversion]

See more B♭ chords in the
Chords for Two Hands section

F
Chords

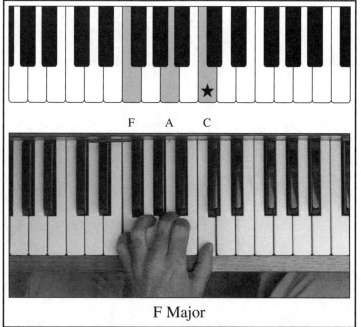

F Major

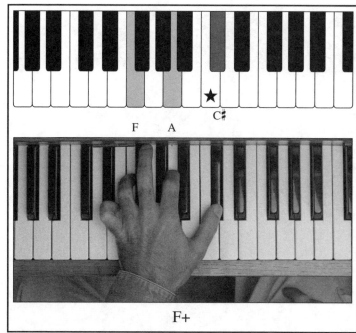

F+

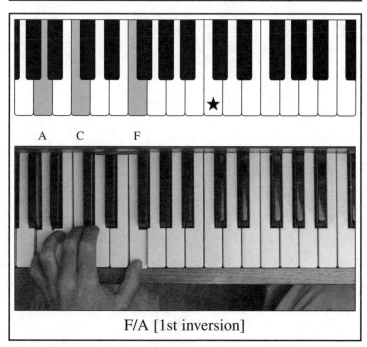

F/A [1st inversion]

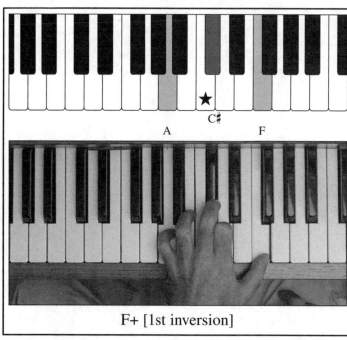

F+ [1st inversion]

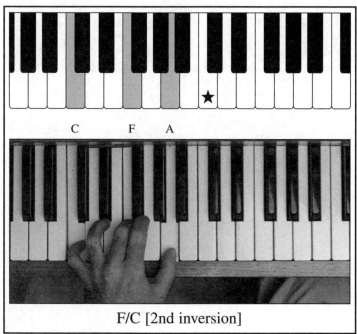

F/C [2nd inversion]

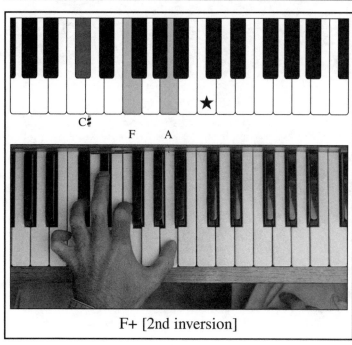

F+ [2nd inversion]

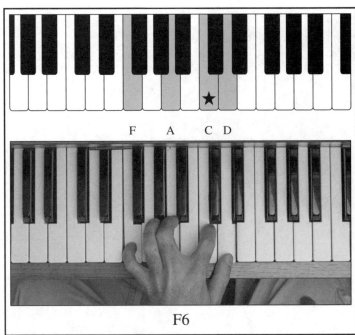

Fsus4

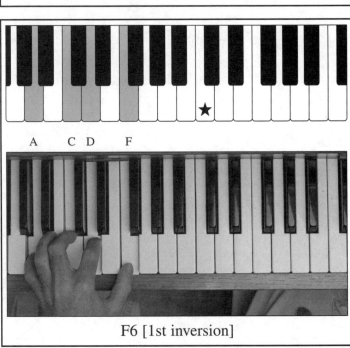

F6

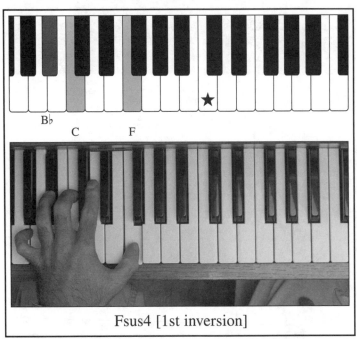

Fsus4 [1st inversion]

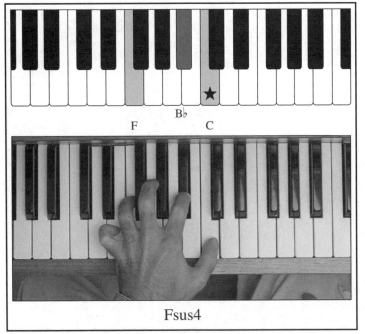

F6 [1st inversion]

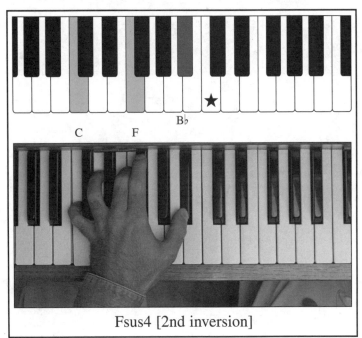

Fsus4 [2nd inversion]

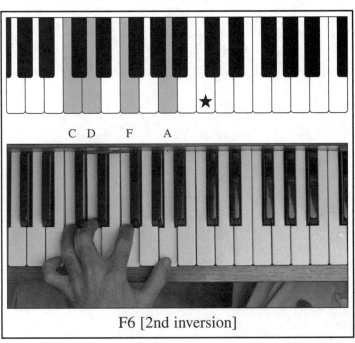

F6 [2nd inversion]

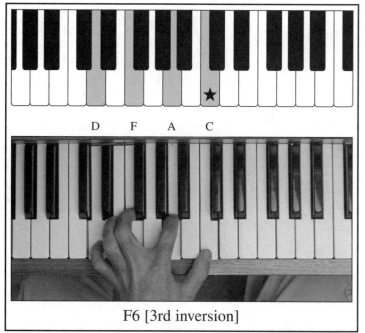

D F A C

F6 [3rd inversion]

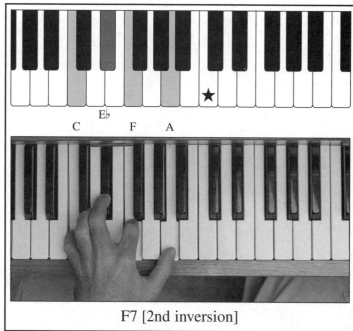

Eb C F A

F7 [2nd inversion]

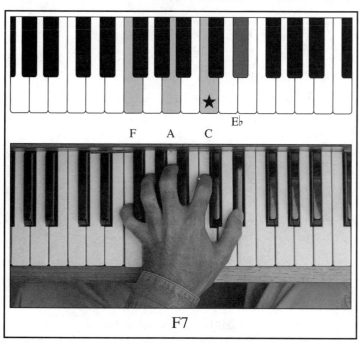

F A C Eb

F7

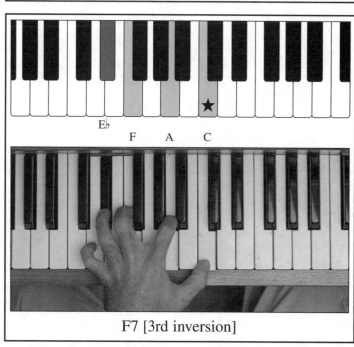

Eb F A C

F7 [3rd inversion]

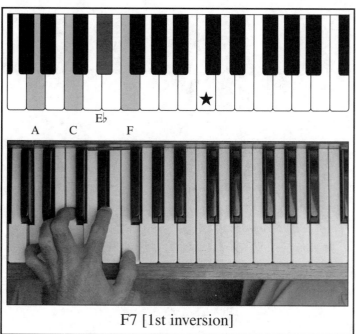

A C Eb F

F7 [1st inversion]

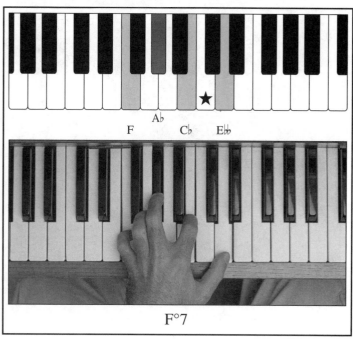

F Ab Cb Ebb

F°7

109

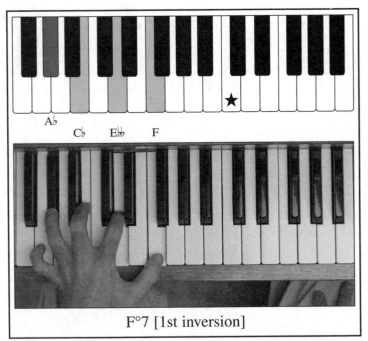

F°7 [1st inversion]

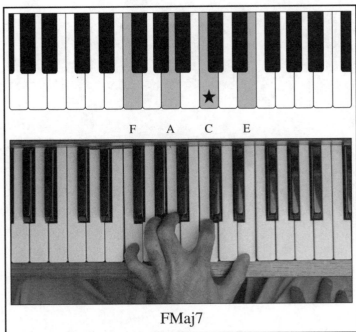

FMaj7

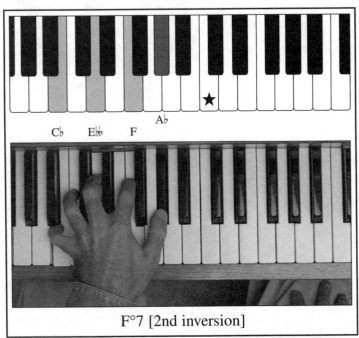

F°7 [2nd inversion]

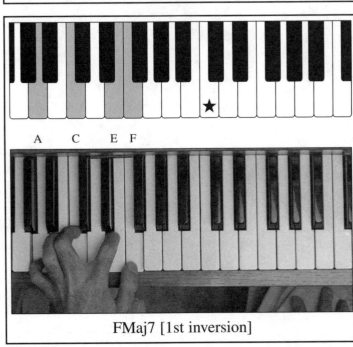

FMaj7 [1st inversion]

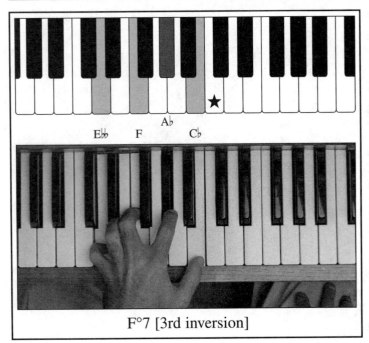

F°7 [3rd inversion]

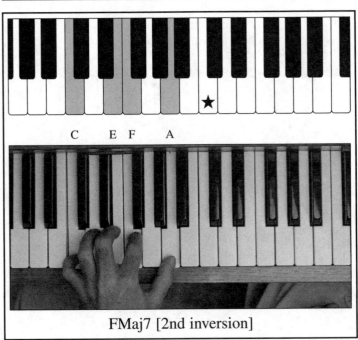

FMaj7 [2nd inversion]

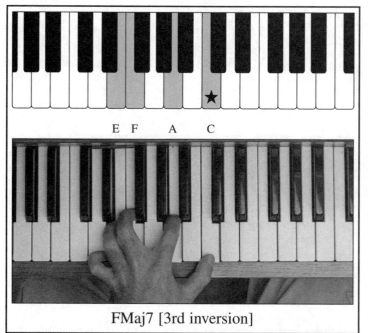

FMaj7 [3rd inversion]

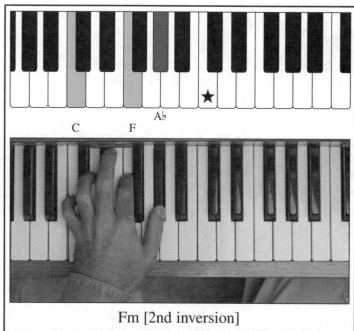

Fm [2nd inversion]

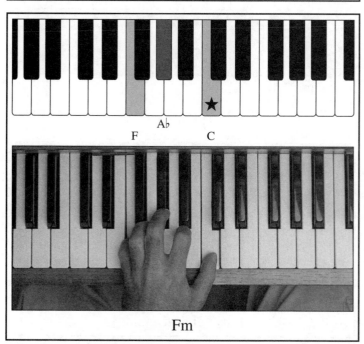

Fm

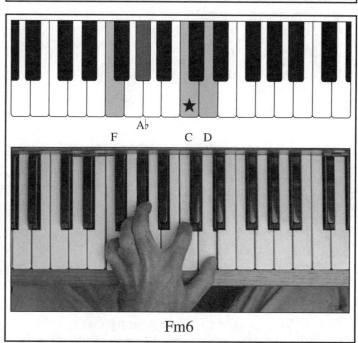

Fm6

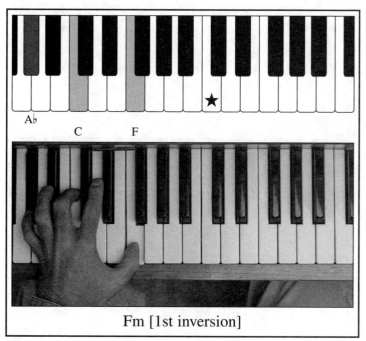

Fm [1st inversion]

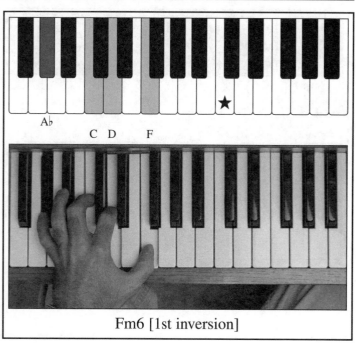

Fm6 [1st inversion]

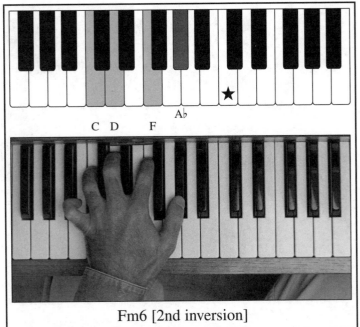

Fm6 [2nd inversion]

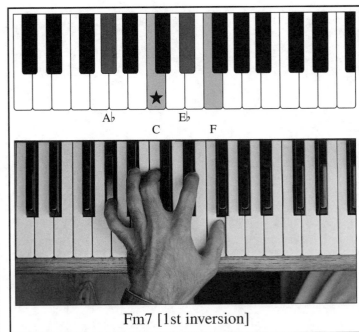

Fm7 [1st inversion]

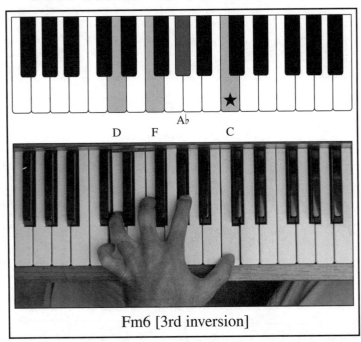

Fm6 [3rd inversion]

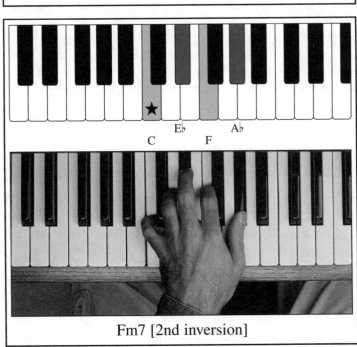

Fm7 [2nd inversion]

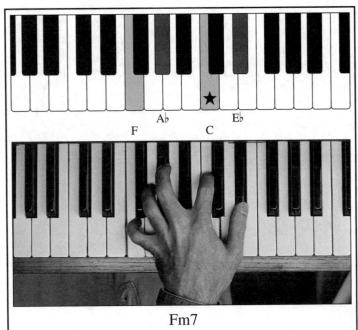

Fm7

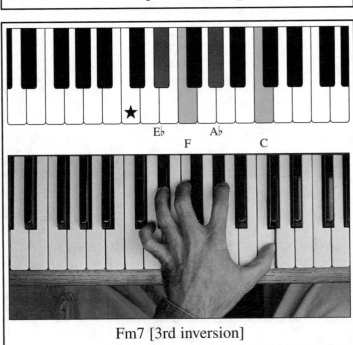

Fm7 [3rd inversion]

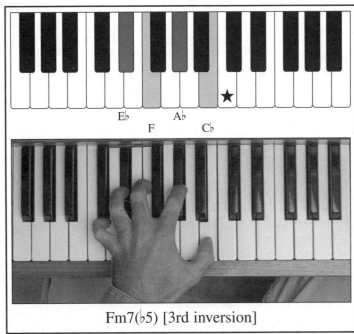

Fm7(♭5)

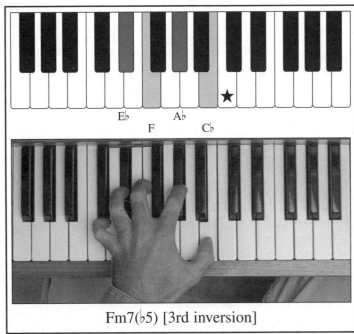

Fm7(♭5) [3rd inversion]

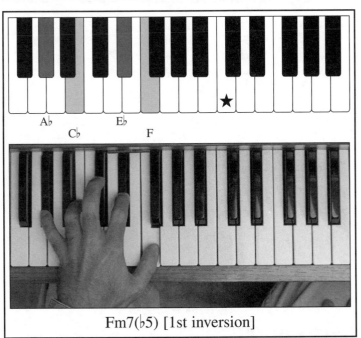

Fm7(♭5) [1st inversion]

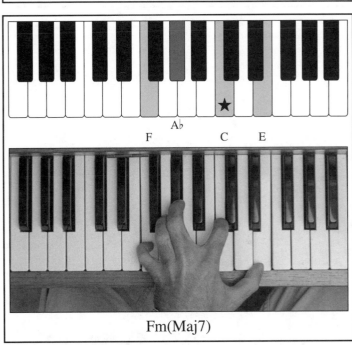

Fm(Maj7)

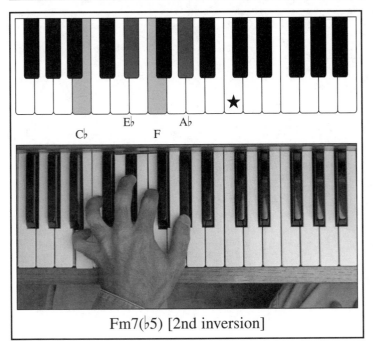

Fm7(♭5) [2nd inversion]

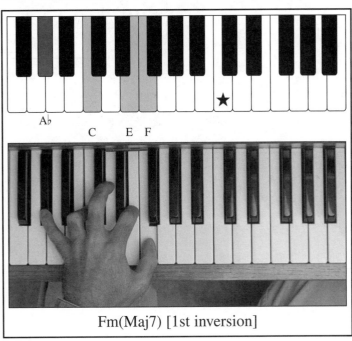

Fm(Maj7) [1st inversion]

113

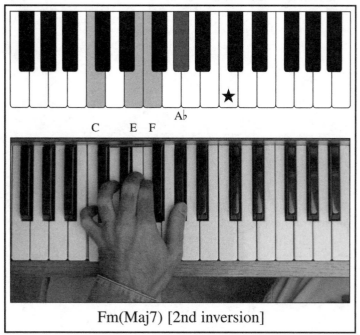

Fm(Maj7) [2nd inversion]

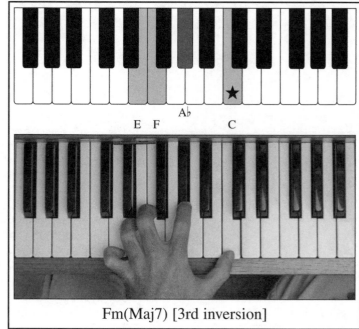

Fm(Maj7) [3rd inversion]

See more F chords in the
***Chords for Two Hands* section**

C
Chords

For Two Hands

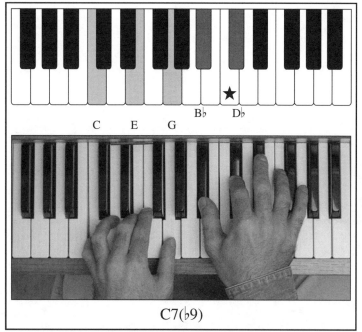

C7(♭9)

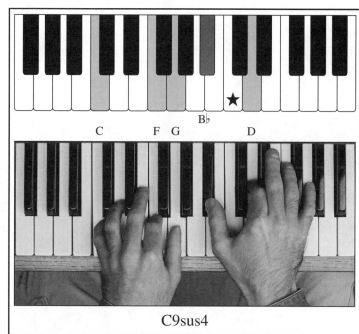

C9sus4

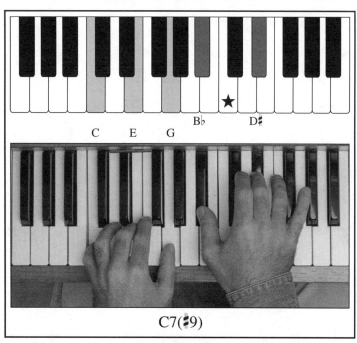

C7(♯9)

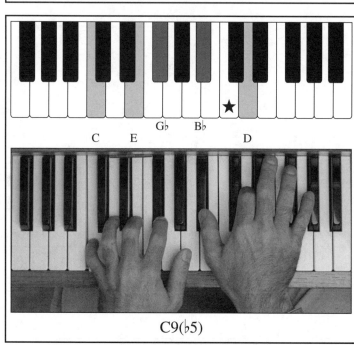

C9(♭5)

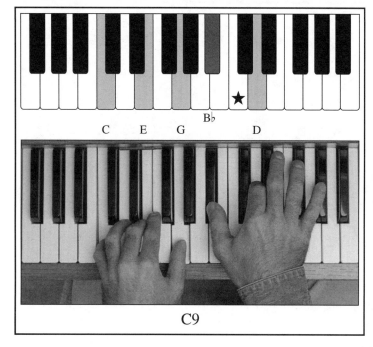

C9

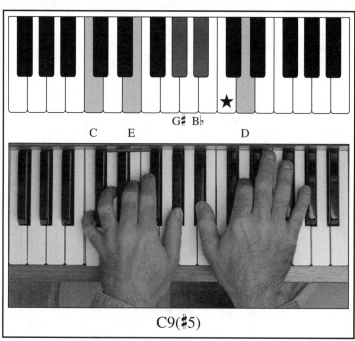

C9(♯5)

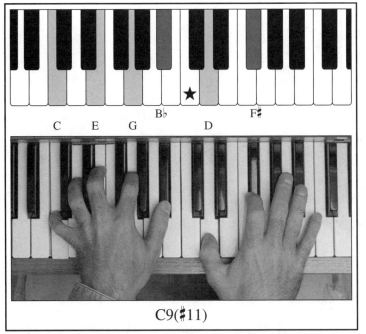

C9(♯11)

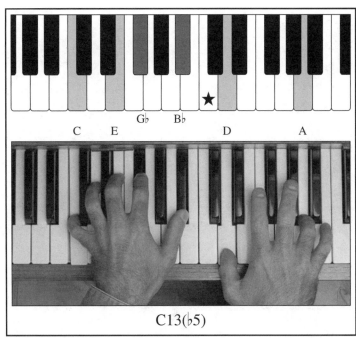

C13(♭5)

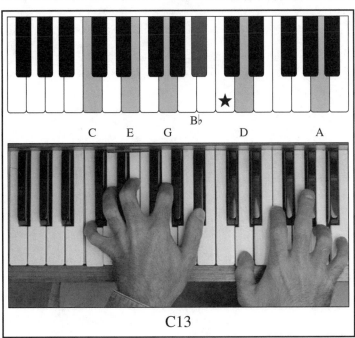

C13

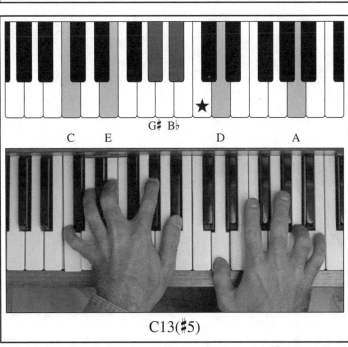

C13(♯5)

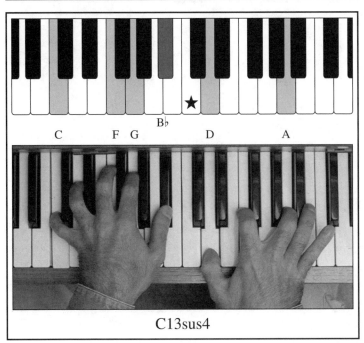

C13sus4

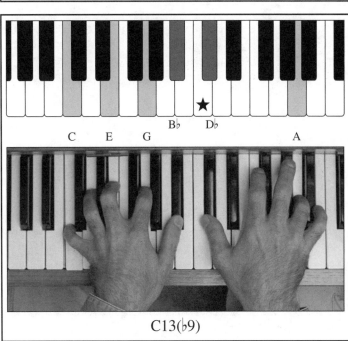

C13(♭9)

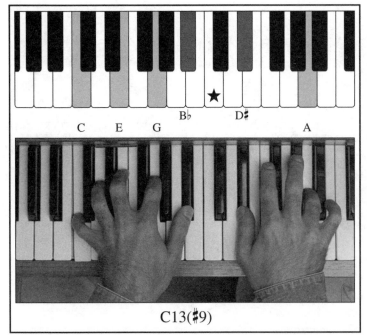

C13(♯9)

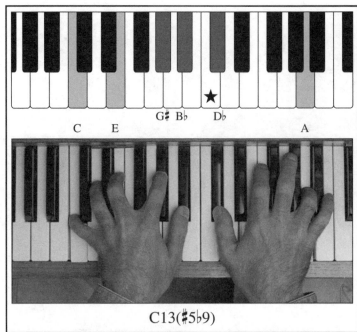

C13(♯5♭9)

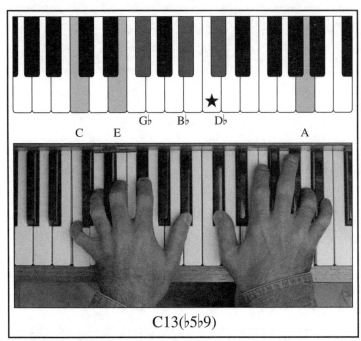

C13(♭5♭9)

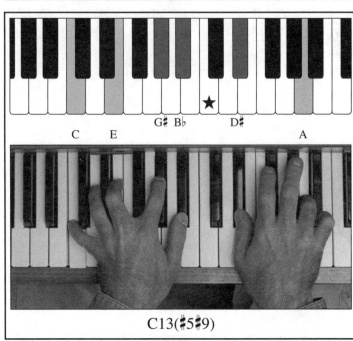

C13(♯5♯9)

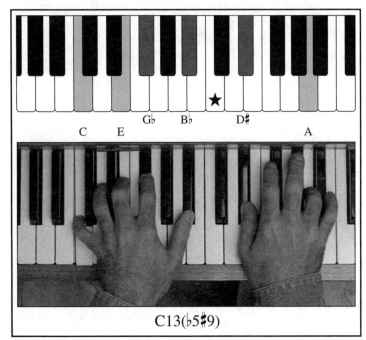

C13(♭5♯9)

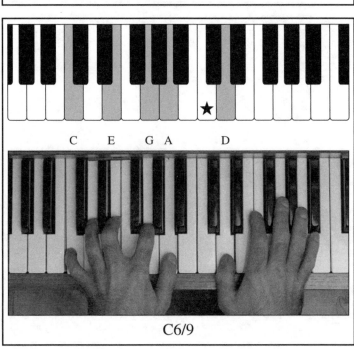

C6/9

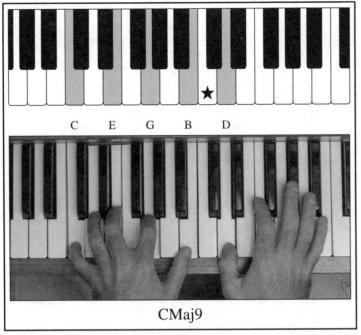

CMaj9

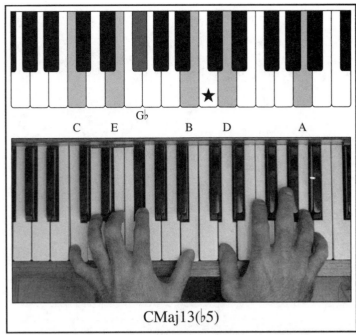

CMaj13(♭5)

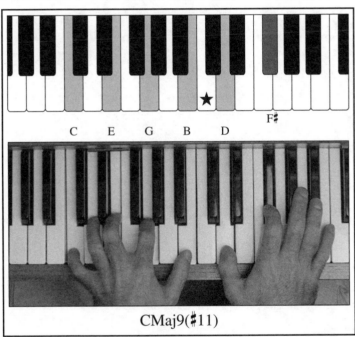

CMaj9(♯11)

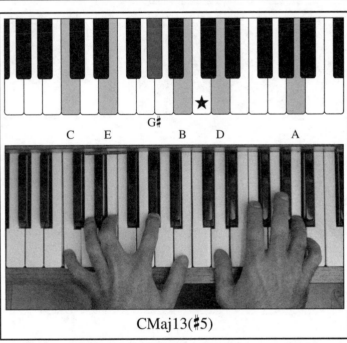

CMaj13(♯5)

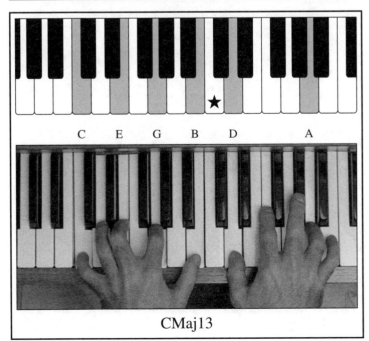

CMaj13

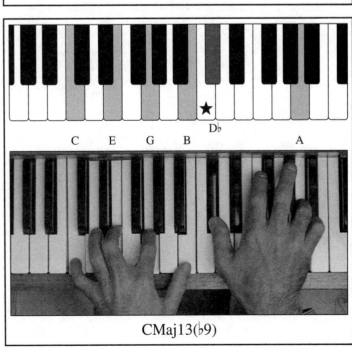

CMaj13(♭9)

119

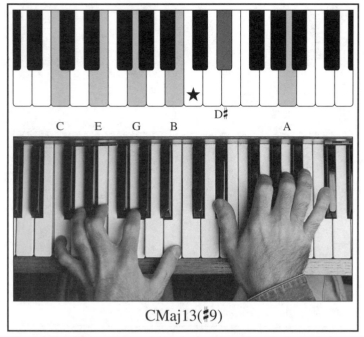

CMaj13(♯9)

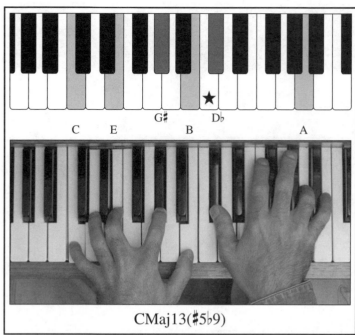

CMaj13(♯5♭9)

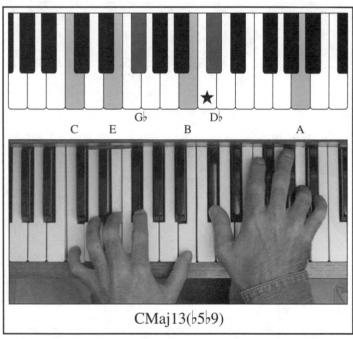

CMaj13(♭5♭9)

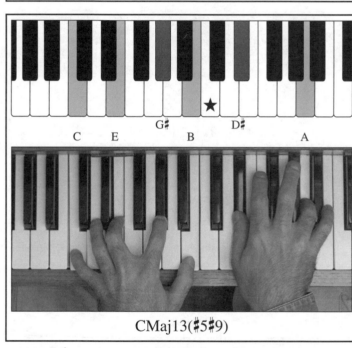

CMaj13(♯5♯9)

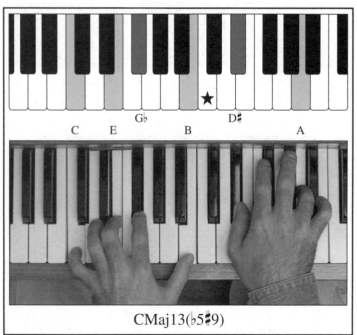

CMaj13(♭5♯9)

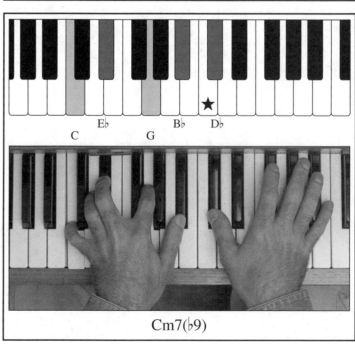

Cm7(♭9)

120

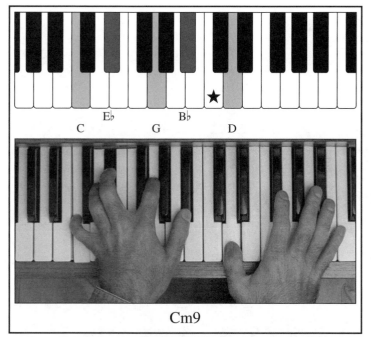

Cm9

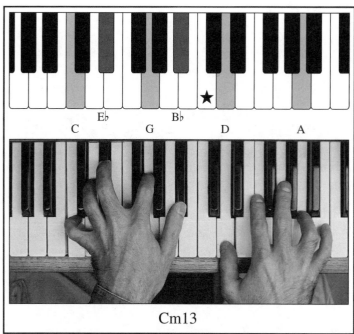

Cm13

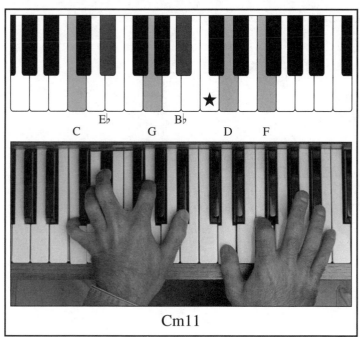

Cm11

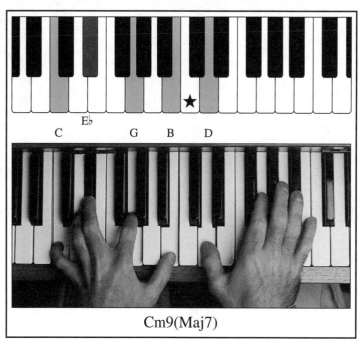

Cm9(Maj7)

G
Chords

For Two Hands

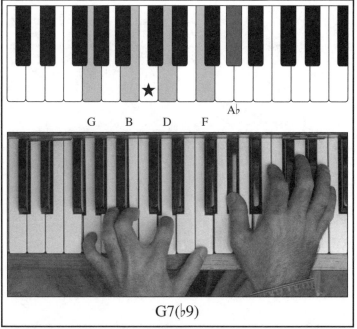

G7(♭9)

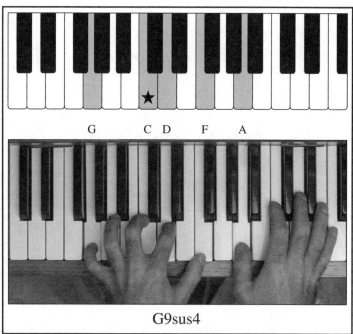

G9sus4

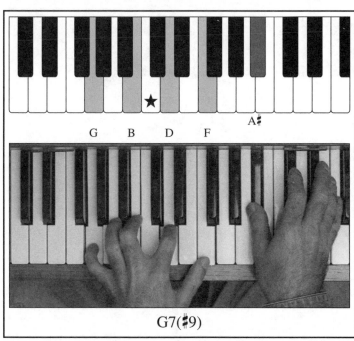

G7(♯9)

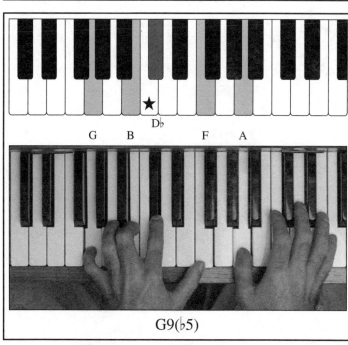

G9(♭5)

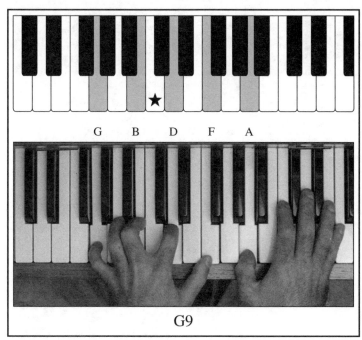

G9

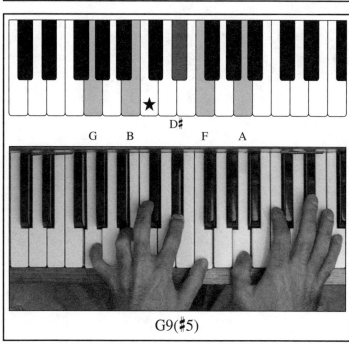

G9(♯5)

123

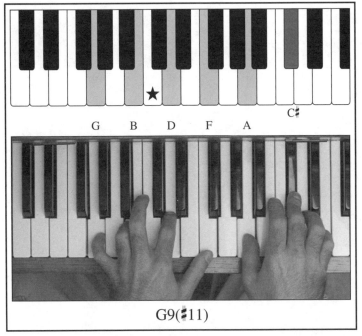

G9(♯11)

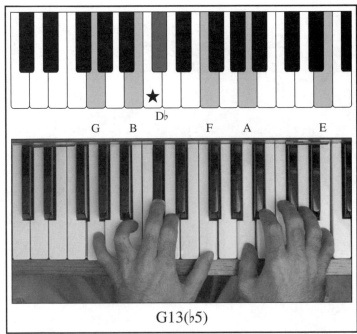

G13(♭5)

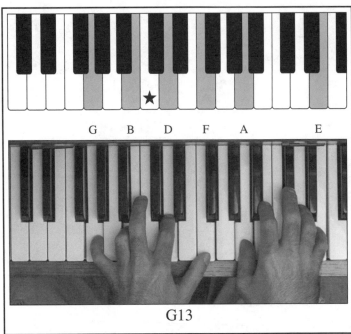

G13

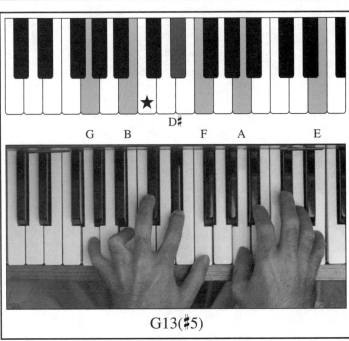

G13(♯5)

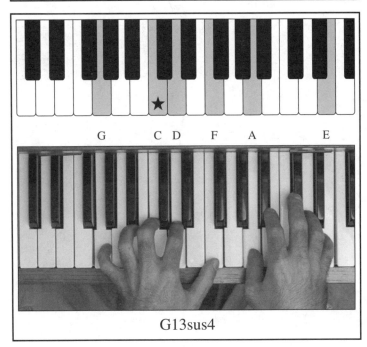

G13sus4

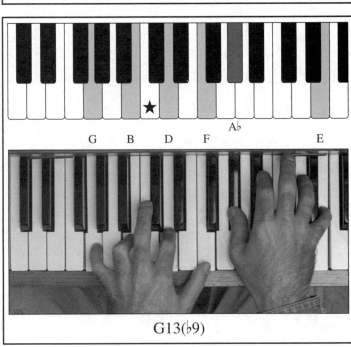

G13(♭9)

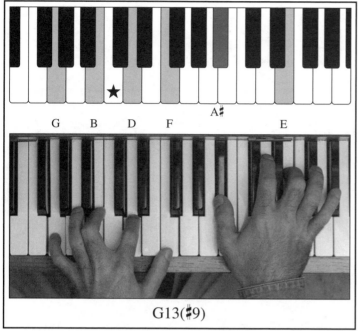

G13(♯9)

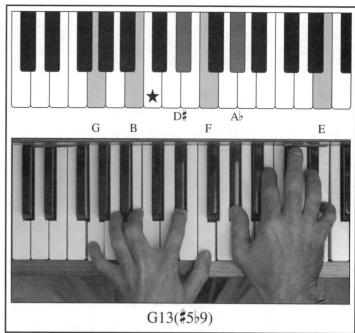

G13(♯5♭9)

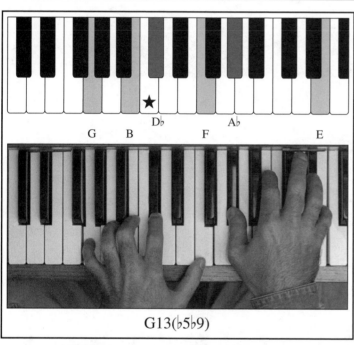

G13(♭5♭9)

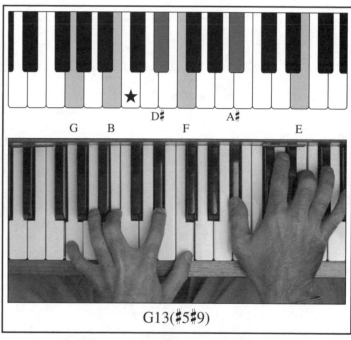

G13(♯5♯9)

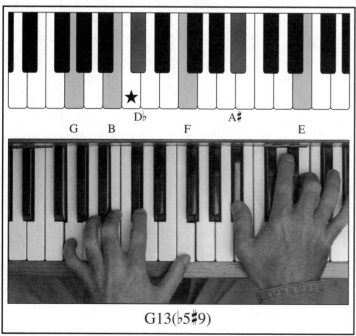

G13(♭5♯9)

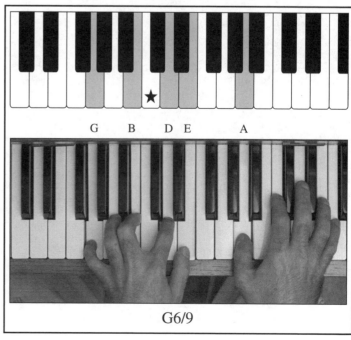

G6/9

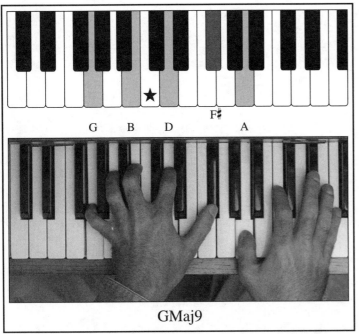

GMaj9

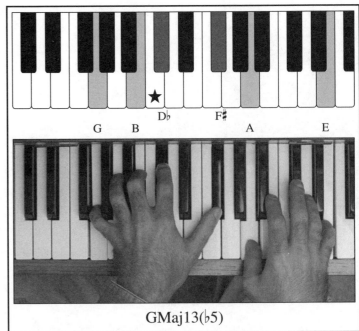

GMaj13(♭5)

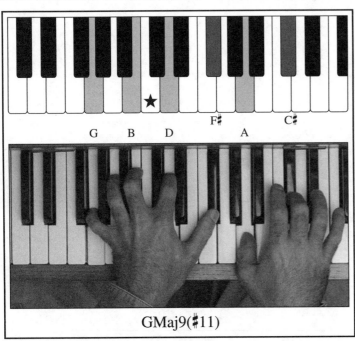

GMaj9(♯11)

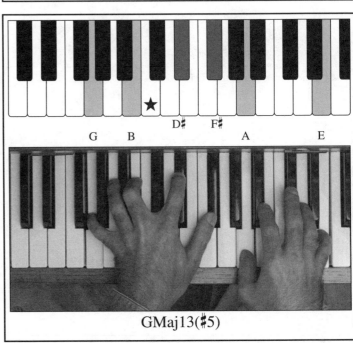

GMaj13(♯5)

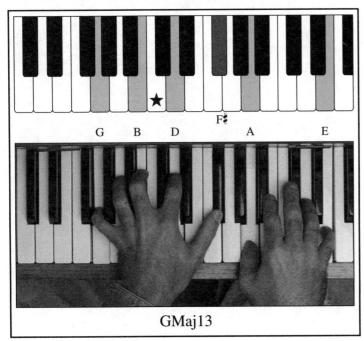

GMaj13

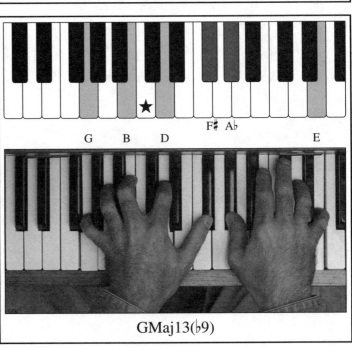

GMaj13(♭9)

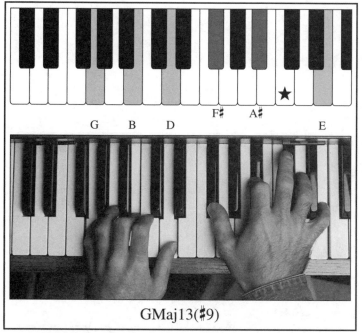

GMaj13(♯9)

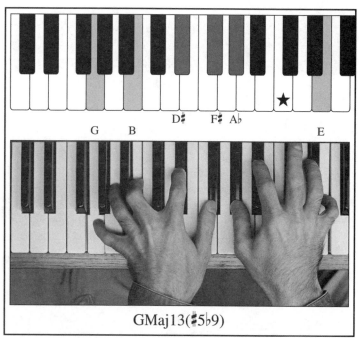

GMaj13(♯5♭9)

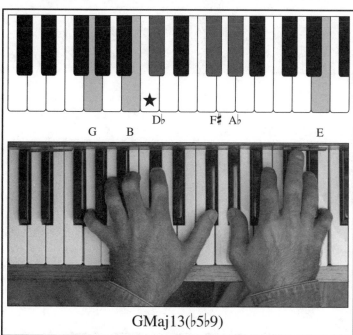

GMaj13(♭5♭9)

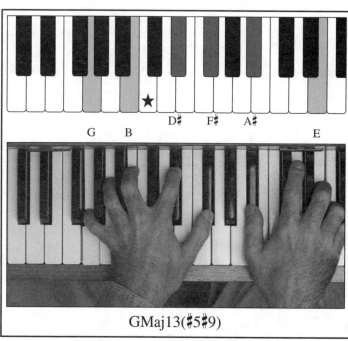

GMaj13(♯5♯9)

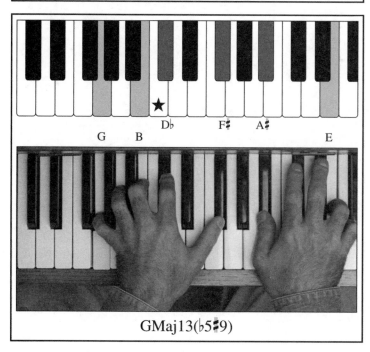

GMaj13(♭5♯9)

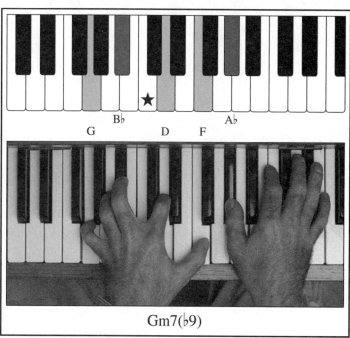

Gm7(♭9)

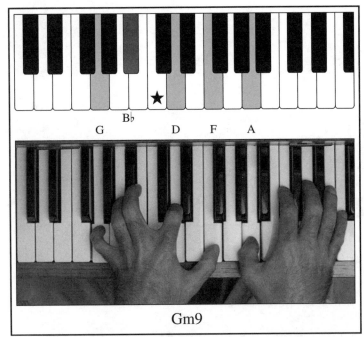

Gm9

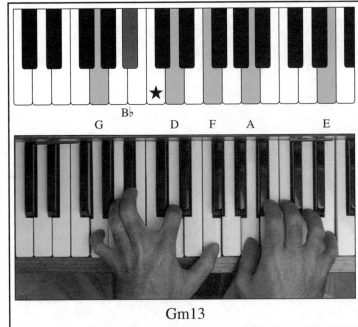

Gm13

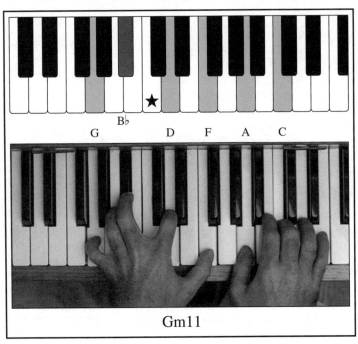

Gm11

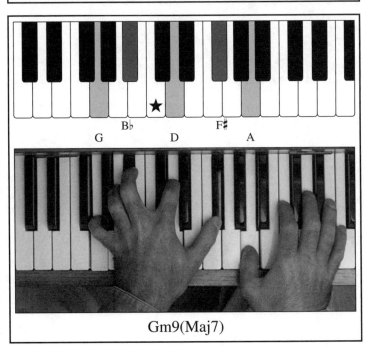

Gm9(Maj7)

D
Chords

For Two Hands

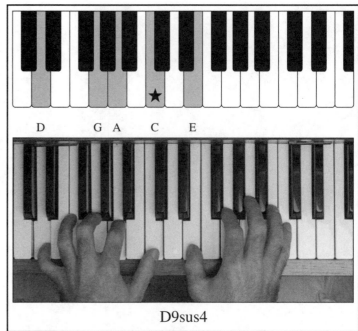

F#   Eb
D   A   C

D7(♭9)

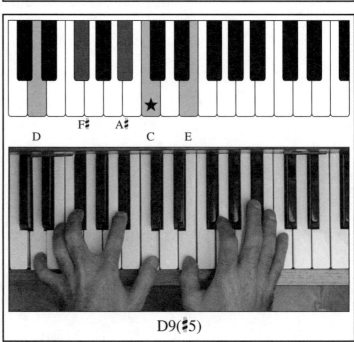

D   G A   C   E

D9sus4

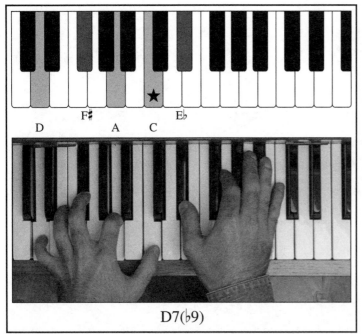

F#   A   C   E#
D

D7(♯9)

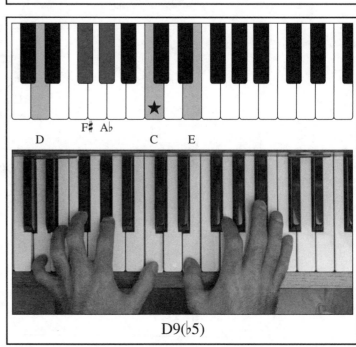

F# A♭   C   E
D

D9(♭5)

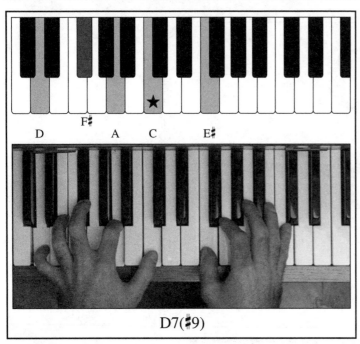

F#
D   A   C   E

D9

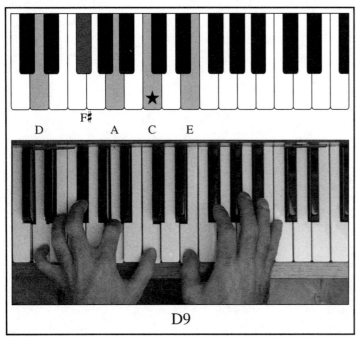

F#   A#   C   E
D

D9(♯5)

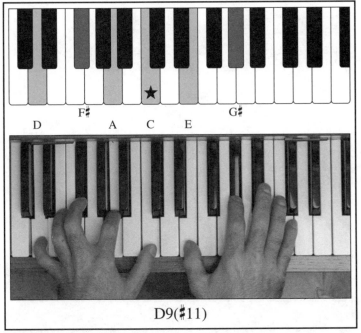

D9(♯11)

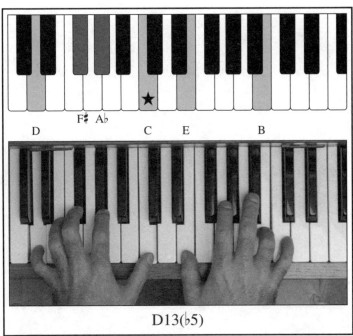

D13(♭5)

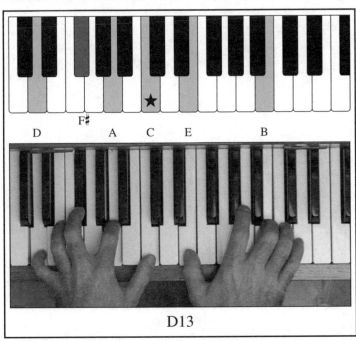

D13

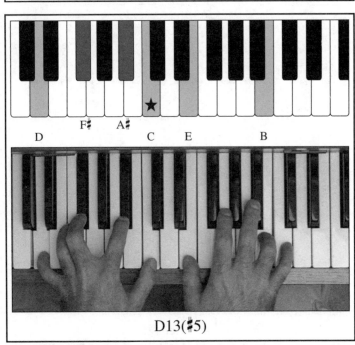

D13(♯5)

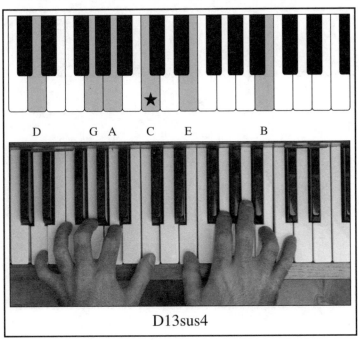

D13sus4

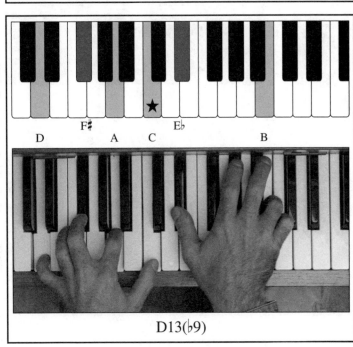

D13(♭9)

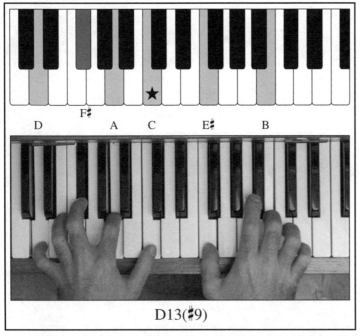

D13(#9)

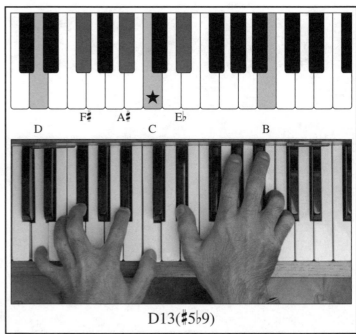

D13(#5♭9)

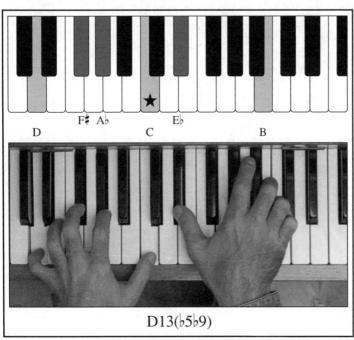

D13(♭5♭9)

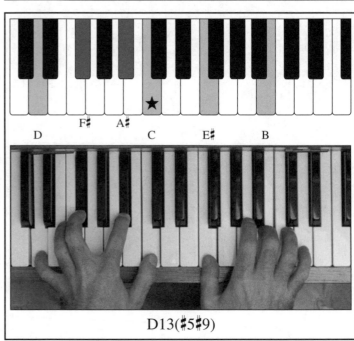

D13(#5#9)

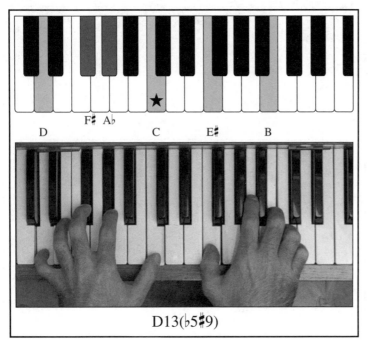

D13(♭5#9)

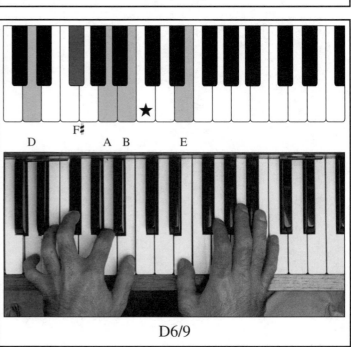

D6/9

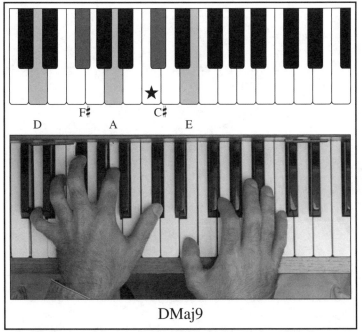

DMaj9

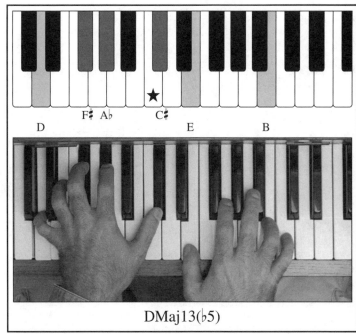

DMaj13(♭5)

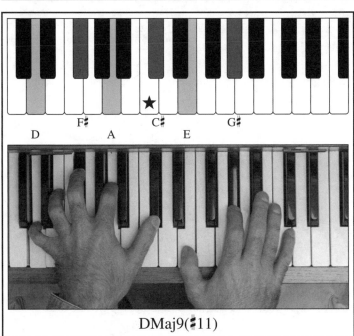

DMaj9(♯11)

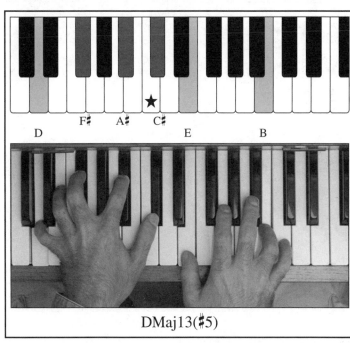

DMaj13(♯5)

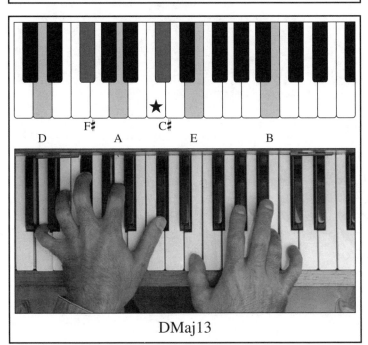

DMaj13

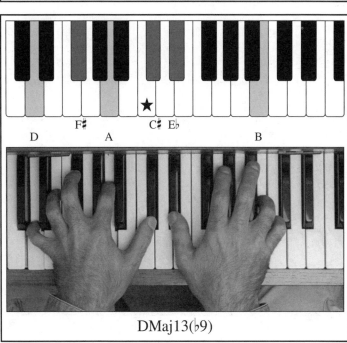

DMaj13(♭9)

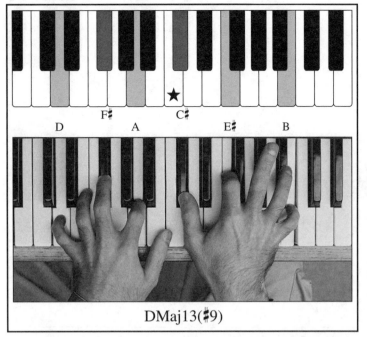

DMaj13(♯9)

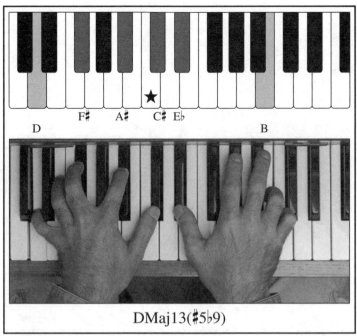

DMaj13(♯5♭9)

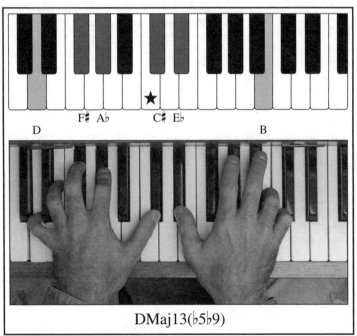

DMaj13(♭5♭9)

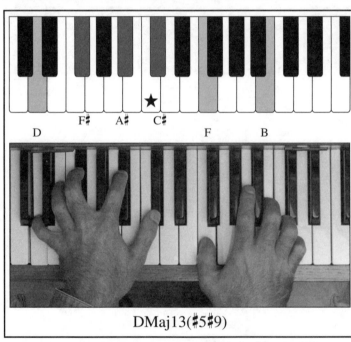

DMaj13(♯5♯9)

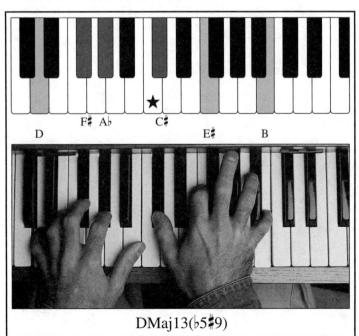

DMaj13(♭5♯9)

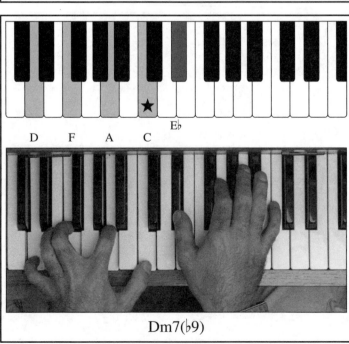

Dm7(♭9)

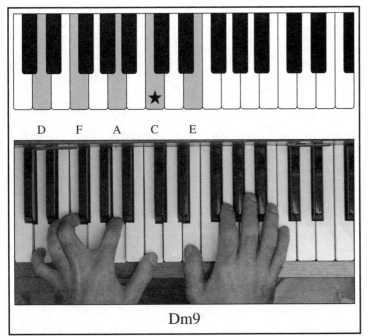

Dm9

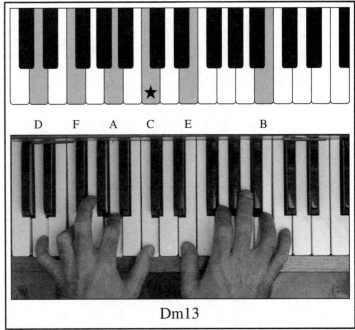

Dm13

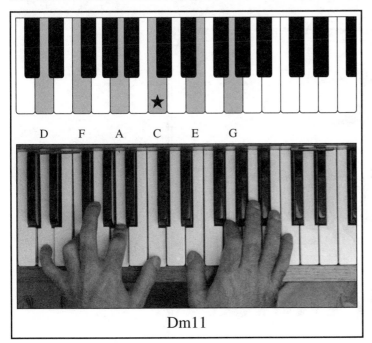

Dm11

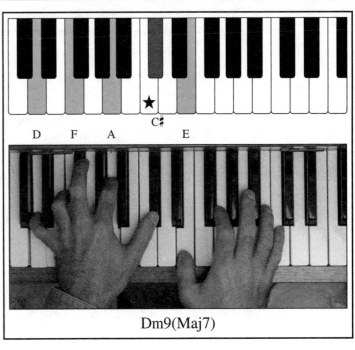

Dm9(Maj7)

135

A
Chords

For Two Hands

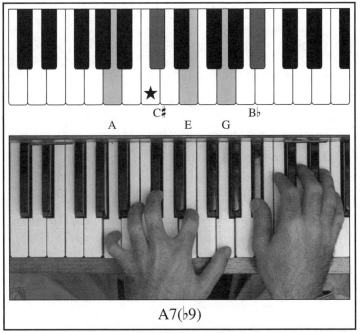

A7(♭9)

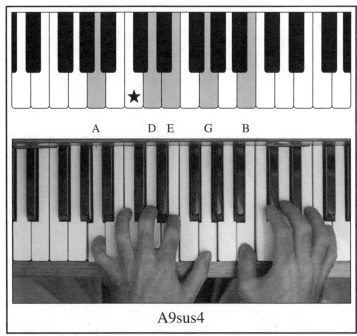

A9sus4

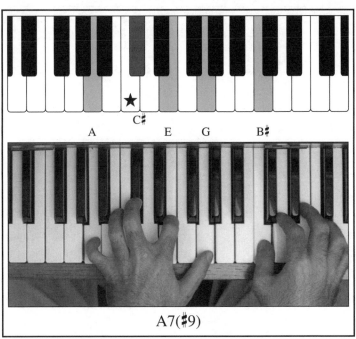

A7(♯9)

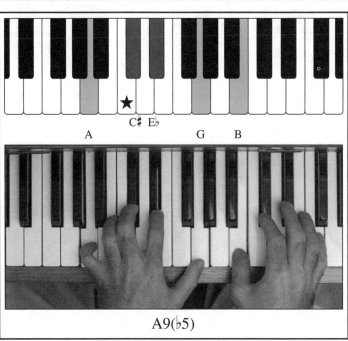

A9(♭5)

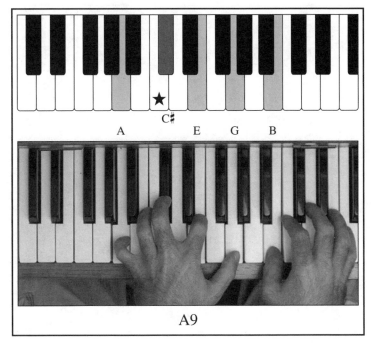

A9

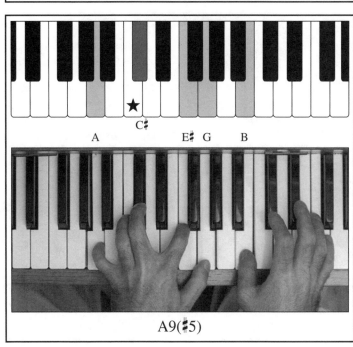

A9(♯5)

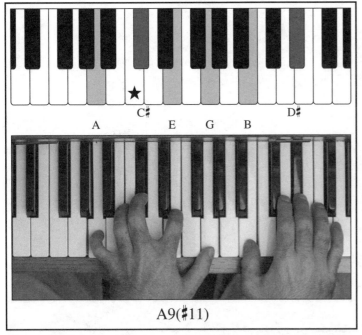

A9(♯11)

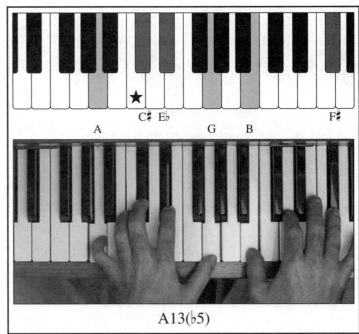

A13(♭5)

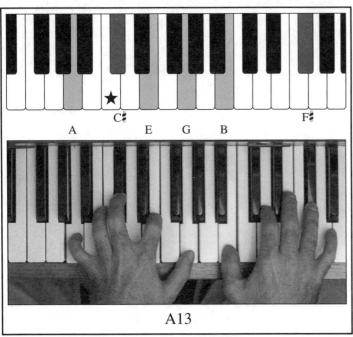

A13

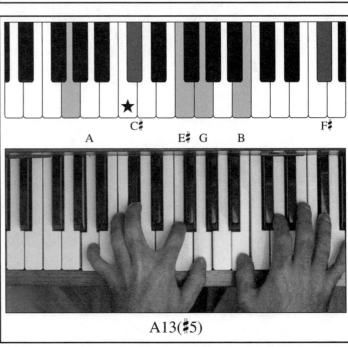

A13(♯5)

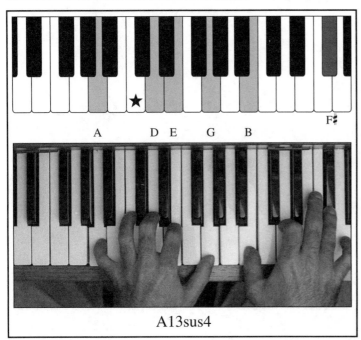

A13sus4

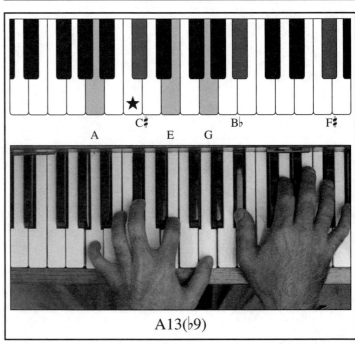

A13(♭9)

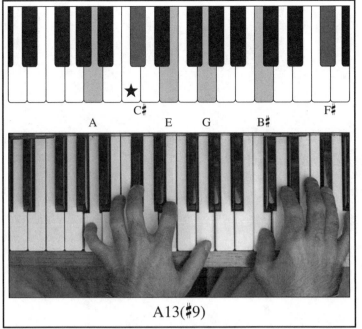

A13(♯9)

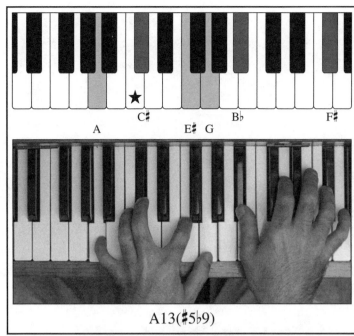

A13(♯5♭9)

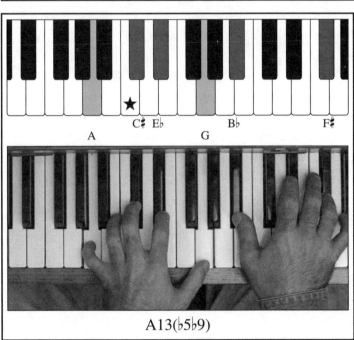

A13(♭5♭9)

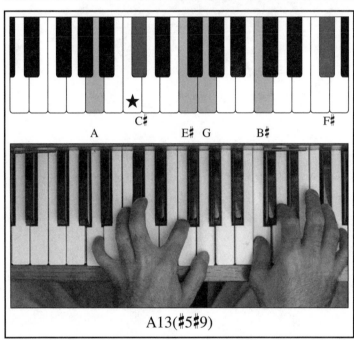

A13(♯5♯9)

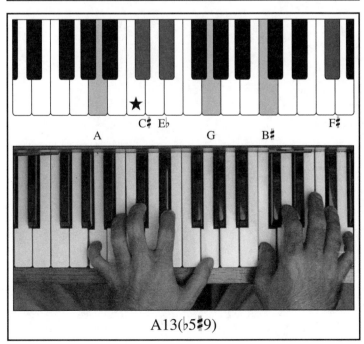

A13(♭5♯9)

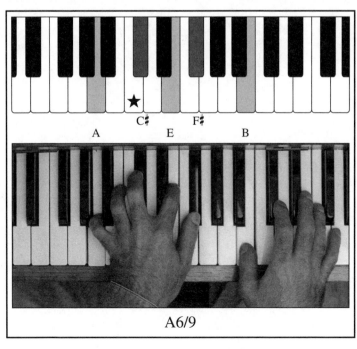

A6/9

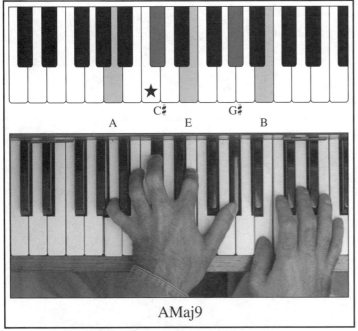

AMaj9

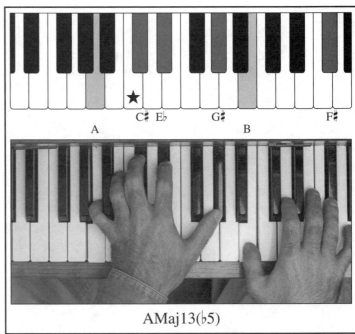

AMaj13(♭5)

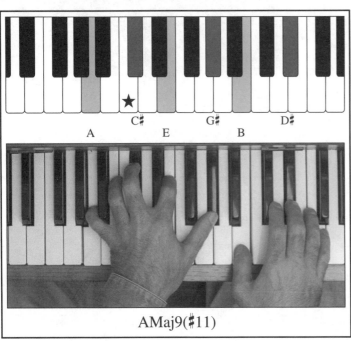

AMaj9(♯11)

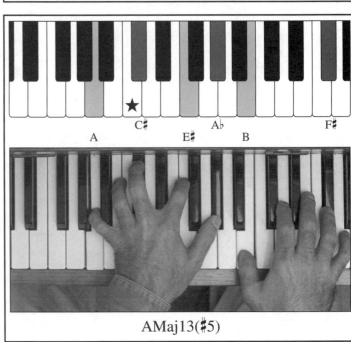

AMaj13(♯5)

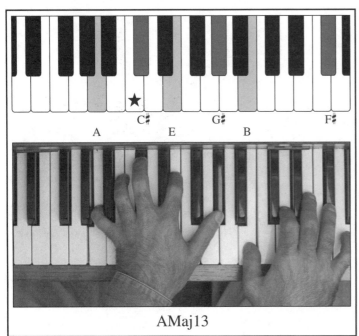

AMaj13

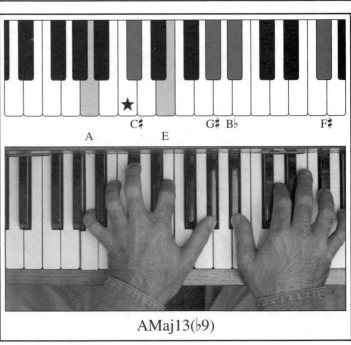

AMaj13(♭9)

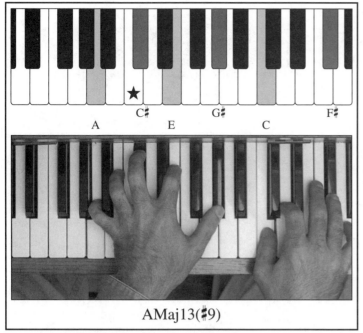

AMaj13(♯9)

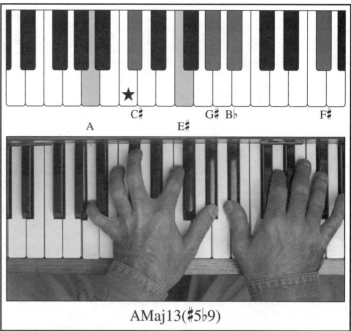

AMaj13(♯5♭9)

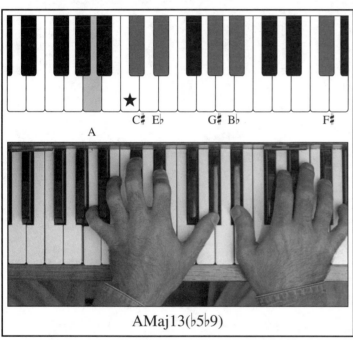

AMaj13(♭5♭9)

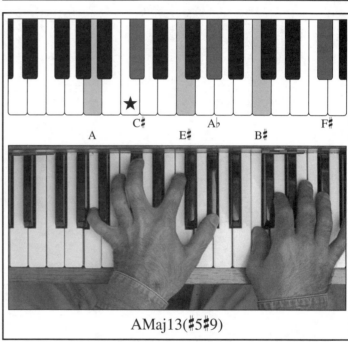

AMaj13(♯5♯9)

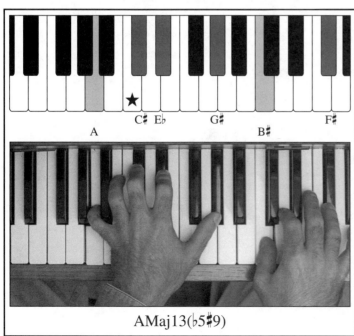

AMaj13(♭5♯9)

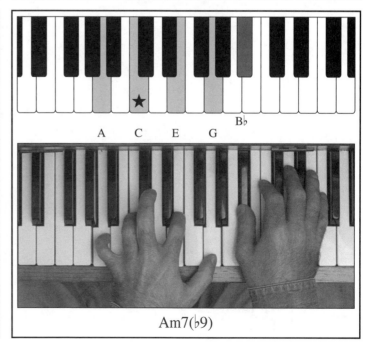

Am7(♭9)

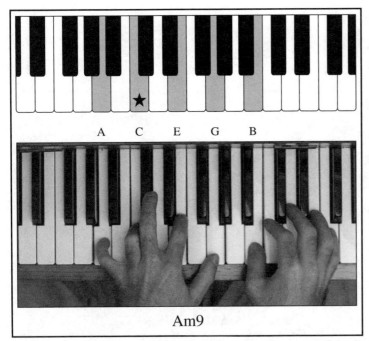

Am9

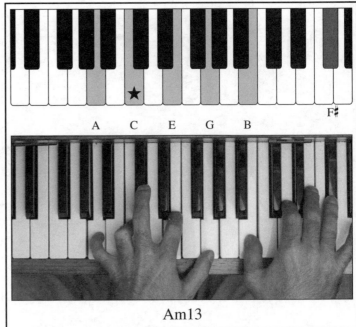

Am13

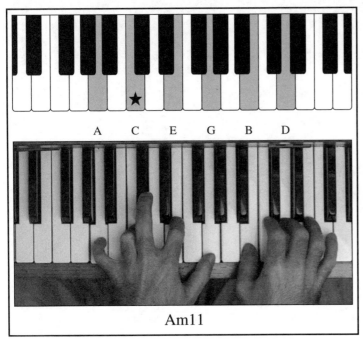

Am11

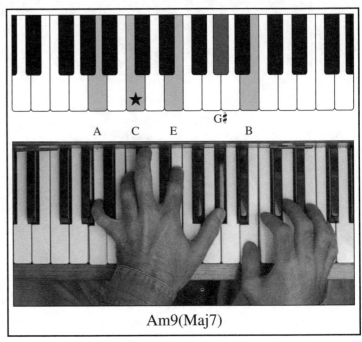

Am9(Maj7)

E
Chords

For Two Hands

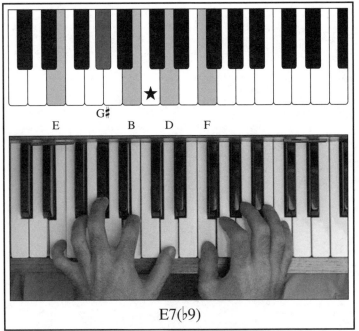

E7(♭9)

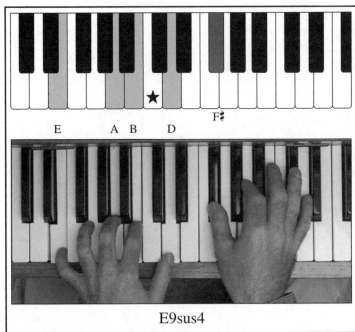

E9sus4

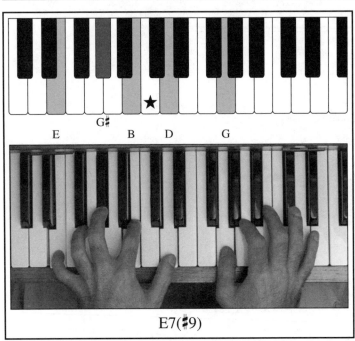

E7(♯9)

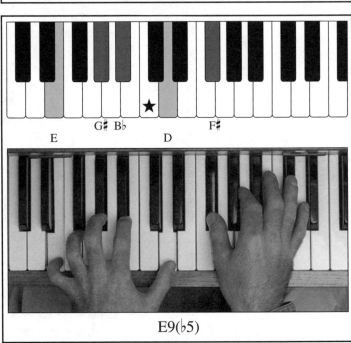

E9(♭5)

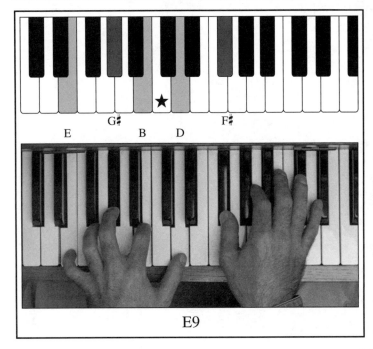

E9

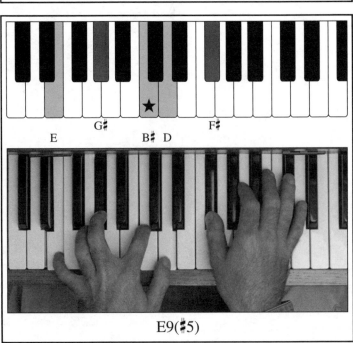

E9(♯5)

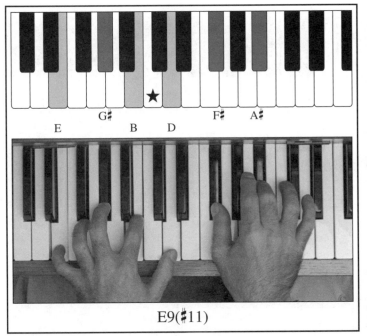

E9(♯11)

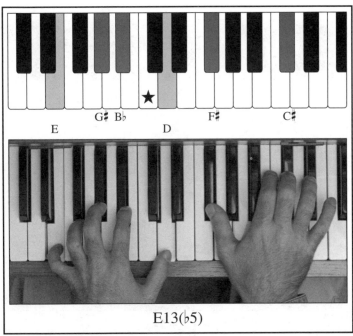

E13(♭5)

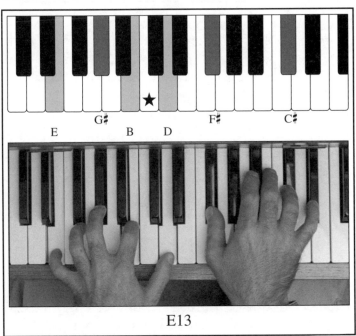

E13

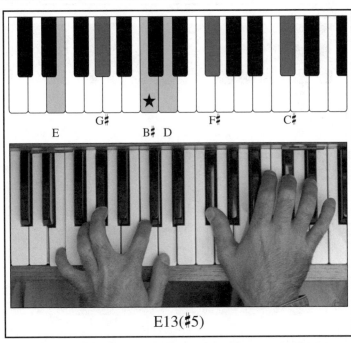

E13(♯5)

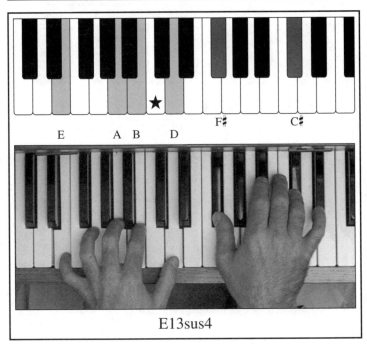

E13sus4

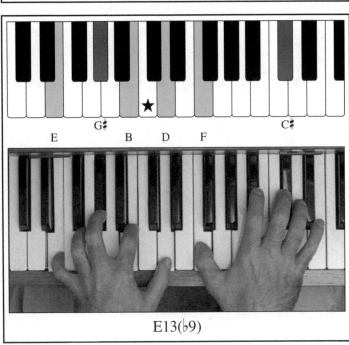

E13(♭9)

145

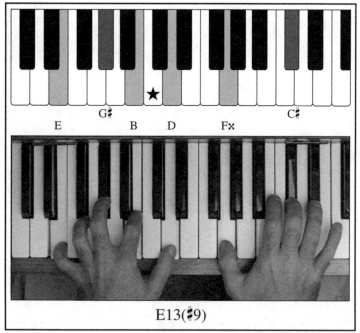

E13(♯9)

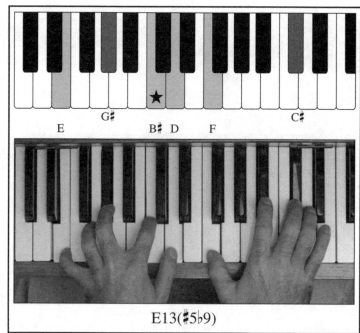

E13(♯5♭9)

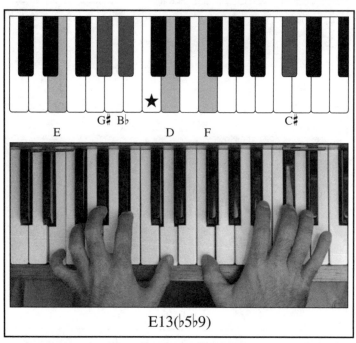

E13(♭5♭9)

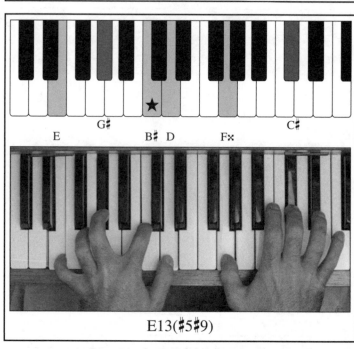

E13(♯5♯9)

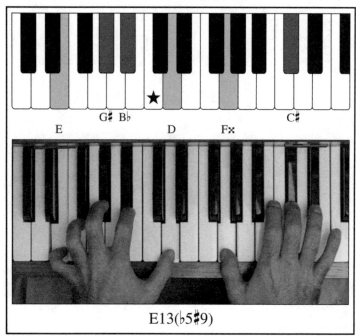

E13(♭5♯9)

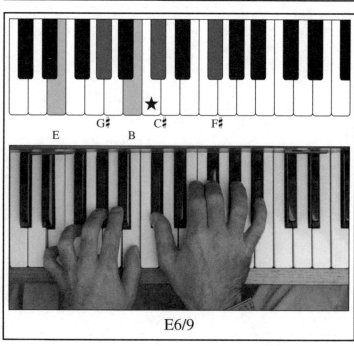

E6/9

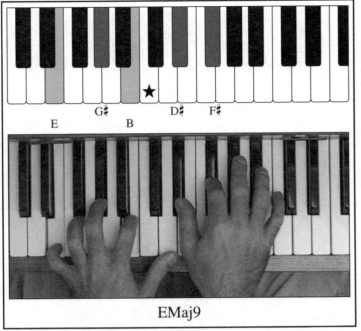

EMaj9

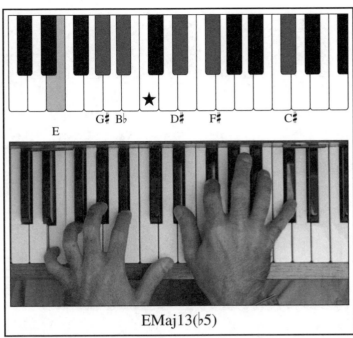

EMaj13(♭5)

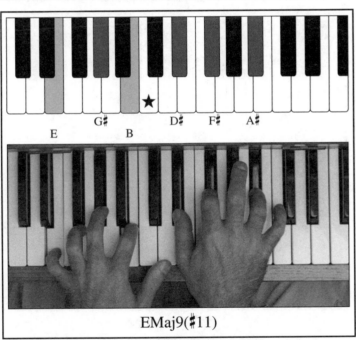

EMaj9(♯11)

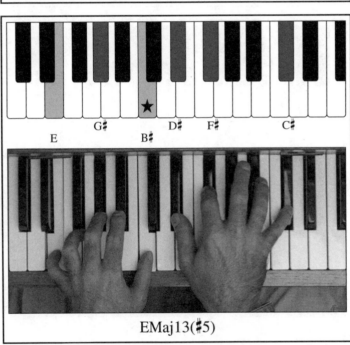

EMaj13(♯5)

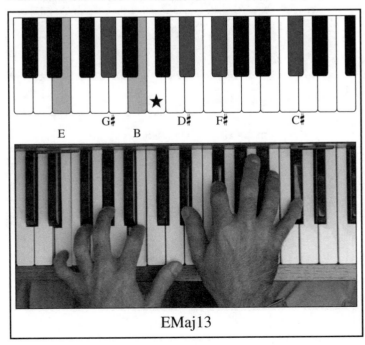

EMaj13

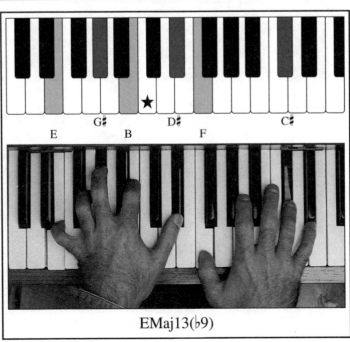

EMaj13(♭9)

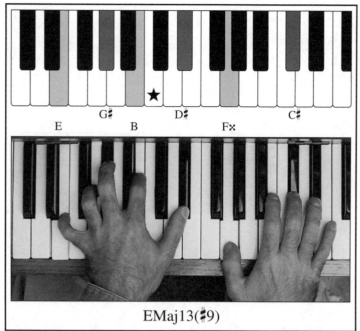

EMaj13(♯9)

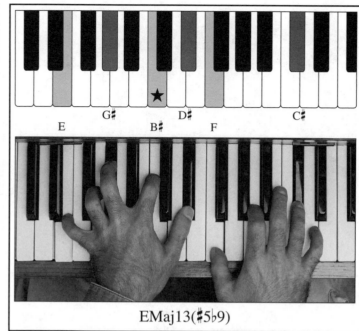

EMaj13(♯5♭9)

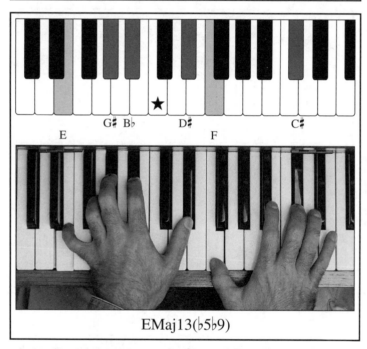

EMaj13(♭5♭9)

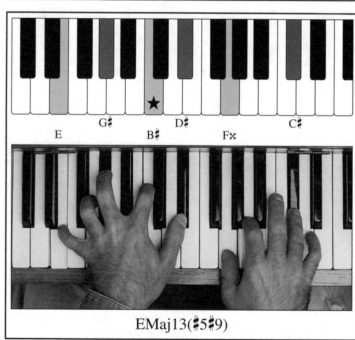

EMaj13(♯5♯9)

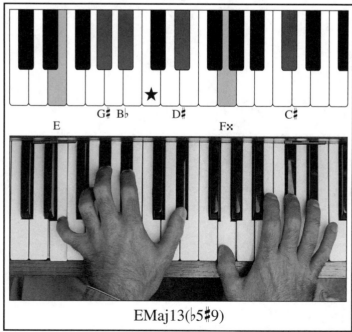

EMaj13(♭5♯9)

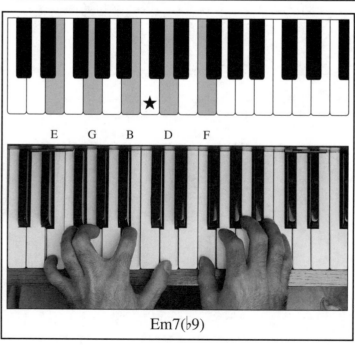

Em7(♭9)

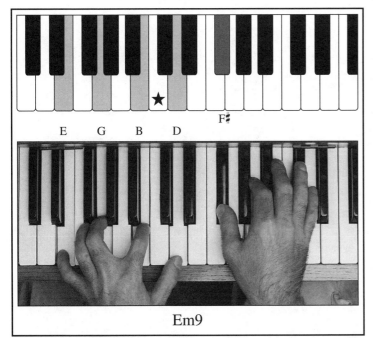

E G B D F#

Em9

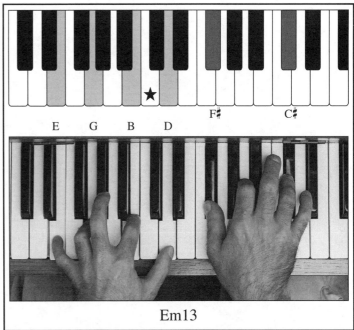

E G B D F# C#

Em13

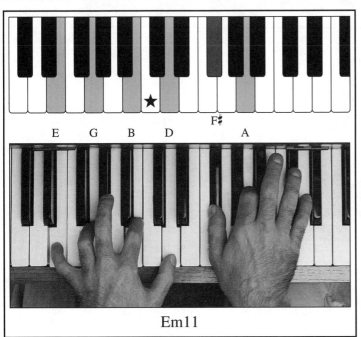

E G B D F# A

Em11

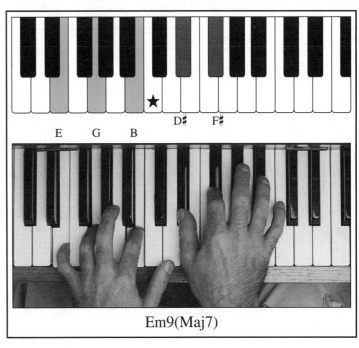

E G B D# F#

Em9(Maj7)

B
Chords

For Two Hands

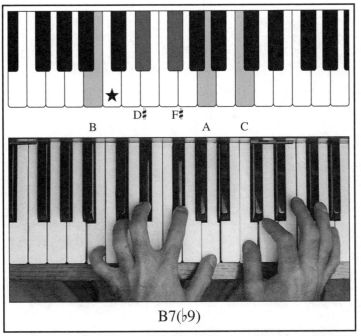

B7(♭9)

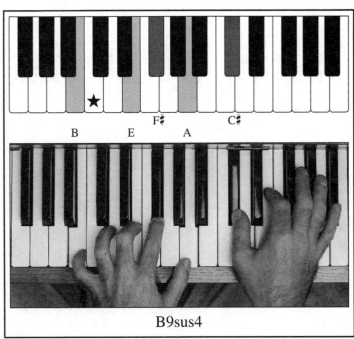

B9sus4

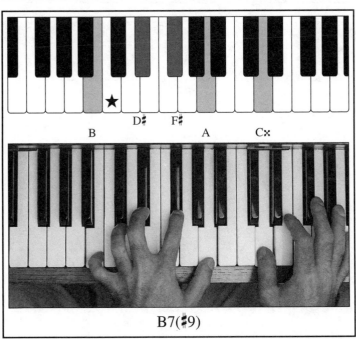

B7(♯9)

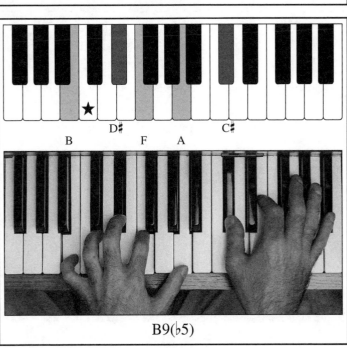

B9(♭5)

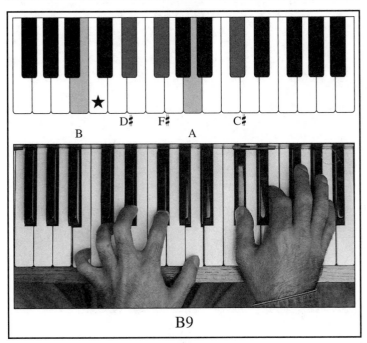

B9

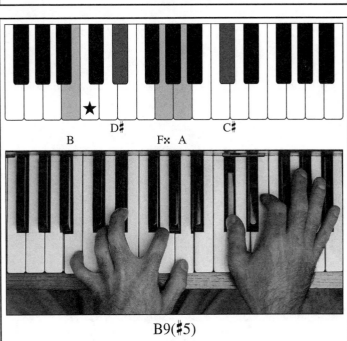

B9(♯5)

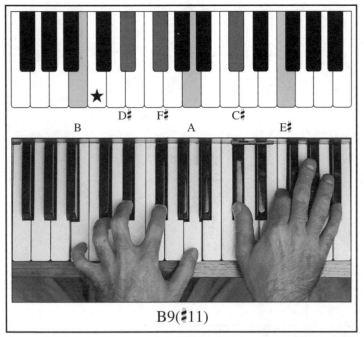

B9(♯11)

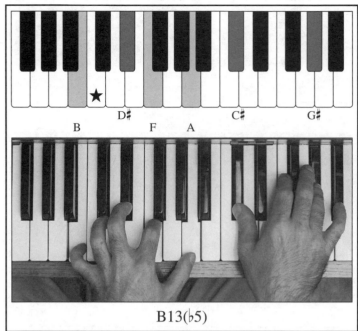

B13(♭5)

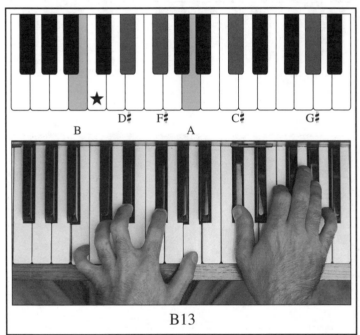

B13

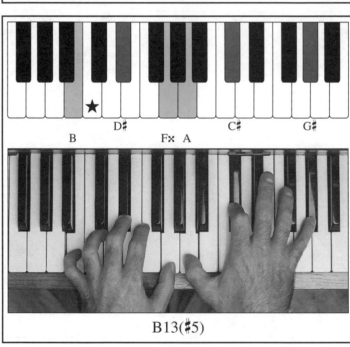

B13(♯5)

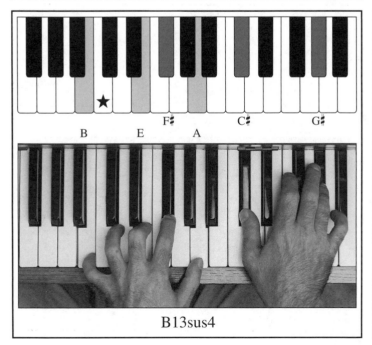

B13sus4

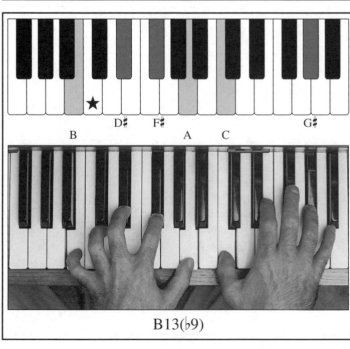

B13(♭9)

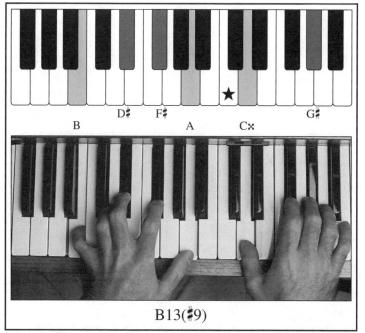

B13(♯9)

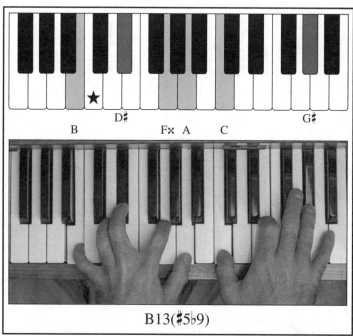

B13(♯5♭9)

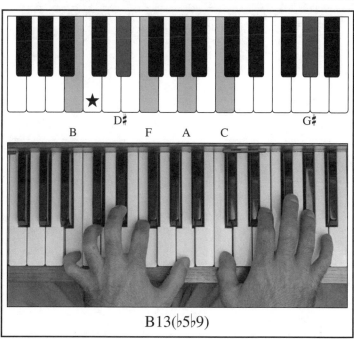

B13(♭5♭9)

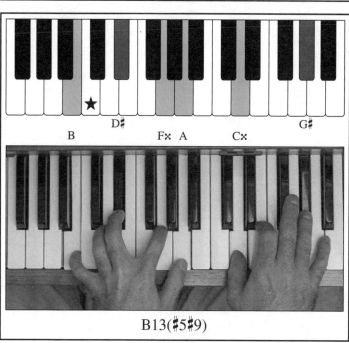

B13(♯5♯9)

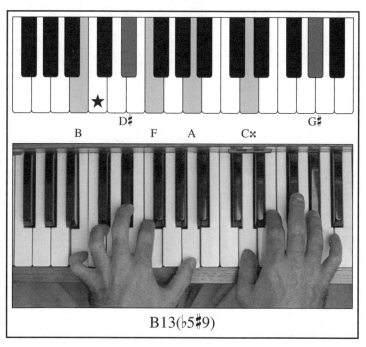

B13(♭5♯9)

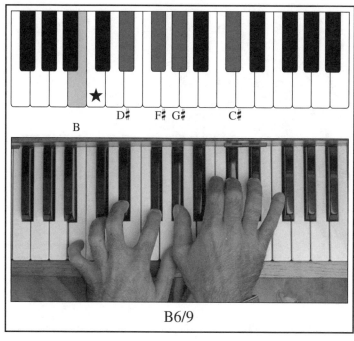

B6/9

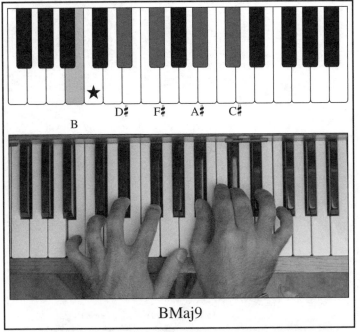

BMaj9

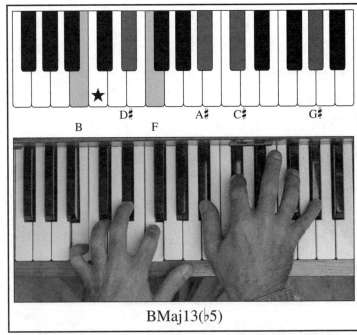

BMaj13(♭5)

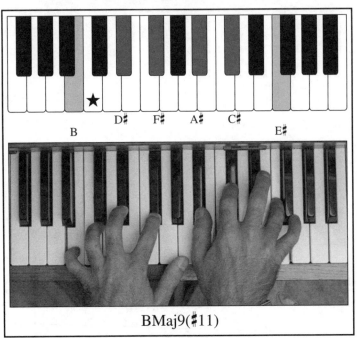

BMaj9(♯11)

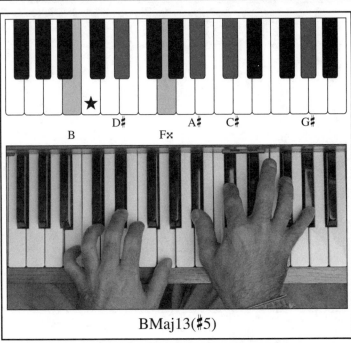

BMaj13(♯5)

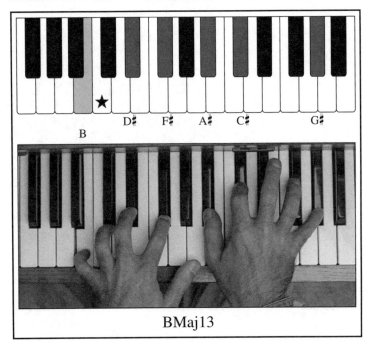

BMaj13

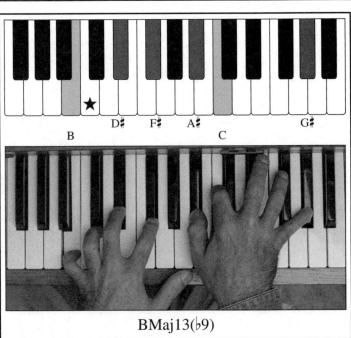

BMaj13(♭9)

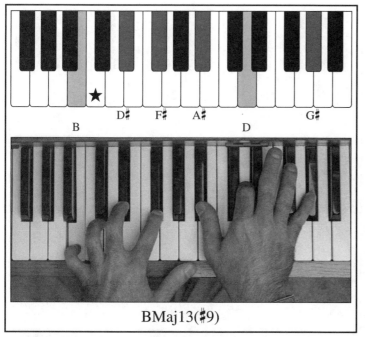

BMaj13(♯9)

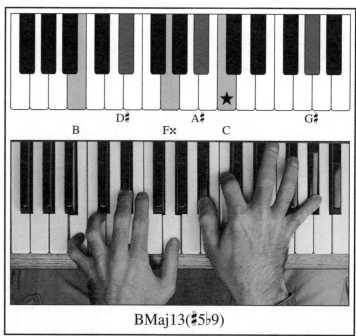

BMaj13(♯5♭9)

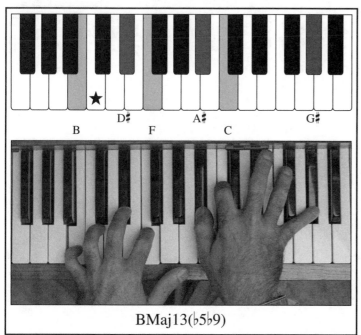

BMaj13(♭5♭9)

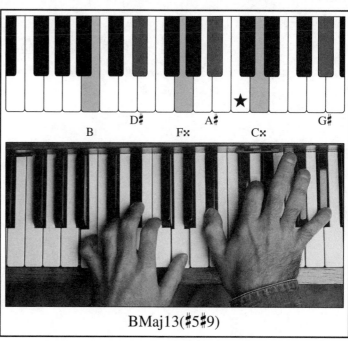

BMaj13(♯5♯9)

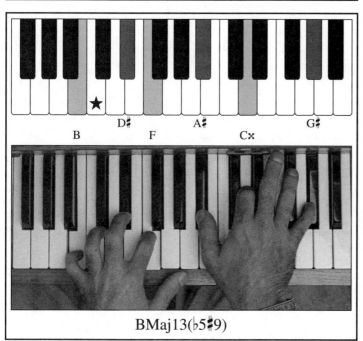

BMaj13(♭5♯9)

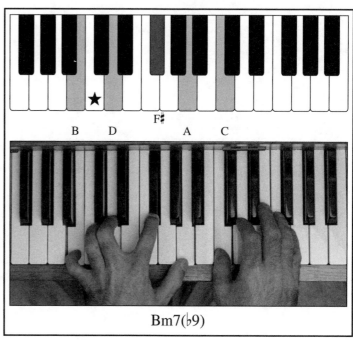

Bm7(♭9)

155

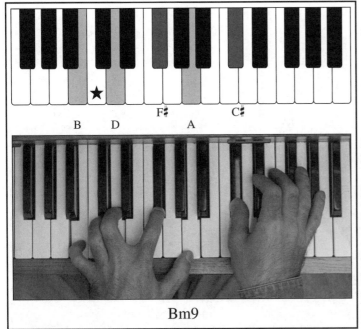

Bm9

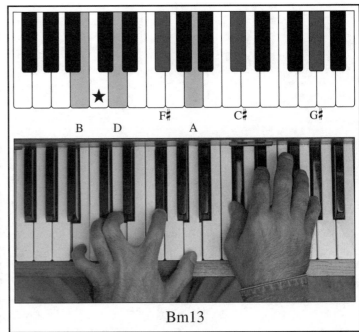

Bm13

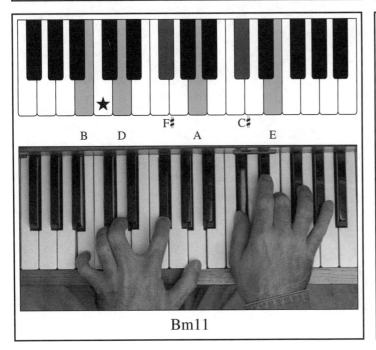

Bm11

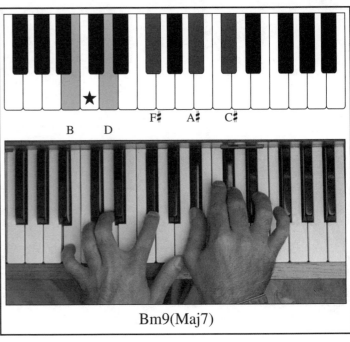

Bm9(Maj7)

F♯
Chords

For Two Hands

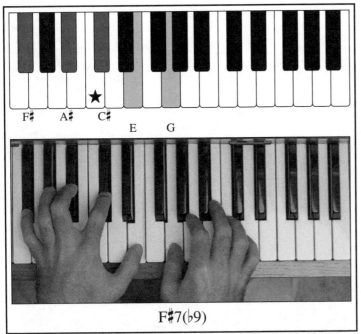

F#7(♭9)

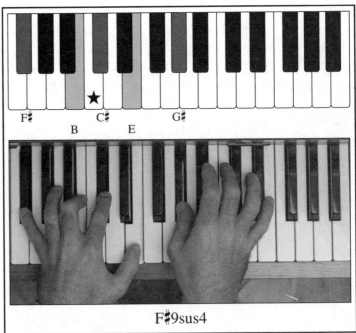

F#9sus4

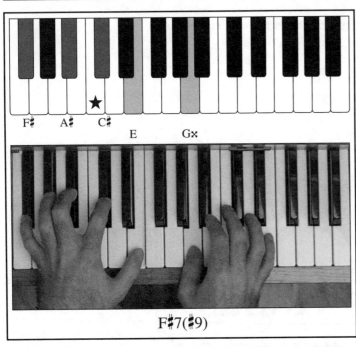

F#7(#9)

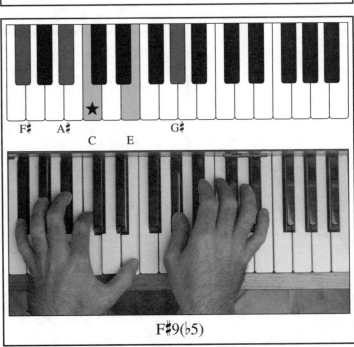

F#9(♭5)

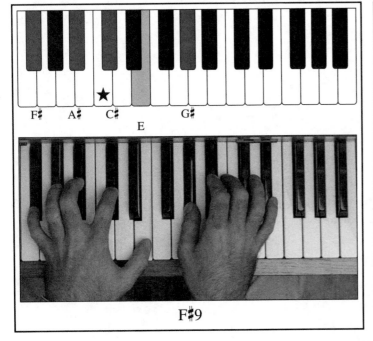

F#9

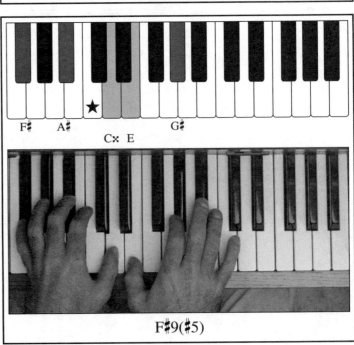

F#9(#5)

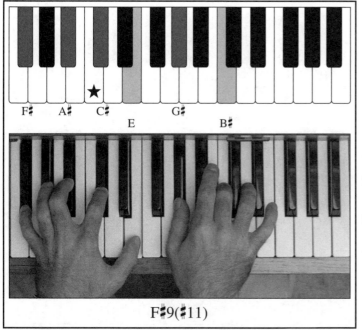

F#9(#11)

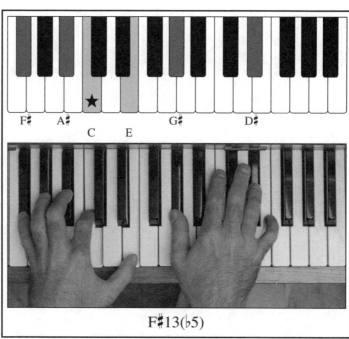

F#13(♭5)

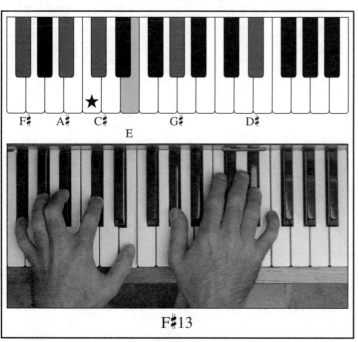

F#13

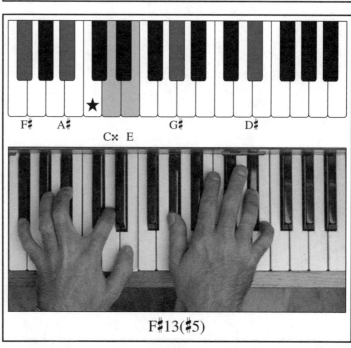

F#13(#5)

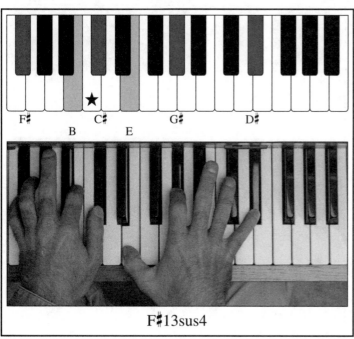

F#13sus4

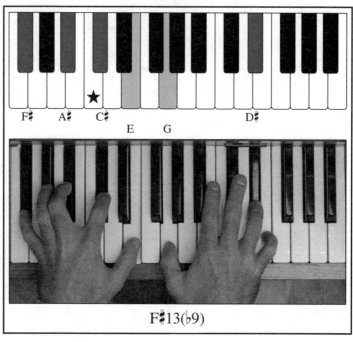

F#13(♭9)

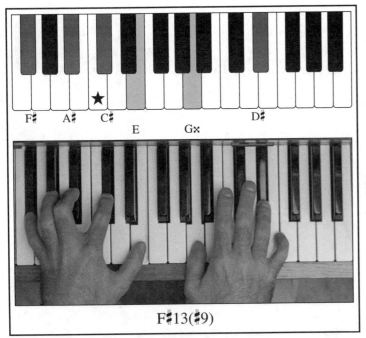

F#13(#9)

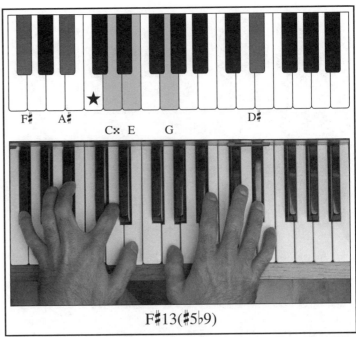

F#13(#5b9)

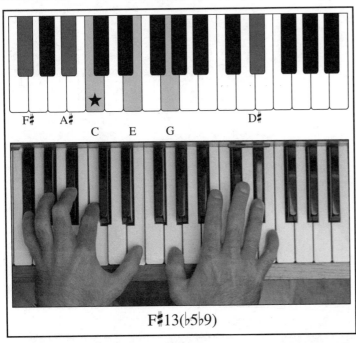

F#13(b5b9)

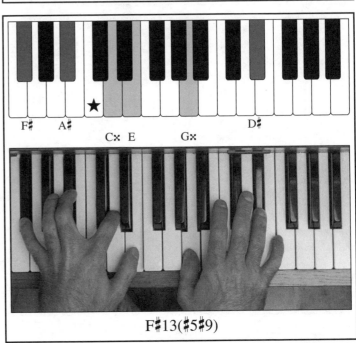

F#13(#5#9)

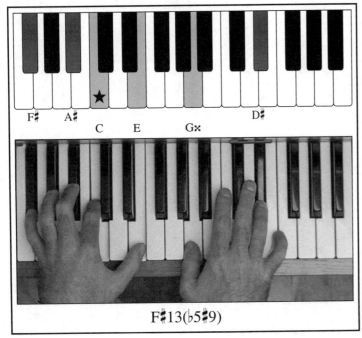

F#13(b5#9)

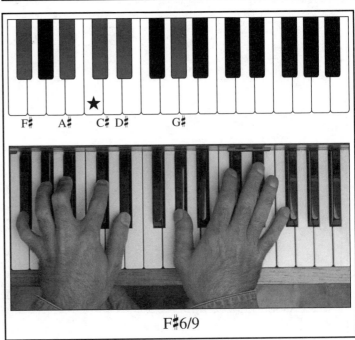

F#6/9

160

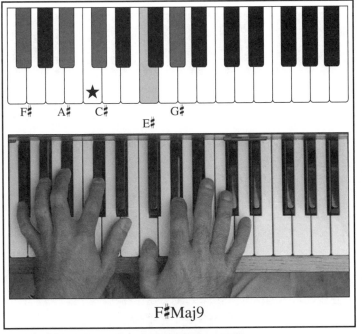

F#Maj9

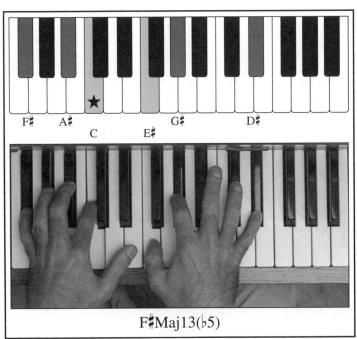

F#Maj13(♭5)

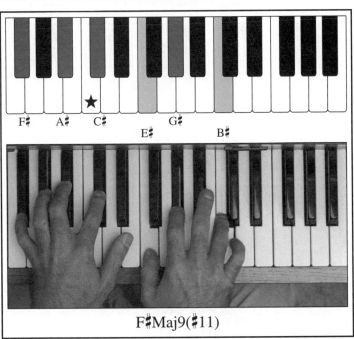

F#Maj9(#11)

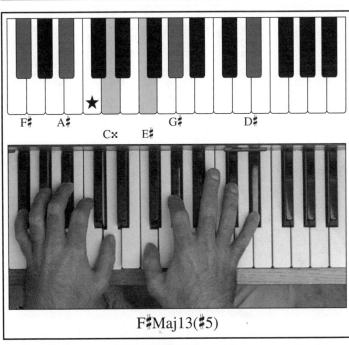

F#Maj13(#5)

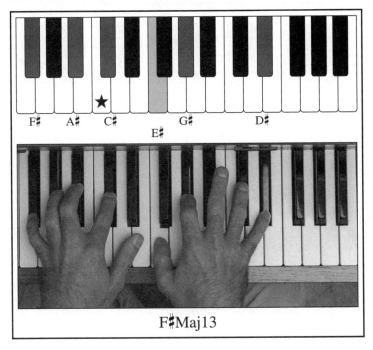

F#Maj13

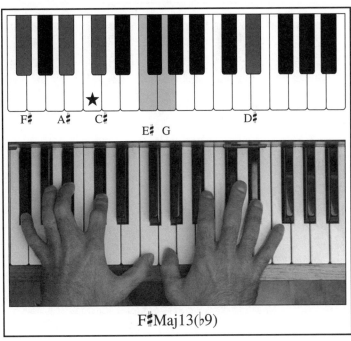

F#Maj13(♭9)

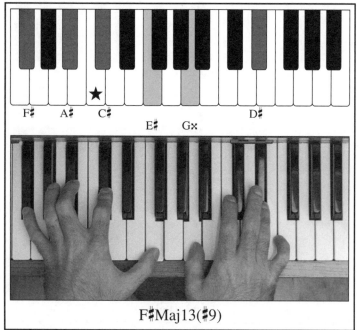

F#Maj13(#9)

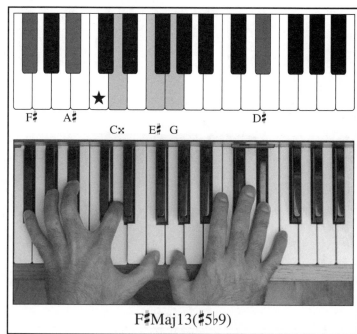

F#Maj13(#5♭9)

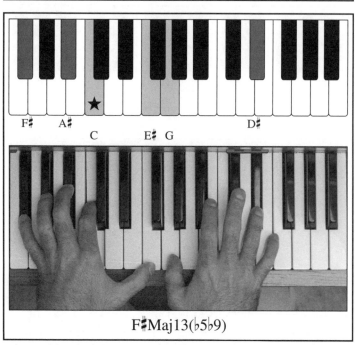

F#Maj13(♭5♭9)

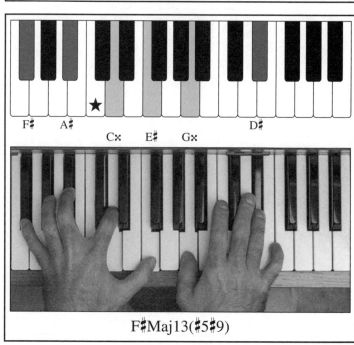

F#Maj13(#5#9)

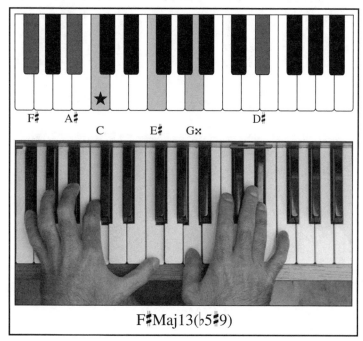

F#Maj13(♭5#9)

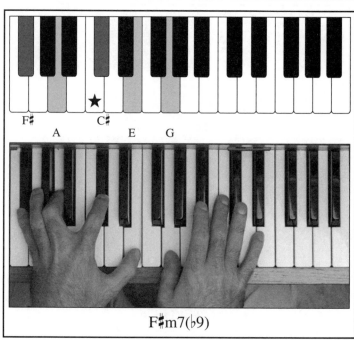

F#m7(♭9)

162

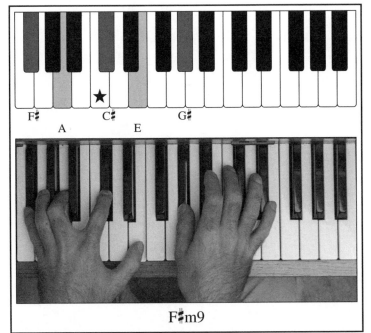

F#m9

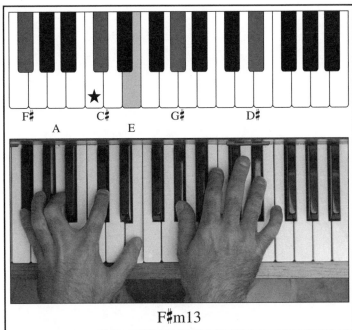

F#m13

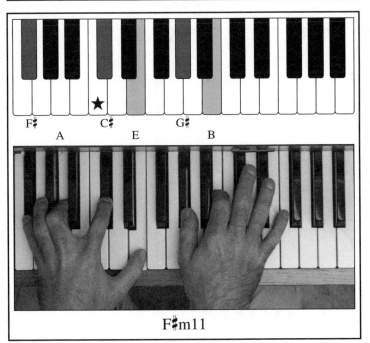

F#m11

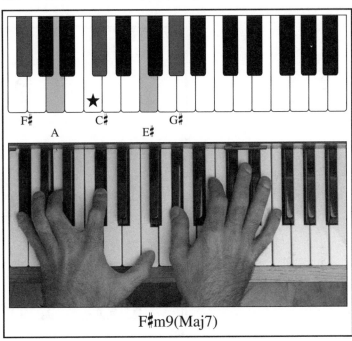

F#m9(Maj7)

163

D♭
Chords

For Two Hands

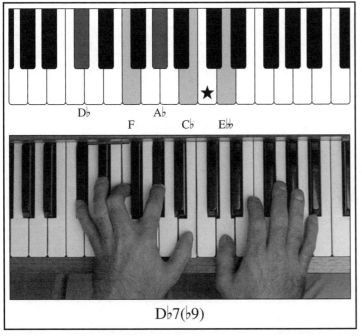

Db7(b9)

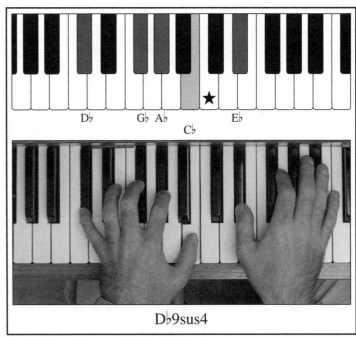

Db9sus4

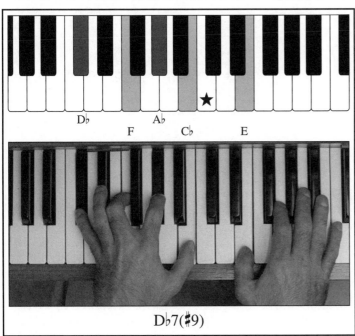

Db7(#9)

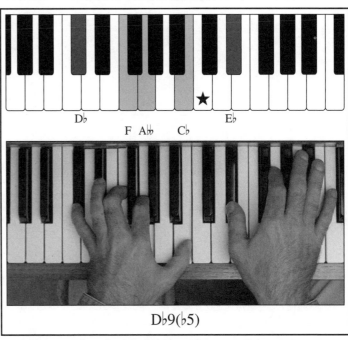

Db9(b5)

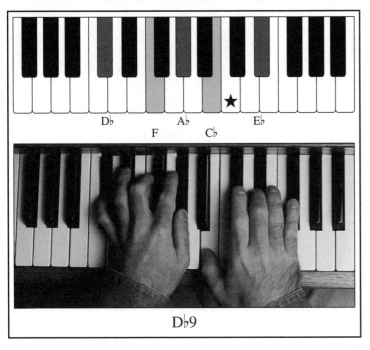

Db9

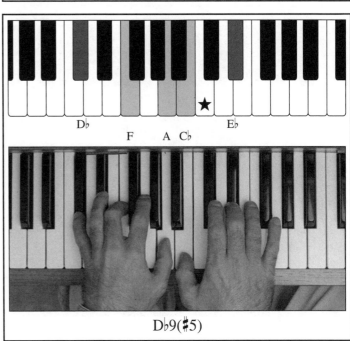

Db9(#5)

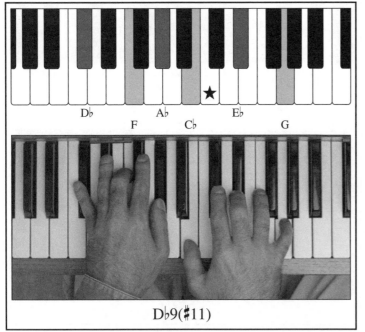

Db9(#11)

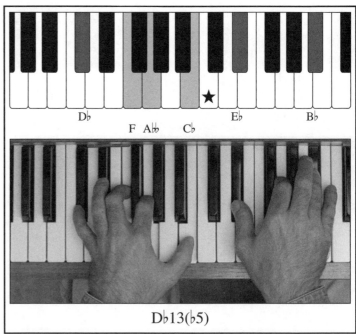

Db13(b5)

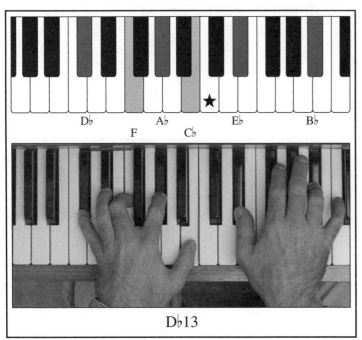

Db13

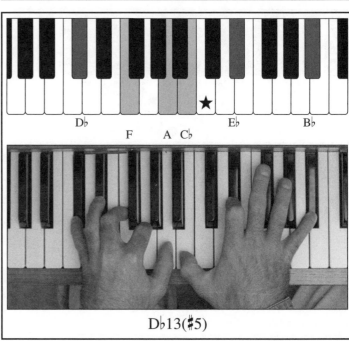

Db13(#5)

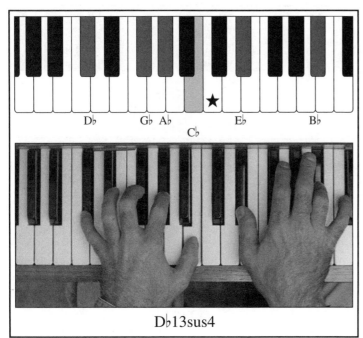

Db13sus4

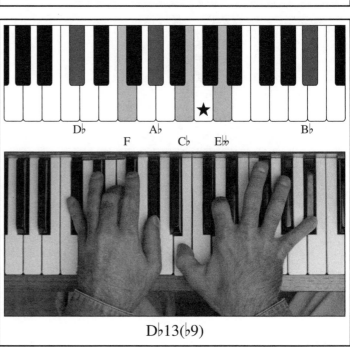

Db13(b9)

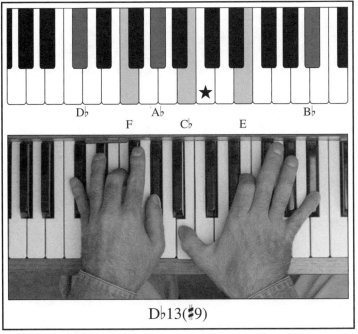

Db13(♯9)

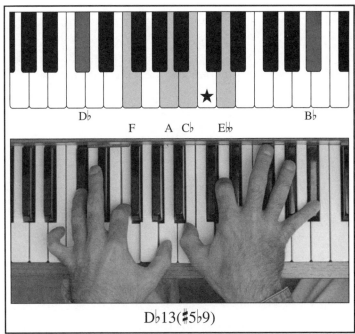

Db13(♯5b9)

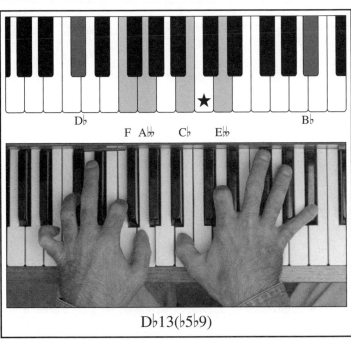

Db13(b5b9)

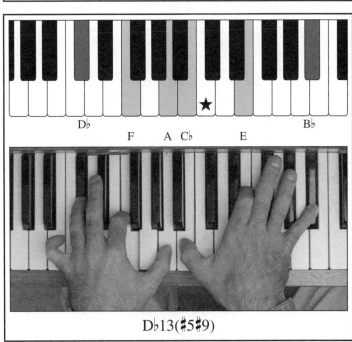

Db13(♯5♯9)

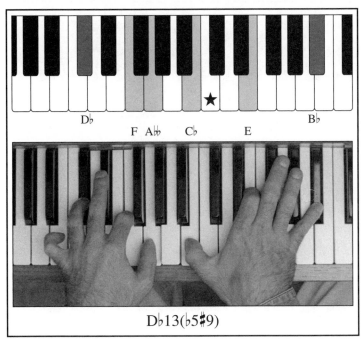

Db13(b5♯9)

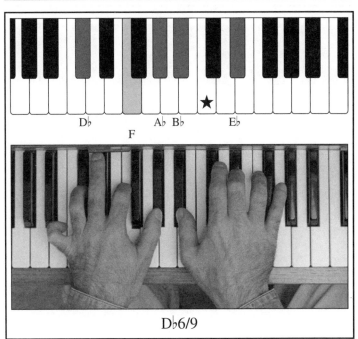

Db6/9

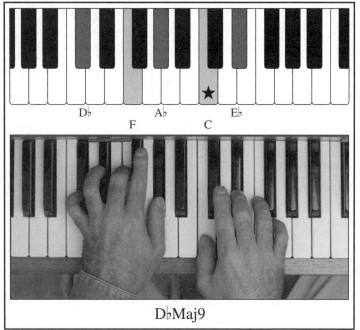

DbMaj9

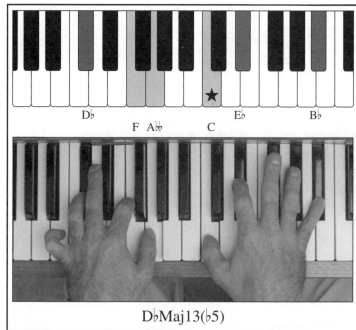

DbMaj13(b5)

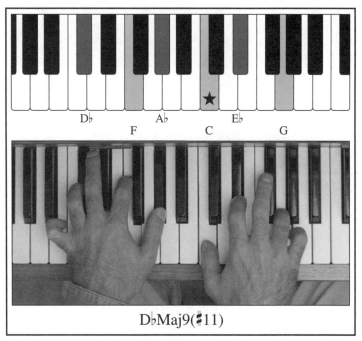

DbMaj9(#11)

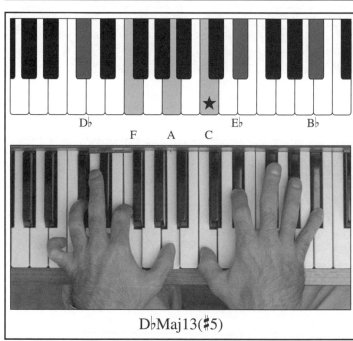

DbMaj13(#5)

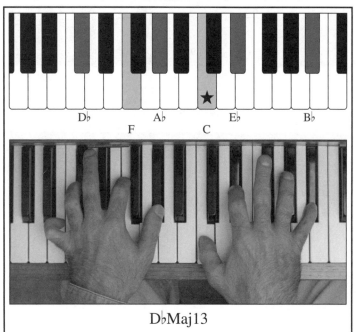

DbMaj13

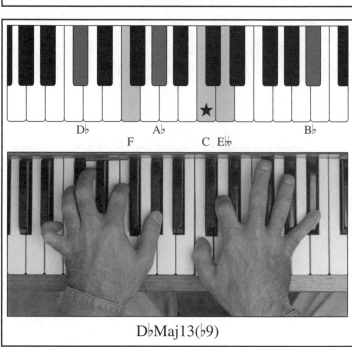

DbMaj13(b9)

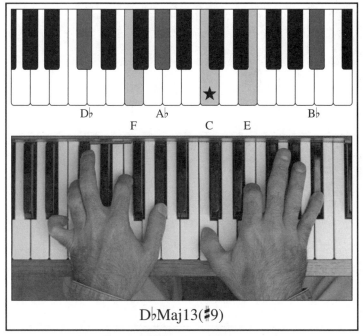

DbMaj13(#9)

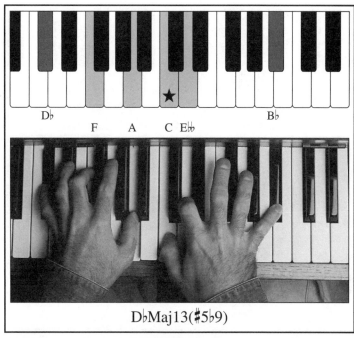

DbMaj13(#5b9)

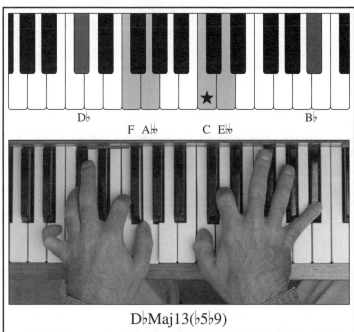

DbMaj13(b5b9)

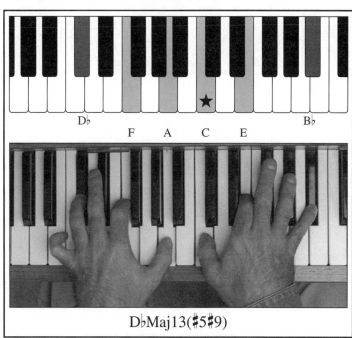

DbMaj13(#5#9)

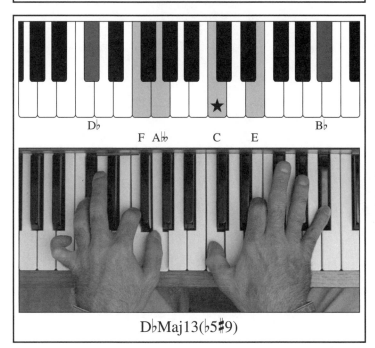

DbMaj13(b5#9)

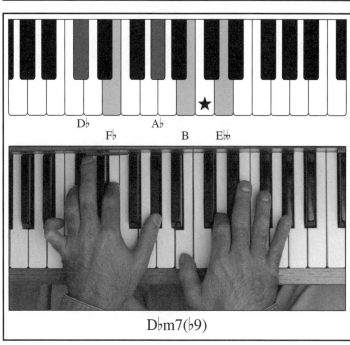

Dbm7(b9)

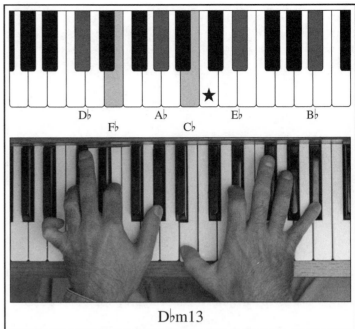

D♭m9

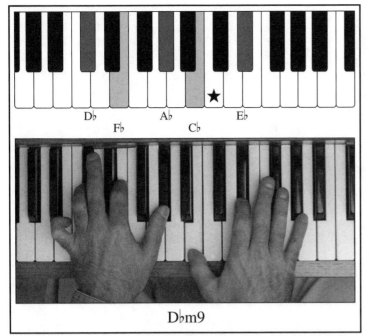

D♭m13

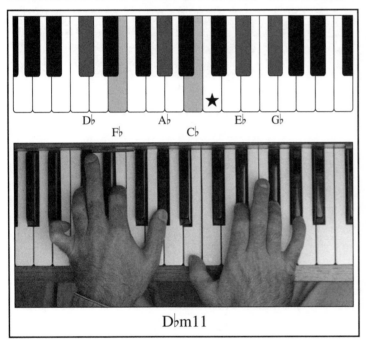

D♭m11

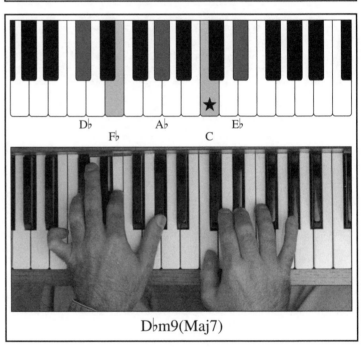

D♭m9(Maj7)

A♭
Chords

For Two Hands

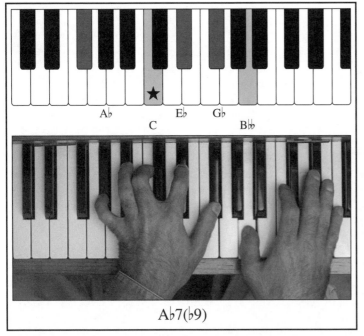

Ab7(b9)

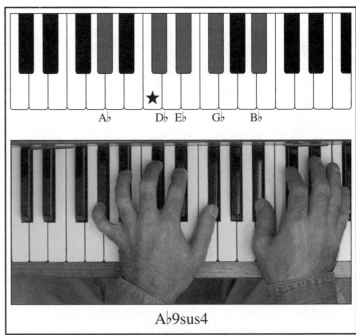

Ab9sus4

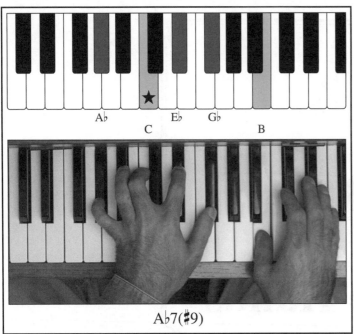

Ab7(#9)

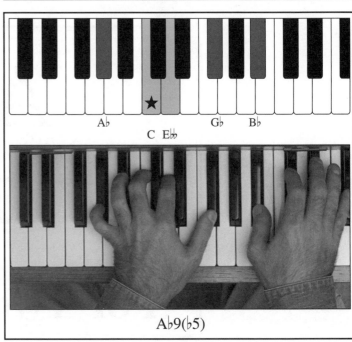

Ab9(b5)

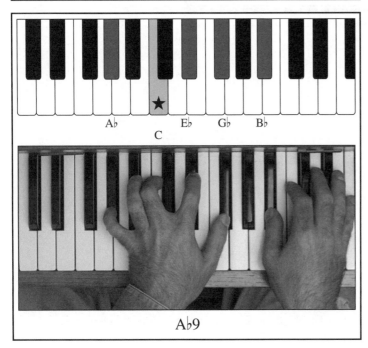

Ab9

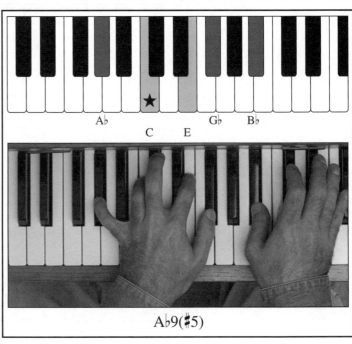

Ab9(#5)

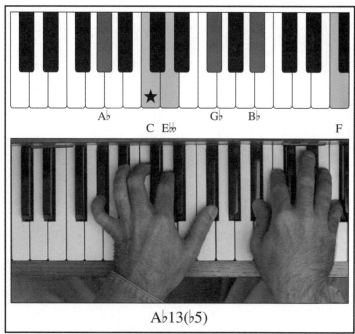

Ab9(#11)

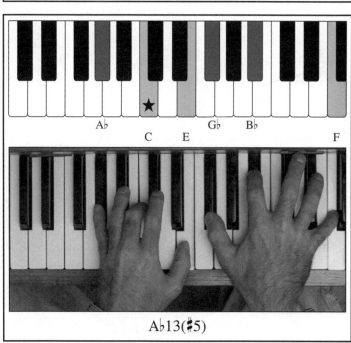

Ab13(b5)

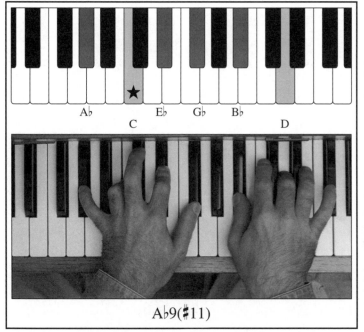

Ab13

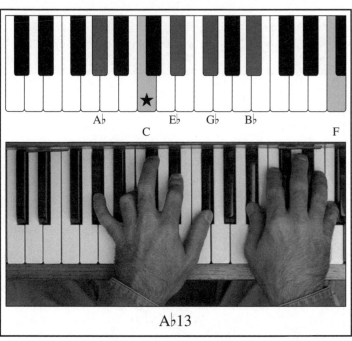

Ab13(#5)

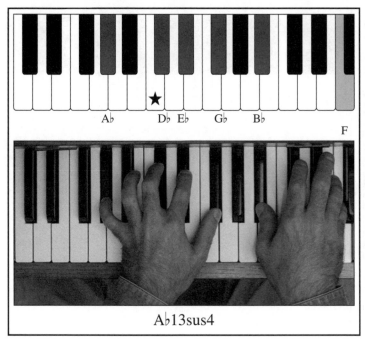

Ab13sus4

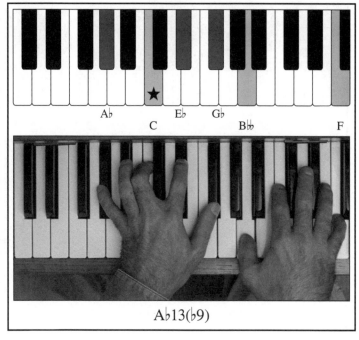

Ab13(b9)

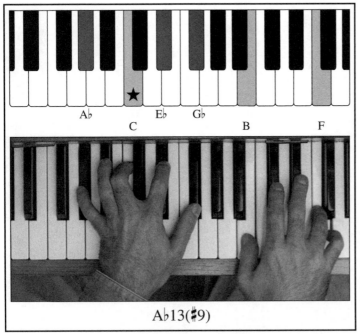

Ab13(#9)

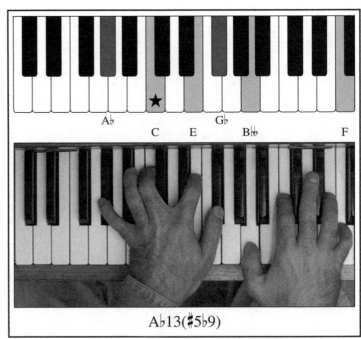

Ab13(#5b9)

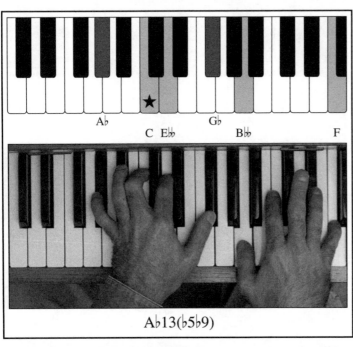

Ab13(b5b9)

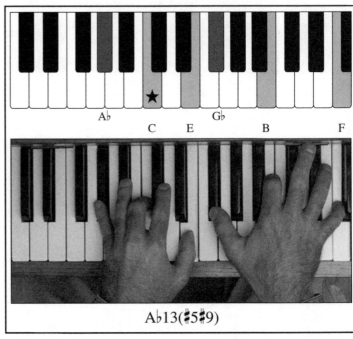

Ab13(#5#9)

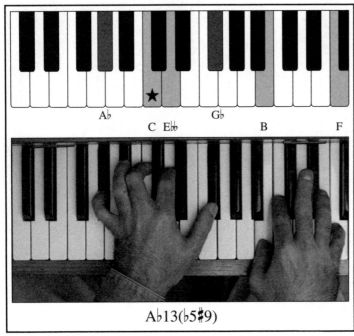

Ab13(b5#9)

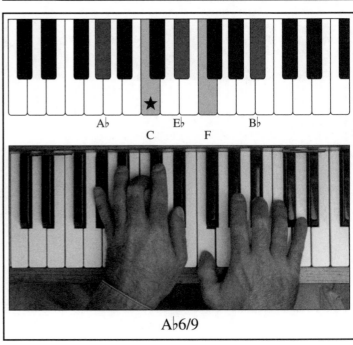

Ab6/9

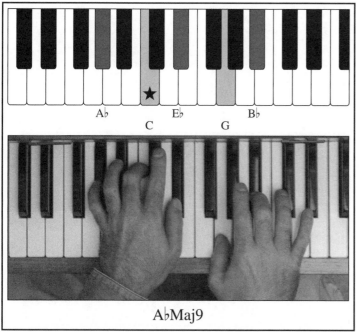

A♭Maj9

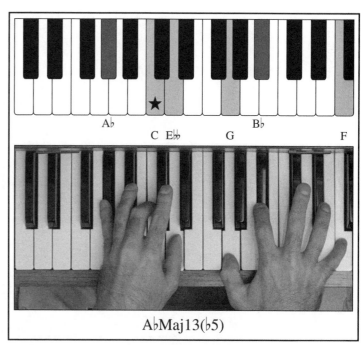

A♭Maj13(♭5)

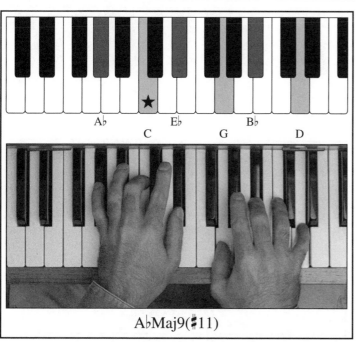

A♭Maj9(♯11)

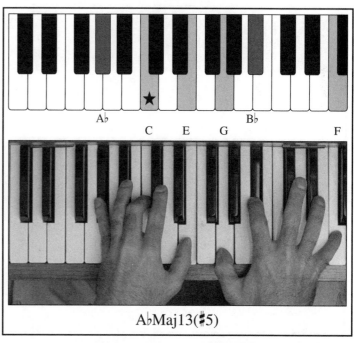

A♭Maj13(♯5)

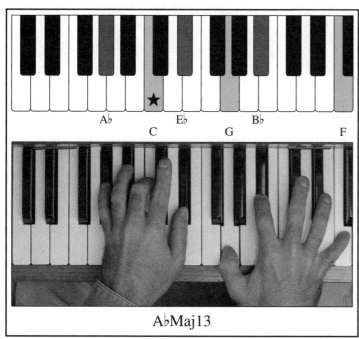

A♭Maj13

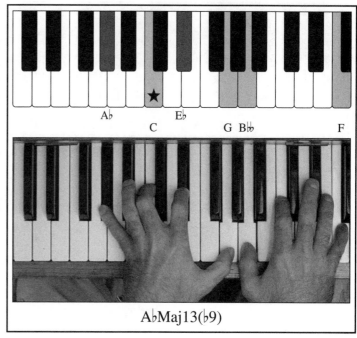

A♭Maj13(♭9)

175

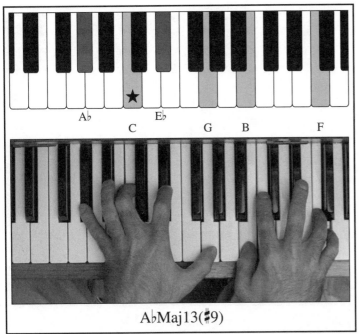

AbMaj13(#9)

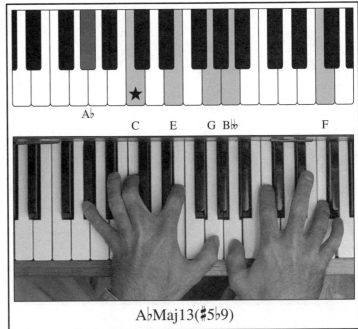

AbMaj13(#5b9)

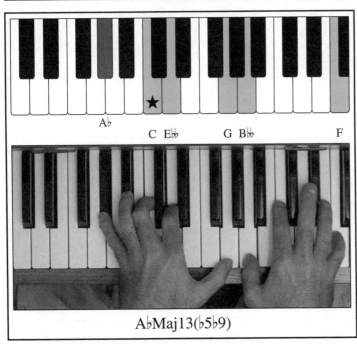

AbMaj13(b5b9)

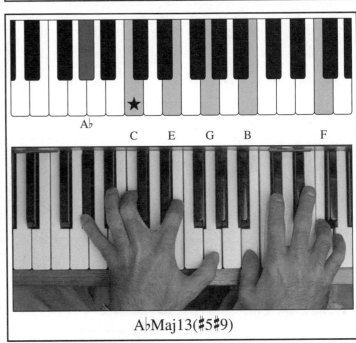

AbMaj13(#5#9)

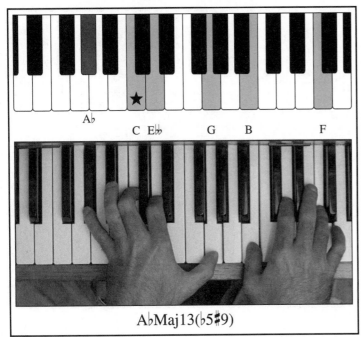

AbMaj13(b5#9)

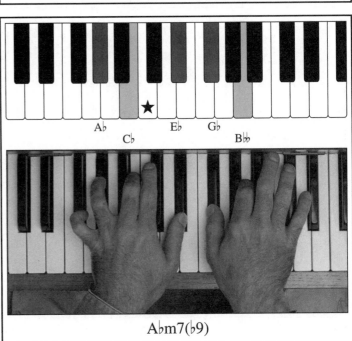

Abm7(b9)

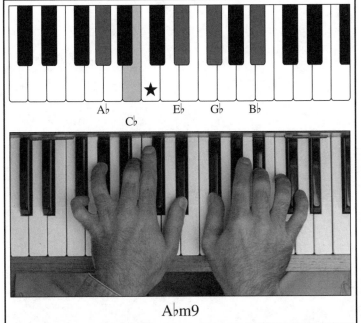

Abm9

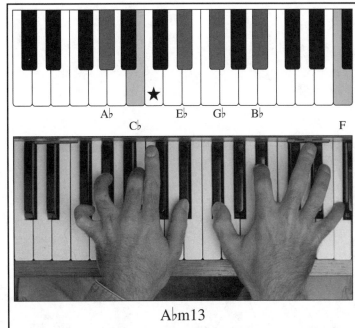

Abm13

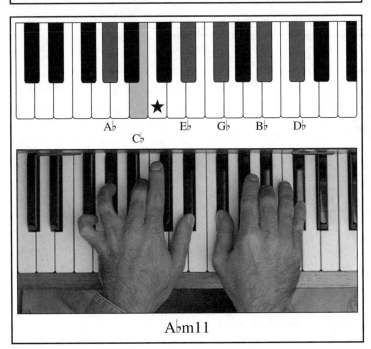

Abm11

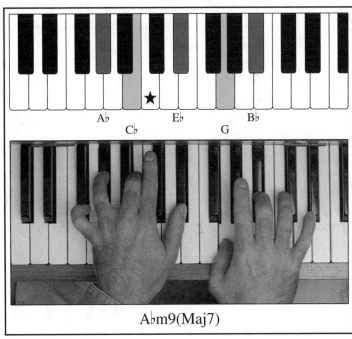

Abm9(Maj7)

E♭ Chords

For Two Hands

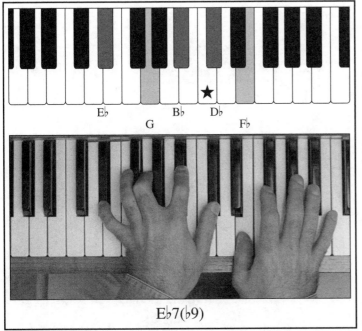

Eb7(b9)

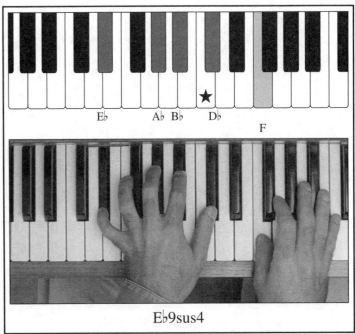

Eb9sus4

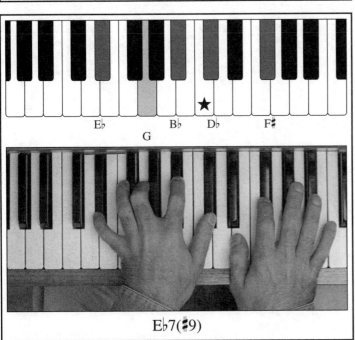

Eb7(#9)

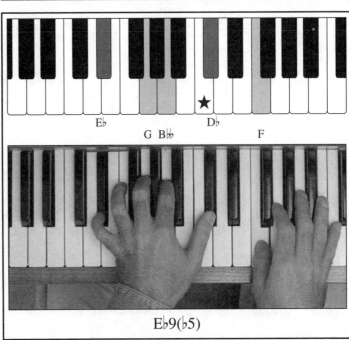

Eb9(b5)

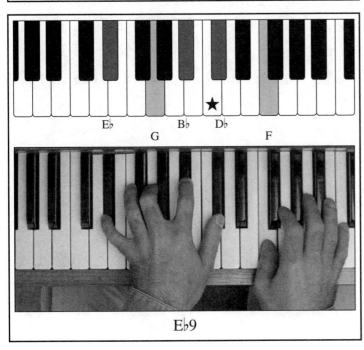

Eb9

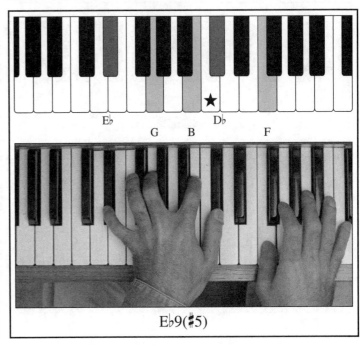

Eb9(#5)

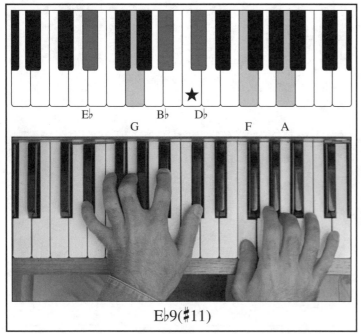

Eb9(#11)

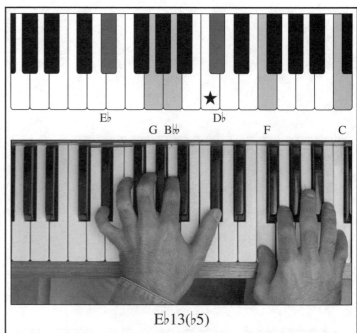

Eb13(b5)

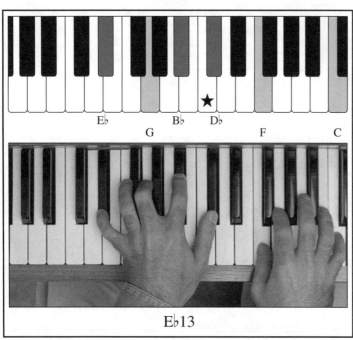

Eb13

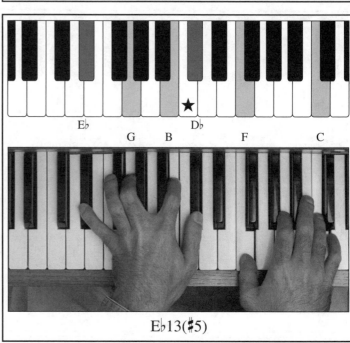

Eb13(#5)

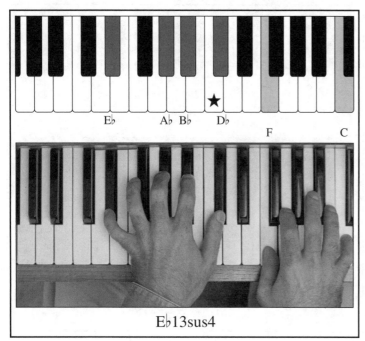

Eb13sus4

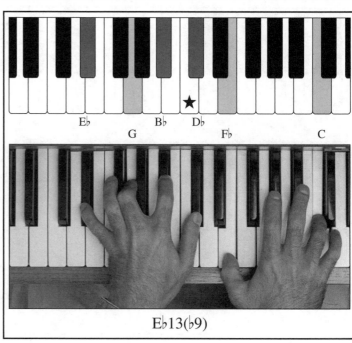

Eb13(b9)

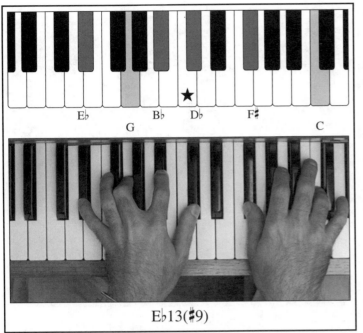

Eb13(#9)

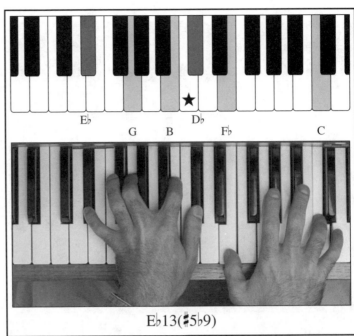

Eb13(#5b9)

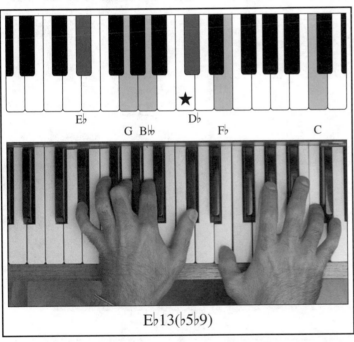

Eb13(b5b9)

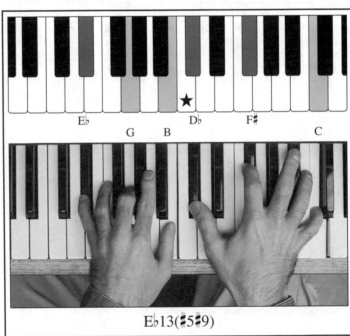

Eb13(#5#9)

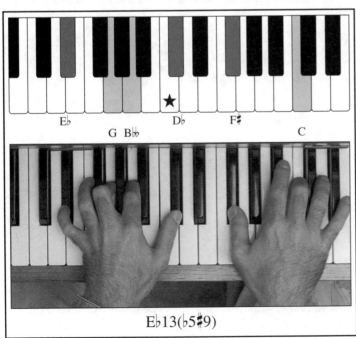

Eb13(b5#9)

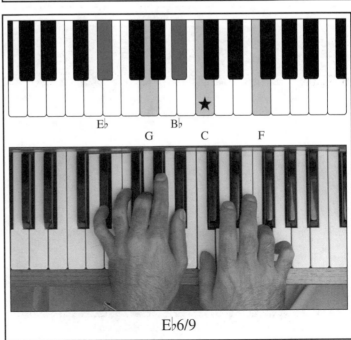

Eb6/9

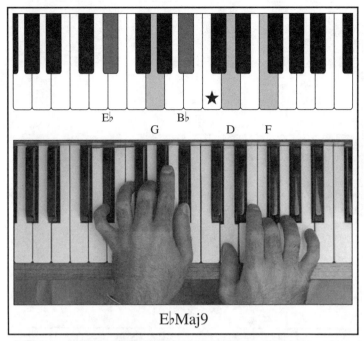

E♭Maj9

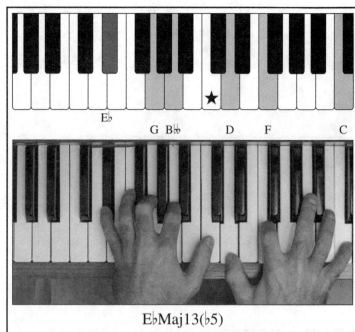

E♭Maj13(♭5)

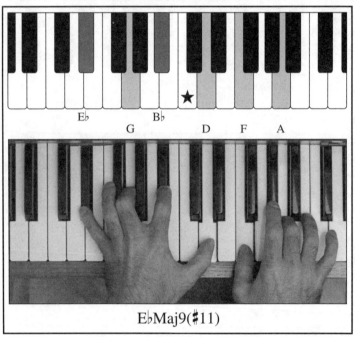

E♭Maj9(♯11)

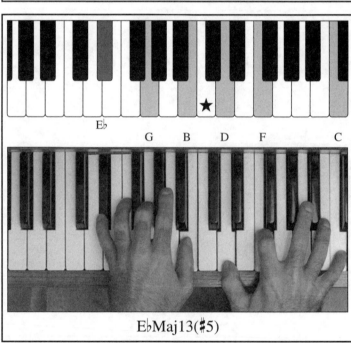

E♭Maj13(♯5)

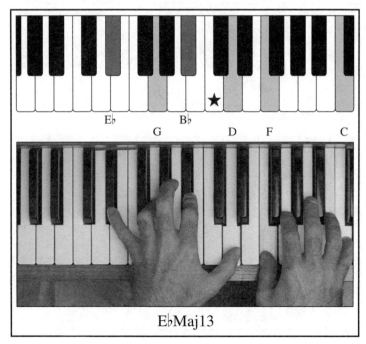

E♭Maj13

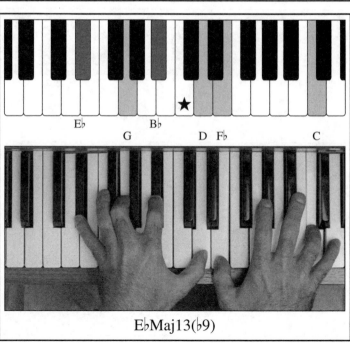

E♭Maj13(♭9)

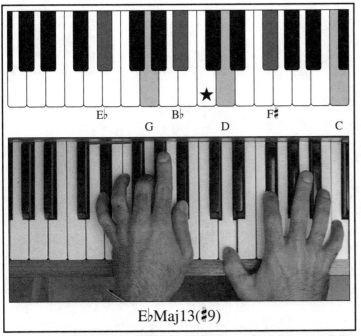

E♭Maj13(♯9)

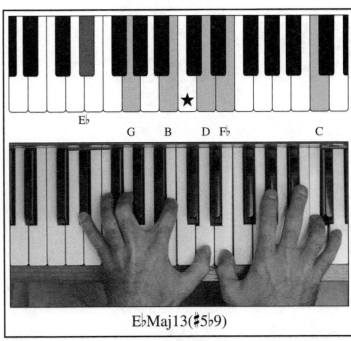

E♭Maj13(♯5♭9)

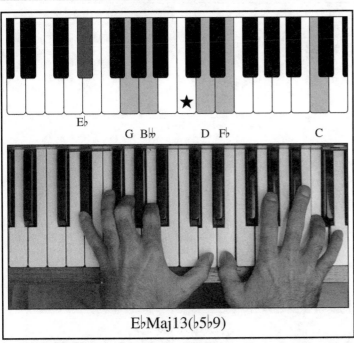

E♭Maj13(♭5♭9)

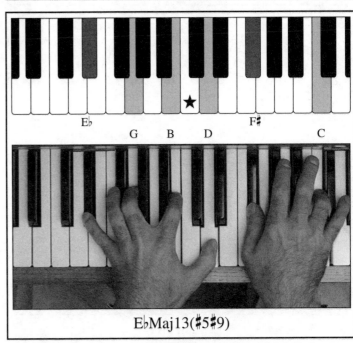

E♭Maj13(♯5♯9)

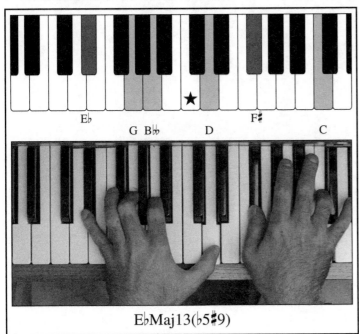

E♭Maj13(♭5♯9)

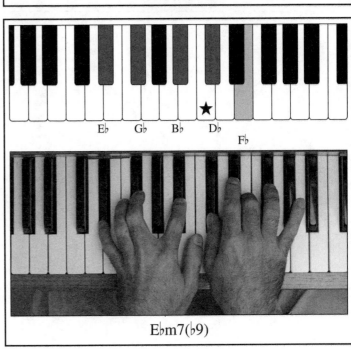

E♭m7(♭9)

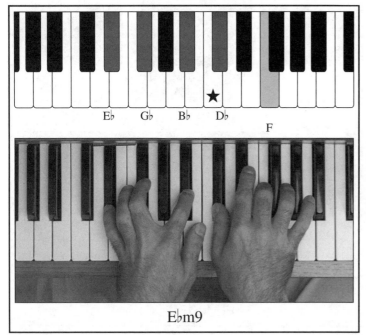

Ebm9

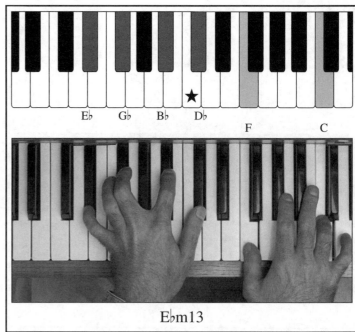

Ebm13

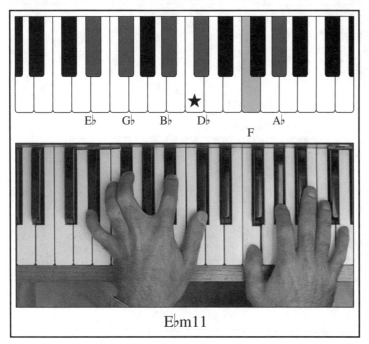

Ebm11

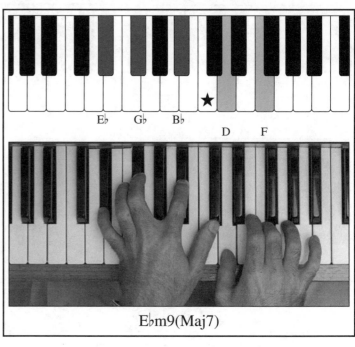

Ebm9(Maj7)

184

B♭
Chords

For Two Hands

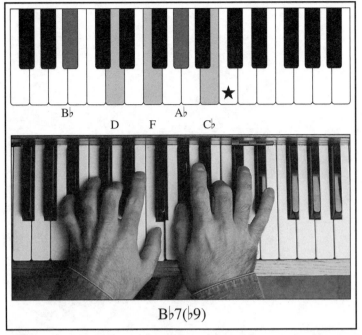

Bb7(b9)

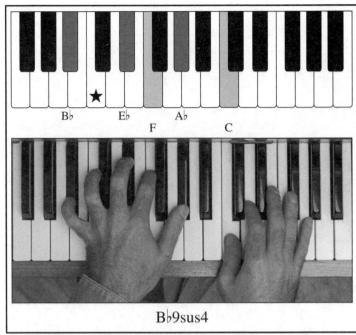

Bb9sus4

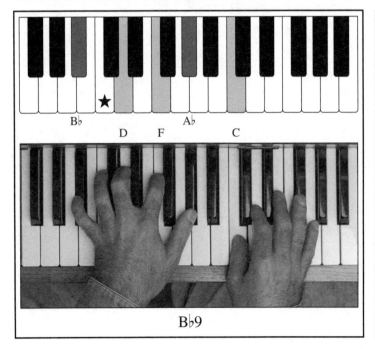

Bb7(#9)

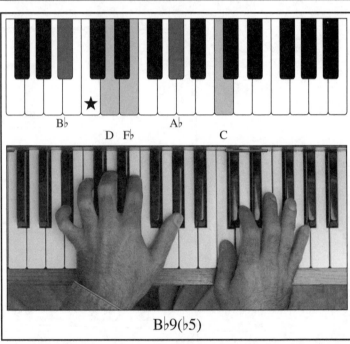

Bb9(b5)

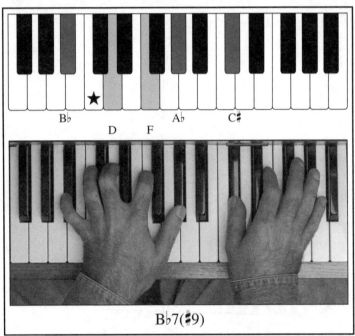

Bb9

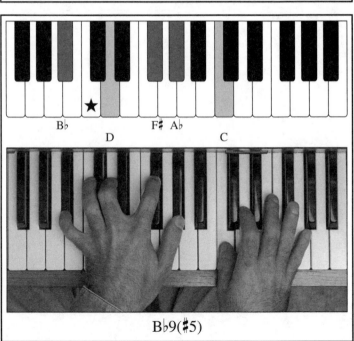

Bb9(#5)

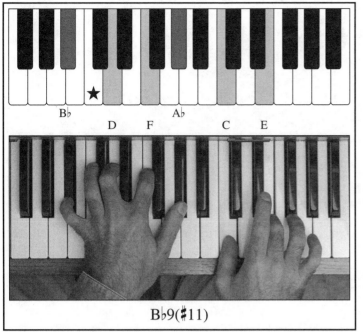

Bb9(#11)

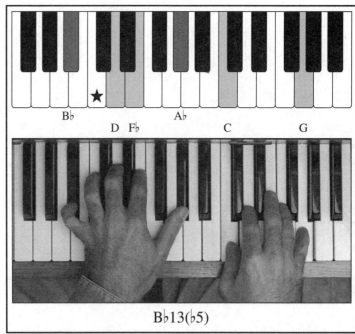

Bb13(b5)

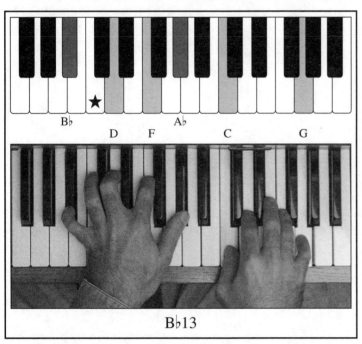

Bb13

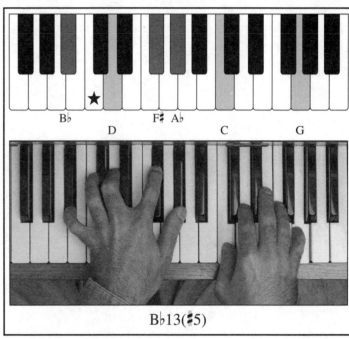

Bb13(#5)

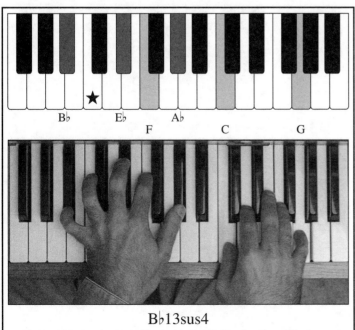

Bb13sus4

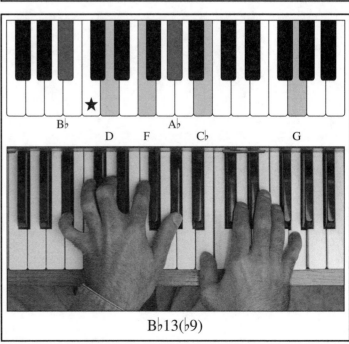

Bb13(b9)

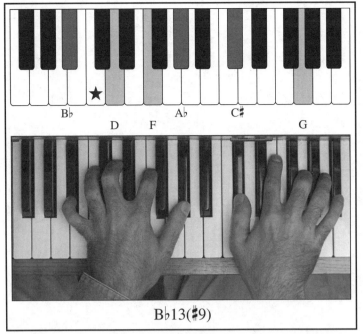

Bb13(#9)

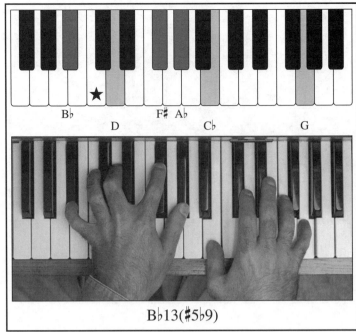

Bb13(#5b9)

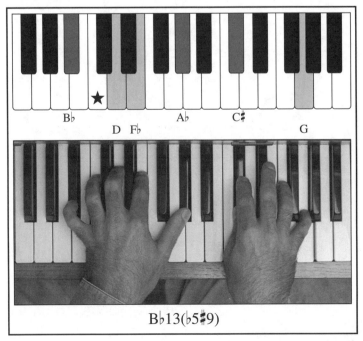

Bb13(b5b9)

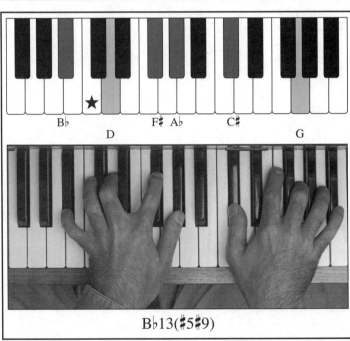

Bb13(#5#9)

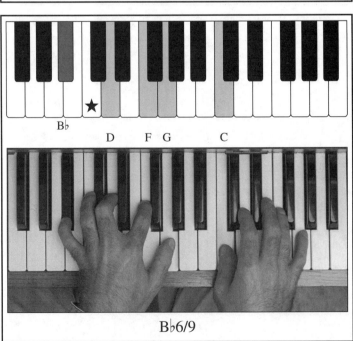

Bb13(b5#9)

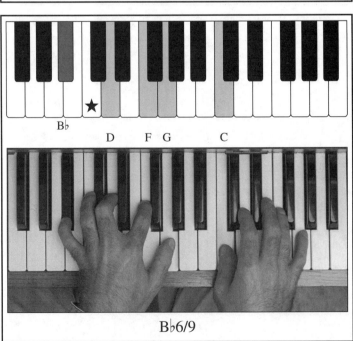

Bb6/9

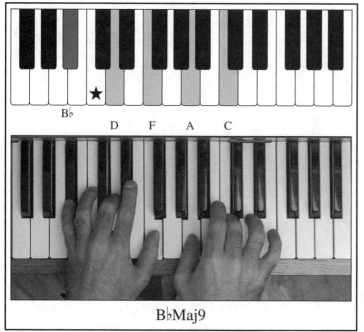

B♭Maj9

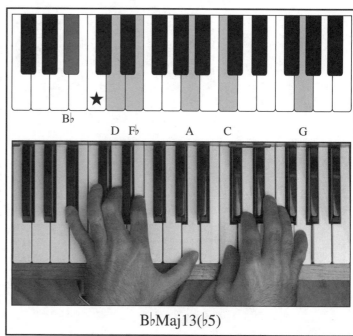

B♭Maj13(♭5)

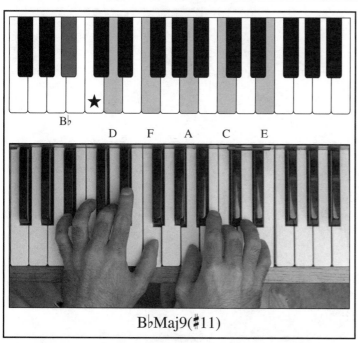

B♭Maj9(♯11)

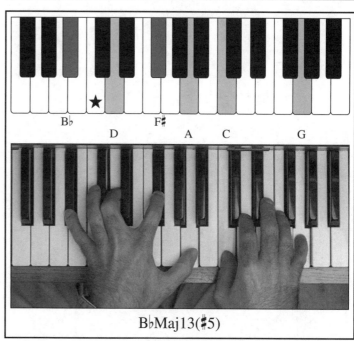

B♭Maj13(♯5)

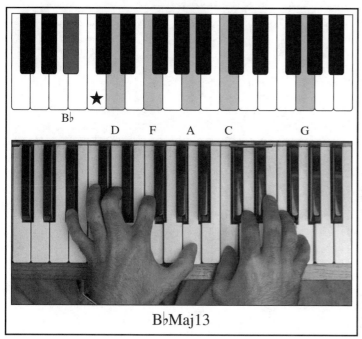

B♭Maj13

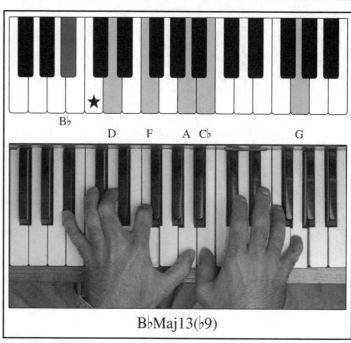

B♭Maj13(♭9)

189

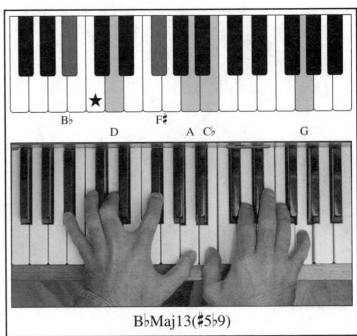

BbMaj13(#9)

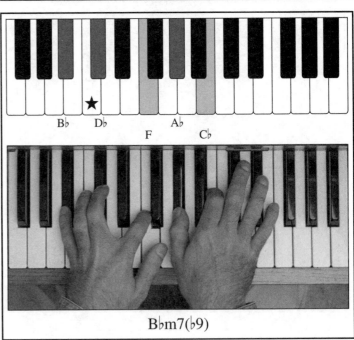

BbMaj13(#5b9)

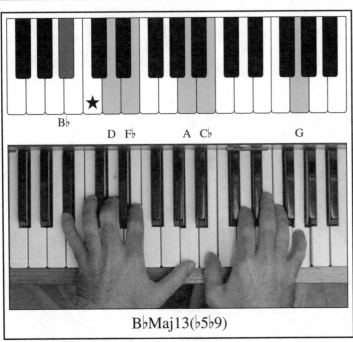

BbMaj13(b5b9)

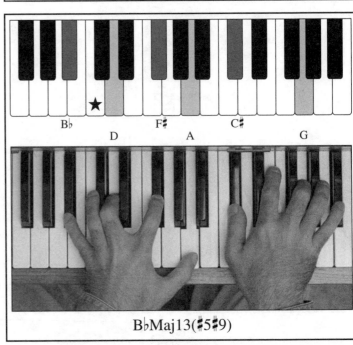

BbMaj13(#5#9)

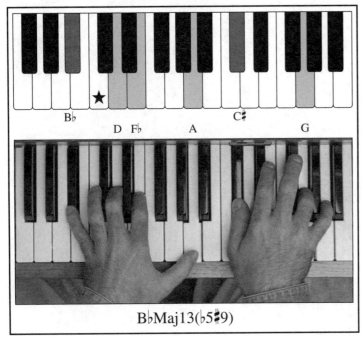

BbMaj13(b5#9)

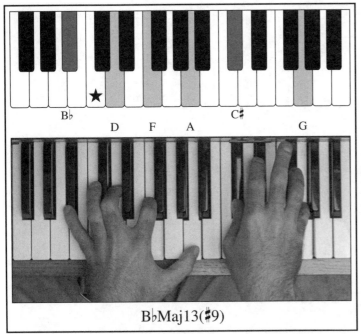

Bbm7(b9)

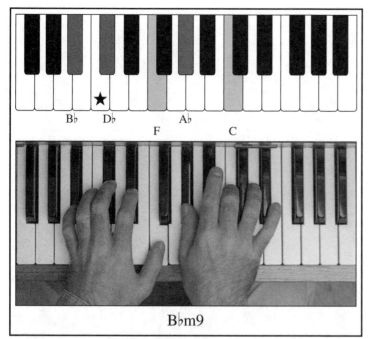

B♭m9

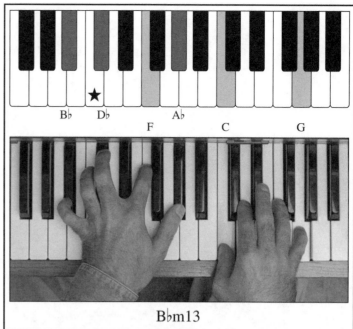

B♭m13

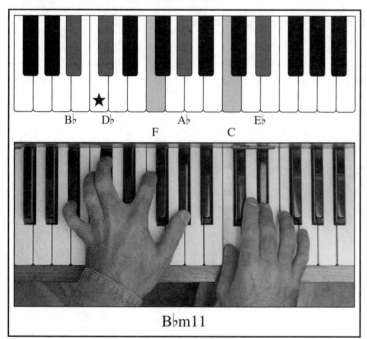

B♭m11

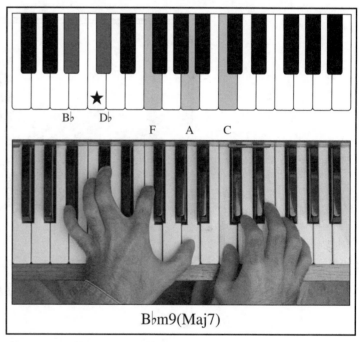

B♭m9(Maj7)

191

F
Chords

For Two Hands

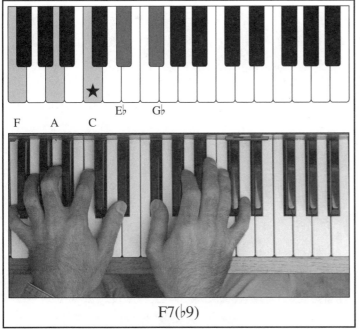

F7(♭9)

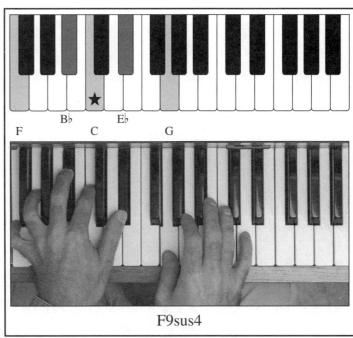

F9sus4

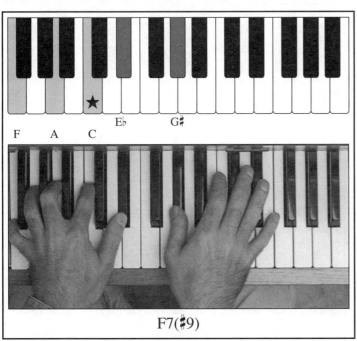

F7(♯9)

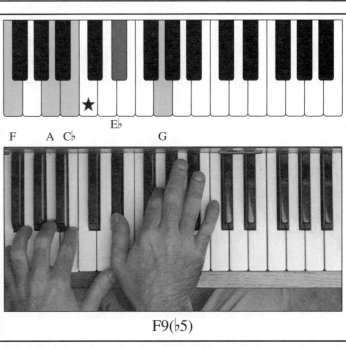

F9(♭5)

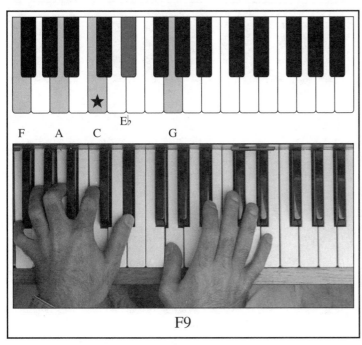

F9

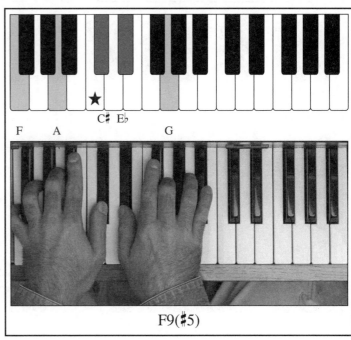

F9(♯5)

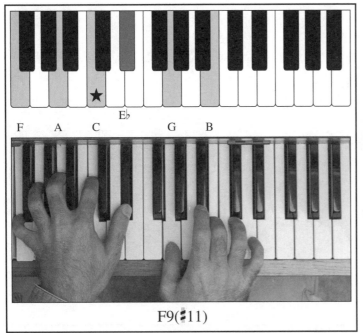

F9(♯11)

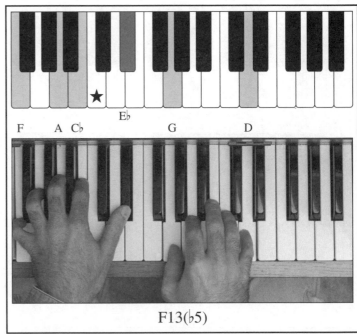

F13(♭5)

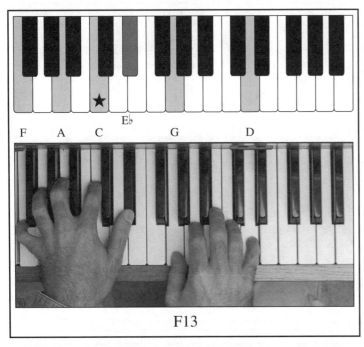

F13

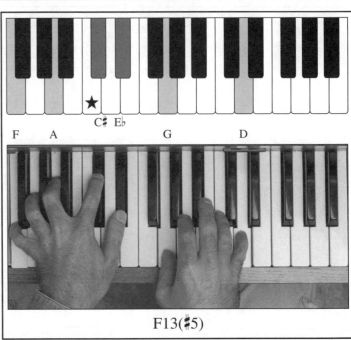

F13(♯5)

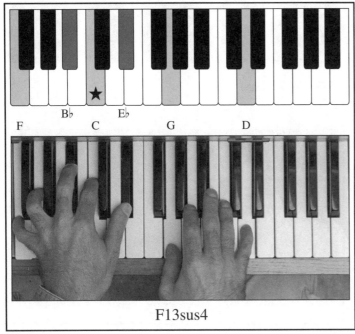

F13sus4

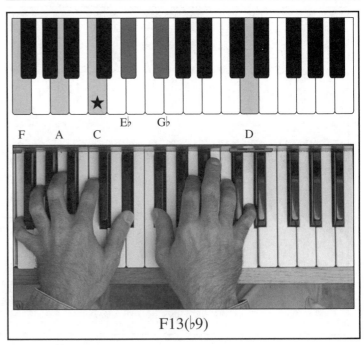

F13(♭9)

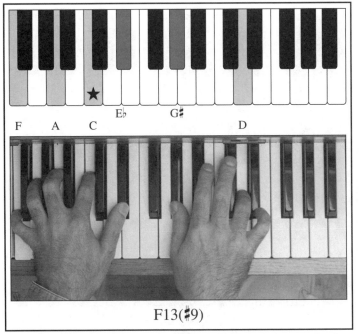

F13(♯9)

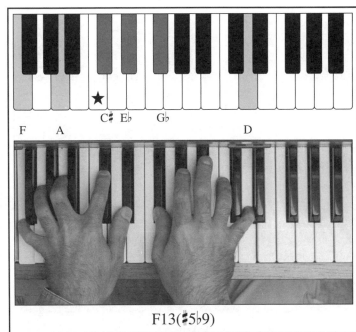

F13(♯5♭9)

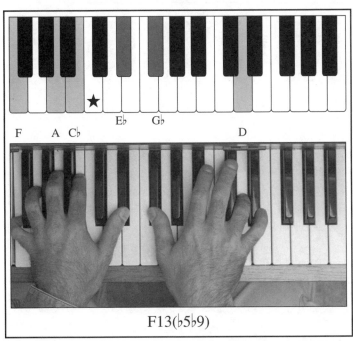

F13(♭5♭9)

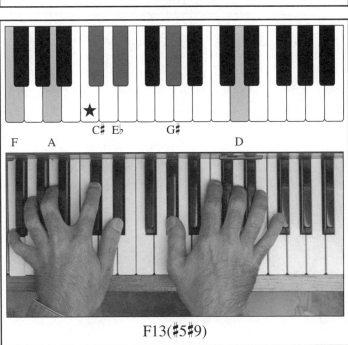

F13(♯5♯9)

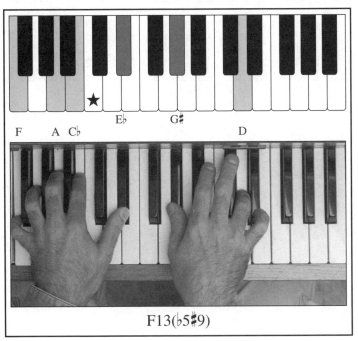

F13(♭5♯9)

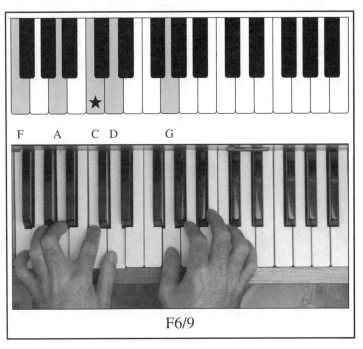

F6/9

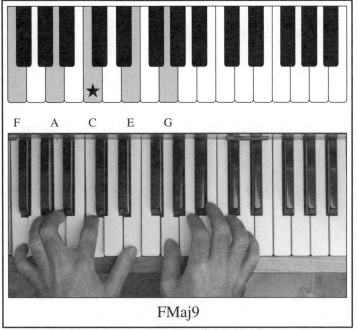

FMaj9

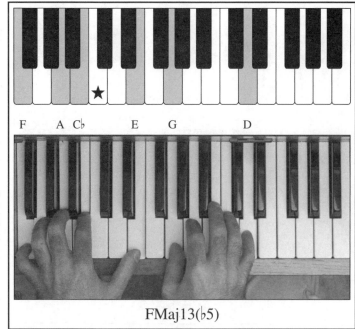

FMaj13(♭5)

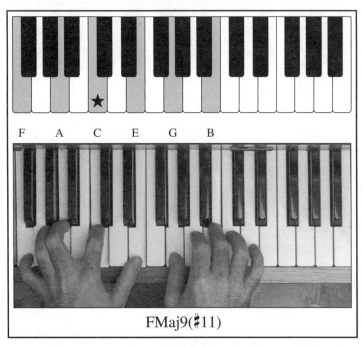

FMaj9(♯11)

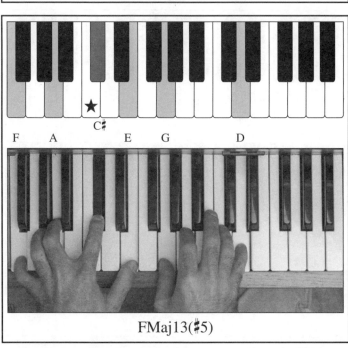

FMaj13(♯5)

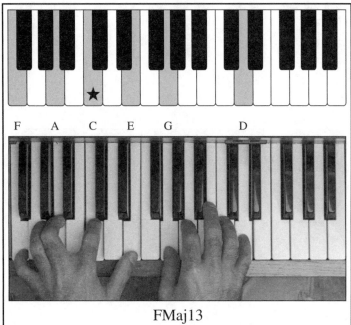

FMaj13

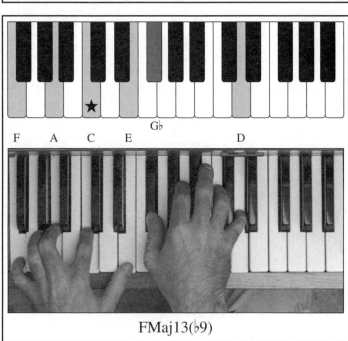

FMaj13(♭9)

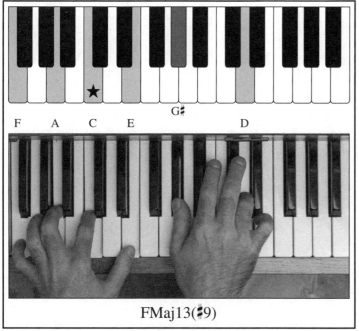

FMaj13(#9)

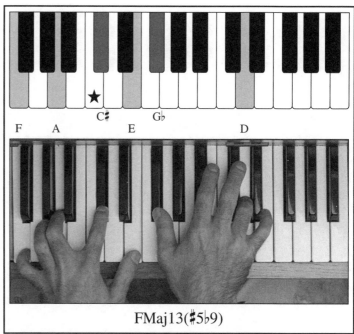

FMaj13(#5♭9)

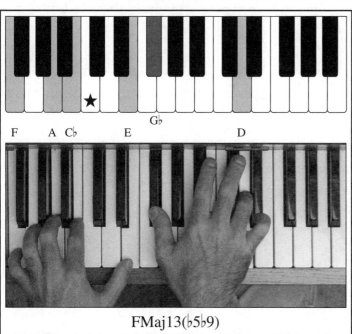

FMaj13(♭5♭9)

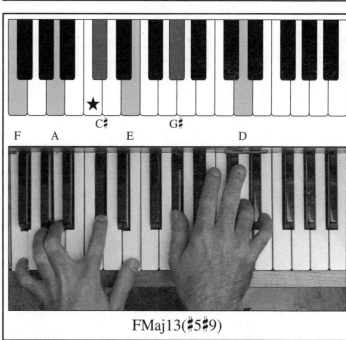

FMaj13(#5#9)

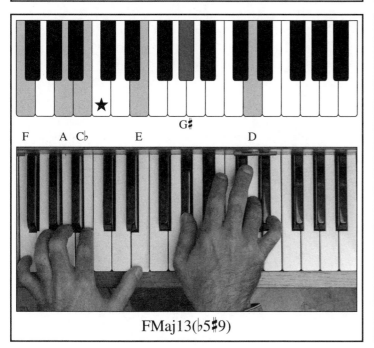

FMaj13(♭5#9)

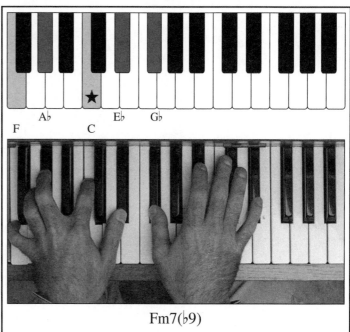

Fm7(♭9)

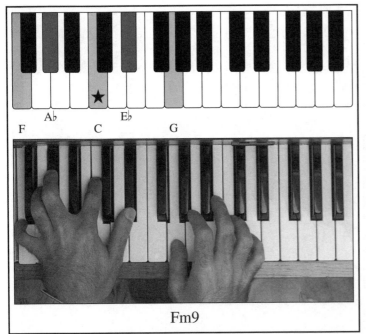

Fm9

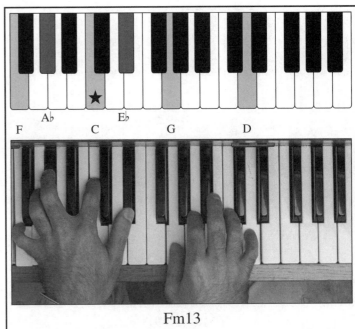

Fm13

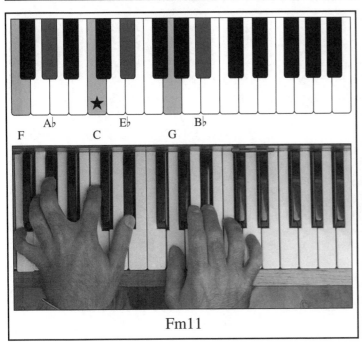

Fm11

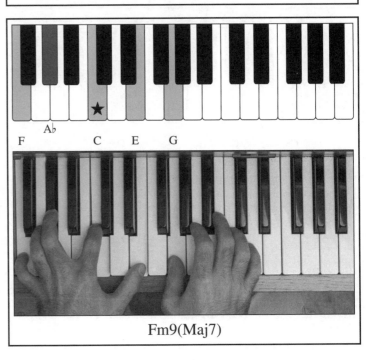

Fm9(Maj7)